Abe· £10.65

Amo

CW01024524

SHAKESPEARE ON THE GERMAN STAGE

VOLUME I: 1586–1914

SHAKESPEARE
ON THE
GERMAN STAGE

Volume 1: 1586–1914

SIMON WILLIAMS

Professor of Dramatic Art
University of California at Santa Barbara

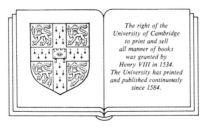

The right of the
University of Cambridge
to print and sell
all manner of books
was granted by
Henry VIII in 1534.
The University has printed
and published continuously
since 1584.

CAMBRIDGE UNIVERSITY PRESS

Cambridge
New York   Port Chester   Melbourne   Sydney

Published by the Press Syndicate of the University of Cambridge
The Pitt Building, Trumpington Street, Cambridge CB2 1RP
40 West 20th Street, New York, NY 10011, USA
10 Stamford Road, Oakleigh, Melbourne 3166, Australia

First published 1990

Printed in Great Britain
at the University Press, Cambridge

British Library cataloguing in publication data
Williams, Simon
Shakespeare on the German stage.
Vol. 1: 1586–1914
1. Drama in English. Shakespeare, William.
Performance, to 1980.
1. Title
792.9'5

Library of congress cataloguing in publication data
Williams, Simon.
Shakespeare on the German stage / Simon Williams.
p.   cm.
Bibliography.
Contents: v. 1. 1586–1914.
ISBN 0–521–34464–6 (v. 1)
1. Shakespeare, William, 1564–1616 – Stage history – Germany.
1. Title.
PR2971.G3W55   1990
792.9'5 0943–dc20   89–9789 CIP

ISBN 0 521 34464 6

For
Euzetta,
with love

Contents

Plates

Preface

There is good reason for regarding Shakespeare as having exercised the most retrograde of influences on the development of English theatre. His monumental presence has for centuries crippled the imagination of playwrights, who have either imitated him inadequately or have been driven to feats of arcane originality in attempts to escape his influence. In Germany, however, Shakespeare has released rather than disabled the imagination of creative writers. Indeed there can be few writers who have had as benign an influence upon a culture not their own as Shakespeare has had upon German-speaking Europe. From the early plays of *Sturm und Drang* through to the epic theatre of Bertolt Brecht and contemporary German playwrights, Shakespeare has constantly served German playwrights as a model that has encouraged them to produce not slavish imitations of his work but a drama that has its own identity and life. His presence in the German repertoire has grown over the years. Perhaps it is greater today than it has been at any time over the last two centuries. A brief glance at the yearly performance statistics of German theatres issued by periodicals such as *Theater Heute* will show that, despite changes in taste, Shakespeare, rather than Goethe, Schiller or Brecht, is usually the most frequently performed playwright in any given season.

So substantial is the contribution made to German culture by Shakespeare's plays, it would be impossible to do it justice within the limits of a relatively short book. Hence the focus of this study is the adaptation and performance of Shakespeare's plays on the German stage before the modern period. Nevertheless, it would be incomplete without some attention being paid to the crucial impact of Shakespeare on German critical thinking and on Germany's great contribution to Shakespeare criticism, not only because such material is of consequence in itself, but because it can also lead us to an appreciation of both the achievement and the shortcomings of the German theatre in rising to the challenge of Shakespeare's plays. The point of gravity of this study is, therefore, the remarkable rise of interest in Shakespeare that occurred at the end of the eighteenth and the beginning of the nineteenth centuries. This was the period during which Shakespeare's works were first absorbed by German critics, first imitated by Germany's playwrights, first translated into German by writers of great accomplishment, and first staged by Germany's major theatre companies. As this was the classical period of German literature, Shakespeare has acquired symbolic status as a nurturing presence during the most fruitful and crucial stage of the country's cultural growth.

Centring this historical study of theatrical performance around a critical and literary debate that occurred over a period of approximately sixty years, from 1750 to 1810, accounts for the seemingly odd, unchronological organisation of the material. Only two chapters, chapters 2 and 10, do not draw significantly from material from this period. All other chapters either explore Shakespeare during the German classical period or discuss how the vision of Shakespeare during this period influenced later performances and productions of his work. Even chapter 10 discusses performances that, as I have argued, represent a culmination of a theatrical process begun back in the late eighteenth century. So that the reader may acquire some idea of the order of the events through which Shakespeare was assimilated into the German theatre, I have appended a brief timeline at the end of the book.

Some chapters have been adapted, often considerably, from previously published articles. Parts of chapters 1 and 5 are based on 'Shakespeare and Weimar Classicism: A Study in Cross-Purposes', *Essays in Theatre*, 5, 1 (November 1986), 27–46; some of the material for chapter 4 was drawn from 'The "Great Guest" Arrives: Early German *Hamlets*', *Theatre Journal*, 38, 3 (October, 1986), 290–308; chapter 6 was taken in part from 'Shakespeare at the Burgtheater: From Heinrich Anschütz to Josef Kainz', *Shakespeare Survey* 35 (1982), 21–9; and chapter 9 is an extended version of 'The "Shakespeare-Stage" in Germany', which first appeared in *Shakespeare and the Victorian Stage*, ed. Richard Foulkes (Cambridge, 1986), pp. 210–22. I would like to thank both the editors and publishers of the journals and the book for their permission to use this material. Some of the material was also delivered, in 1985 and 1987, in lectures at the Universities of East Anglia, Glasgow, Kent, Manchester, Sheffield, and Warwick, at Portsmouth Polytechnic, and at the Goethe Institut in Glasgow.

I have many to thank for the completion of this book. First, my studies were greatly aided by the Regents of the University of California, who awarded me three consecutive Humanities Fellowships, enabling me to devote three complete summers to this project. I travelled to libraries and archives in Austria and Germany through an award from the University of California Senate Research Committee. I would like to acknowledge the help I have received from Roswitha Flatz, Micaela Giesing, Wolfgang

Greisenegger, Heinrich Huesmann and Eckehart Nölle, all of whom did everything they could to provide me both with relevant material and the most stimulating comments on my project. I also benefited from the indefatigable help of the staffs of Theater Museum of the University of Cologne, the German Theatre Museum in Munich, the Theatre Collection at the University of Hamburg and the Theatre Collection at the National Library in Vienna. Closer to home, my work was facilitated by Cheryl La Guardia and Kitty Uthe of the Interlibrary Loan Department and Connie Dowell of the Reference Department of UCSB library; they responded readily to some requests, made at the most outrageous short notice. My manuscript was read, in extracts or complete, by Robert Egan, William Grange, Gerhart Hoffmeister, Robert Potter and Mark Rose. Their comments have been more helpful than perhaps they might guess. I would particularly like to acknowledge Bert States, for his companionship, for conversations on Shakespeare, and his acute appreciation of the work of Dingelstedt. I am especially indebted to Sandy Hortmann of the University of Duisburg, first for his marvellous hospitality, secondly for his reading of the final manuscript, and finally for his authorship – he will be completing the companion volume to this one, taking the story of Shakespeare in the German theatre up to the present day. One could not ask for a better co-author.

The dedication indicates to whom I owe everything else.

I

The literature of Shakespeare in eighteenth-century Germany

For over half the action of Goethe's novel *Wilhelm Meisters Lehrjahre* (*Wilhelm Meister's Apprenticeship*), the young hero takes an uncommonly idealistic view of the theatre. He sees it as the agency for potential social change. Through it he hopes that 'the generous, noble feelings, worthy of mankind' that can be communicated by the performer to the spectator might grow into 'a fellow-feeling with all that is human'.[1] Hence, through theatre, divisions in society might be bridged. Wilhelm sees theatre as a means of personal cultivation as well. Only on stage, he claims, does he, a merchant's son, have the freedom to polish his manners so as to develop a fine aristocratic bearing and escape from the narrow confines of his upbringing. In the course of his theatrical odyssey, Wilhelm encounters the plays of Shakespeare and at once recognises their superiority to all other drama that he has seen or read. Logically, therefore, one might assume that Shakespeare's plays will be powerfully instrumental in the fulfilment of Wilhelm's theatrical ideals. However they are not. This is partly because, as the novel progresses, Wilhelm's ideals about theatre are revealed as fallible. More critically, however, the plays come to be seen as suited neither to Wilhelm's view of theatre's mission nor to the exigencies of theatrical representation.

This is immediately apparent from the way in which he responds to the plays when he first reads them, during his stay at the Count's castle with a troupe of travelling players. For a start, the man who suggests he should read Shakespeare, the officer Jarno, has, as Wilhelm has observed with distress, little tolerance for theatrical performance. Jarno recommends Shakespeare to Wilhelm as an antidote first to his unconvincing enthusiasm for Racine and the French tragedians, then to his more convincing

---

[1] Johann Wolfgang von Goethe, *Wilhelm Meisters Lehrjahre, Goethes Werke*, ser. 1, 55 vols. (Weimar, 1887–1918), vol. 21, p. 165. Translations from the German are my own, unless otherwise indicated.

attachment to the theatre itself. Reading Shakespeare, Jarno argues, may abate Wilhelm's ardour for the theatre, leading him to rechannel his energies towards different and, it is implied, more productive interests. Wilhelm's initial reaction to Shakespeare's plays confirms what Jarno has said. While reading them, he avoids the public life of the theatre, retiring to one of the most removed rooms in the Count's castle, where only the Harper and Mignon, who has an active dislike of theatre, are allowed to visit him. The reading is a deeply private experience. Through it, Wilhelm becomes aware for the first time of the wealth of his perceptions and the abundance of his imagination. Shakespeare works on him like a magician who entirely possesses his mind.

> One hears of magicians who by magic formulae draw a huge throng of spiritual forms into their cell. The spells are so powerful that they soon fill up the whole space of the room ... Every corner is crammed full and every ledge occupied. Embryos expand themselves and giant forms contract themselves into mushrooms.[2]

But this sense of transformation initially encourages Wilhelm 'to take quicker footsteps forwards into the actual world, to mingle in the flood of destinies that hangs over it'. Only secondarily does it occur to him to use his new experience to enrich the theatre and even then he feels that only fragments of the plays, which he calls 'a few cups from the great ocean of true nature',[3] can be effectively realised on stage. Embodying the whole experience of his reading would seem to be beyond the capacity of theatre.

Goethe suggests several reasons why this is so. For a start, while his description of theatrical life is vivid and engaging, it is clear that he regards most actors as innately incapable of recognising, let alone realising on stage, the richness of Shakespeare's world. Either, like Philine, they are given to the pleasures of the moment, or they prize acting as a means of self-display, or, like Melina, they are concerned only with the money they can make. In the course of the novel, the image of the theatre as an aggregation of all human foibles, failings and vices grows until, just before his initiation into the Tower Society, Wilhelm passionately renounces it. The theatre is not, it would appear, the place for serious artistic endeavour.

These obstacles to the successful representation of Shakespeare arise, it might be argued, mainly from the underdeveloped condition of German theatre during the 1770s, the decade in which the novel is set. But Goethe extends his enquiry to a consideration of the aesthetic compatibility of Shakespeare and the theatre. This becomes the most persistent theme of the long discussions between Wilhelm and the actor-manager Serlo. Serlo is represented as a competent and effective theatre artist. His actors have a

---

'high, clear understanding of their art',[4] while his own performances are distinguished by their completeness, vigour, conciseness and variety. Consequently, he becomes the guarantor of the theatre as a serious art form. It is therefore the more notable that he has fundamental doubts as to the viability of staging Shakespeare's plays unless the original text, which in this instance we should understand as the prose translations of Wieland,[5] has been radically altered. Most of Serlo's and Wilhelm's discussions revolve around *Hamlet*, the production of which Wilhelm makes conditional upon his becoming a professional actor. Serlo eventually succeeds in leading Wilhelm away from his insistence on staging *Hamlet* in its original form, which facilitates production of the play but at the same time means that the stage is not being used to realise objectively the intensely subjective experience of Wilhelm's first reading. The encounter with Shakespeare that so amplified his imaginative life cannot, it would seem, be replicated on stage.

Serlo finds compelling practical reasons for this. He possesses a commercial sense as acute as that of any of his colleagues and avoids staging Shakespeare's plays because their lack of dramaturgical economy places undue stress on 'the number of personnel, on the decorations and theatre machinery, on time, on dialogue, and on the physical strengths of the actor'. Even though these challenges might be met, Serlo does not consider the rewards to be gained from them to be worthwhile, as audiences, represented throughout the novel as superficial in judgement, are accustomed to prizing only beautiful passages. They would fail to appreciate the whole work of art before them. 'The theatre', Serlo concludes acerbically, 'is only something patched up and pieced together.'[6] He therefore sees no problem in adapting the plays to appeal to their deficient tastes.

Wilhelm comes to accept the need for adaptation, but for different reasons. He acknowledges the limitations posed by Serlo, but argues that the main reason for adapting *Hamlet* is to remedy an aesthetic flaw. This he identifies as an incongruity between the inner and outer actions of the play, between what he defines as

> the great inner relationships of the persons and of the events, the powerful effects arising from the characters and actions of the main figures [and] the external relationships of the persons by which they are brought from one

---

[4] *Ibid.*, vol. 22, p. 84.

[5] Wieland's translations of twenty-two of the plays were published between 1762 and 1766. The first volume of the verse translations of A. W. Schlegel, which became the standard version of Shakespeare in Germany, was not published until 1797. At any point in this study, the term 'original' should be understood as referring to the plays as they appear in the First Folio, translated into German and published in a version that at any given time was generally considered to be complete and unchanged.

[6] *Goethes Werke*, ser. 1, vol. 22, p. 157.

place to another or are bound together in this way or that through certain coincidental events.[7]

While Wilhelm insists that the former, the 'inner action' of the play, must remain untouched, he is quite happy to tamper with the latter, which he regards as little more than dispensable framework. His resulting adaptation is a fairly plausible version of *Hamlet* in which the various toings-and-froings of the action all take place between Denmark and Norway in a political context that the audience will understand with ease. In the place of the apparent external disunity of Shakespeare's play there is now unity, in place of untidiness there is now tidiness, and of confusion clarity.

By the standards of the eighteenth century, in which stage adaptations of classics were the universal rule, Wilhelm's version of *Hamlet*, given only in plot summary, is quite commendable. In contrast to the only version of *Hamlet* that was performed in Germany until the end of the century – by Friedrich Ludwig Schröder, the original for the character of Serlo[8] – Goethe's fictional hero has made some intelligent choices. He retains both Rosencrantz and Guildenstern, where Schröder had cut Rosencrantz; he is fully aware of the importance of all the scenes with the Players, while Schröder had cut all but the play scene itself: above all, he has both Laertes and Hamlet die at the end, while Schröder, obedient to the tastes of the late eighteenth century that disliked undeserved deaths, did not.

But even though Wilhelm's adaptation is closer to the original, for two reasons the very act of adaptation violates his initial attachment to Shakespeare. First the piece has been tailored to accord with the model of French neoclassical tragedy,[9] whereas Wilhelm's initial reading of Shakespeare had been in reaction to that model. Secondly, as Serlo points out, the new version does not require the audience to use their imagination. This he approves of, as he considers that any appeal to the imagination will make the audience's responses uncertain, a circumstance he is altogether unwilling to introduce into his theatre.[10] Though Serlo does not expound on this, no doubt he suspects such an appeal for it might loosen the hold he ideally wishes the stage to have over the spectator. Yet Shakespeare's plays first appealed to Wilhelm by their power to kindle his imagination, giving him both a greater sense of his individuality and a greater understanding of the world around him. His plays awoke in him 'a thousand feelings and abilities ... of which he had previously had no understanding nor presentiment'[11] and confirmed 'everything [he had] anticipated about mankind and its destiny'.[12] In the circumscribed world of the new *Hamlet*

---

[7] *Ibid.*, pp. 158–9.   [8] See chapter 4.
[9] Jane K. Brown, 'The Theatrical Mission of the *Lehrjahre*', in *Goethe's Narrative Fiction*, ed. William J. Lillyman (Berlin and New York, 1983), p. 75.
[10] *Goethes Werke*, ser. 1, vol. 22, p. 161.   [11] *Ibid.*, vol. 21, p. 299.   [12] *Ibid.*, p. 310.

adaptation, there is order and clarity; both audience and actors can feel at ease with the material as they are sure about what is happening. However, the potency and breadth of Shakespeare's original appeal to Wilhelm has been severely reduced.

But even in adaptation one aspect of Shakespeare's work has an intense, even a disturbing influence over the actor: this is his power of characterisation. In the course of the discussions on *Hamlet*, Wilhelm observes that the play approximates more to the novel than to the drama as Hamlet's lack of an assertive character retards rather than forwards the action. Shakespeare's hero, according to Wilhelm, does not have the substance that harnesses him to 'the fate that hurries humanity without their intervention through outwardly unconnected circumstances to an unforeseen catastrophe'.[13] In other words, the play lacks dramatic momentum and a sense of inevitability, features definitive of the dramaturgy of neoclassical tragedy.[14] Instead, Shakespeare's action, being comparatively unhurried, allows the audience to contemplate the action at their leisure and to concentrate more completely than they could do in neoclassical tragedy on the characters represented on stage. Whether this is desirable is questionable, for Shakespeare's characters, in contrast to those in the average drama of the time, are complete and lifelike. As they can embody corrupt as well as wholesome traits of personality, they can have a potentially degenerating effect both upon those who act them and, implicitly, on their audience too.

This is most clearly demonstrated through a rather bizarre chain of events. While the production of *Hamlet* is still being discussed, Aurelie, Serlo's sister, questions Wilhelm about Ophelia. Wilhelm quickly realises that she identifies his account of Ophelia's rejection by Hamlet with her own situation after she had been abandoned by her lover Lothario. Later Aurelie questions the propriety of Ophelia's songs during the mad-scenes: 'What do ribaldry and lewd stupidity have to do in the mouth of this noble maiden?' she asks.[15] Wilhelm justifies the songs as the expression of desires that had previously been hidden. At this moment, Serlo grabs a dagger lying on Aurelie's dressing-table, leading to a passionate confrontation between brother and sister. Serlo has associated the talk of Ophelia with Aurelie's suicidal tendencies arising from her abandonment; undoubtedly he feels that such matters should not be discussed, either on stage or off. At issue too is his unease at Aurelie using a dramatic character

[13] *Ibid.*, vol. 22, p. 178.
[14] A long discussion of the seemingly clear but ultimately deceptive differences between the drama and the novel can be found in chapter 5 of Eric A. Blackall's *Goethe and the Novel* (Ithaca and London, 1976).
[15] *Goethes Werke*, ser. 1, vol. 22, p. 91.

to express the pain of her betrayal.[16] It is clear that by the manner in which he had Aurelie die Goethe also found the identification of the actor with the character to be destructive. She dies from an illness caused by a further row between her and her brother, after she has frankly acted on stage the pain of another character who has suffered sexual betrayal, Orsina in Lessing's *Emilia Galotti*.

The personal identification of the actor with the role is especially possible in Shakespeare because of his exceptional powers of characterisation. Due to the leisurely course of his action, the character could draw more attention than the action itself. This has its dangers for it threatens to violate the boundary between the artificial world of art and the realm of private emotions. While art, from the humane viewpoint of the Enlightenment, should moderate any aberrant or excessive emotions, Shakespeare's characters would seem to activate, even feed them. Goethe confines his narrative to the influence of Shakespeare on the performer, but by implication the spectator can be affected too. This disturbing, visceral influence therefore contradicts the highest purpose of theatre as advocated by Wilhelm, that as a communal art it should help create a cohesive society by encouraging each class to respect the other and by arousing in the audience that 'fellow-feeling for all that is human'.[17] But through Shakespeare, the theatre seems to have a diametrically opposed function, as his plays are capable of feeding, perhaps even generating isolation and despair. They can also stimulate egotism. Though Wilhelm does not end his life like Hamlet, the irony is that he is in fact greatly prone to identify himself with a dramatic character and therefore to use the theatre to indulge himself rather than to achieve positive social change. His famous interpretation of Hamlet as a flawlessly noble and sensitive young man placed in a situation that is intolerable for him is flatteringly closer to his image of himself than to the more unpalatable original in Shakespeare's play. He only begins to move away from Hamlet and from the theatre as a whole when he comes to see himself as being different from his original perception of Hamlet.[18]

The issue of the performability of Shakespeare is never resolved, nor can we expect it to be. *Wilhelm Meisters Lehrjahre* is fiction not criticism, so

[16] A detailed description of the identity between Ophelia and Aurelie is provided by Mark Evan Bonds, 'Die Funktion des *Hamlet*-Motivs in *Wilhelm Meisters Lehrjahre*', *Goethe-Jahrbuch*, 96 (1979), 103–4.

[17] *Goethes Werke*, ser. 1, vol. 21, p. 165.

[18] For discussions of the relationship between Wilhelm and Hamlet, see Stefan Blessin, 'Die radikal-liberale Konzeption von *Wilhelm Meisters Lehrjahre*', *Deutsche Vierteljahrschrift für Literaturwissenschaft und Geistesgeschichte*, 49 (Sonderheft) (1975), esp. 200–4; Blackall, *Goethe and the Novel*, pp. 121–2; David Roberts, 'Wilhelm Meister and Hamlet: The Inner Structure of Book III of *Wilhelm Meisters Lehrjahre*', *Publications of the English Goethe Society*, ser. 2, 45 (1975), 64–100; and Clark S. Muenzer, *Figures of Identity: Goethe's Novels and the Enigmatic Self* (University Park and London, 1984), esp. pp. 55–9.

Wilhelm's dealings with Shakespeare and the theatre are indicative of his personal growth and development, not of a finished critical judgement by Goethe. Nevertheless, Goethe's ambivalent attitudes towards the suitability of Shakespeare in the theatre are pertinent as he held them persistently. They can be found virtually unchanged in the first and generally very different draft of the novel, *Wilhelm Meisters Theatralische Sendung* (*Wilhelm Meister's Theatrical Mission*), which dates from the 1780s but was not published in his lifetime. This draft was written soon after a vigorous and historic debate on Shakespeare and his importance to the German theatre and people had received a tremendous impetus through the writings of *Sturm und Drang*. Goethe had been a leading figure of this group. The theatre had been slow in responding to this debate, but when *Wilhelm Meisters Lehrjahre* was published in 1795 and 1796, Shakespeare's plays were coming to be seen more frequently than before on German stages. Few works of literature were more widely read in Germany during the first years of the nineteenth century than *Wilhelm Meisters Lehrjahre*,[19] and like all popular and important literature the novel both reflected and influenced public opinion. This suggests that Goethe's curious reticence over Shakespeare cannot be dismissed as mere idiosyncrasy. Indeed it may not implausibly be taken to articulate tastes and concerns over Shakespeare that were widely shared in Germany at that time.

SHAKESPEARE AND THE GERMAN ENLIGHTENMENT

Although severely eviscerated versions of Shakespeare's plays had been seen in Germany since the early seventeenth century, there is no evidence that his name was known there until 1682, when it was mentioned in passing in a handbook on poetry.[20] He did not, however, become the object of critical attention until 1741, when a translation of *Julius Caesar* was published, the first of his plays to appear complete in German translation. This occasioned a major dispute between the Leipzig literary historian and theoretician Johann Christoph Gottsched and the young critic and playwright Johann Elias Schlegel. One of Gottsched's ambitions was to create a native German drama of literary worth by having performed in popular theatres German plays modelled on the French neoclassical drama. Hence audiences in these popular theatres would have the opportunity of seeing drama previously seen only by the aristocracy in

---

[19] See the introduction to *Goethes Wilhelm Meister: Zur Rezeptionsgeschichte der Lehr- und Wanderjahre*, ed. Klaus F. Gille (Königstein, 1979) for a survey of the critical reception and the importance of the novel to German culture.

[20] D. G. Morhof, *Unterricht von der Teutschen Sprache* (Kiel, 1682). See Roy Pascal, ed., *Shakespeare in Germany, 1740–1815* (Cambridge, 1937), p. 37, for the single sentence in which he is mentioned.

the court theatres, at that time the only theatres with any pretensions to high culture in Germany. For Gottsched, therefore, drama was allowable only if it obeyed the three neoclassical unities: if the action followed the laws of probability, if by an elevated tone it encouraged audiences to admire the characters, and if it schooled those audiences to be obedient and virtuous. Tragic action, Gottsched insisted, should be 'capable of arousing pity and fear and stimulating in a moderate way one of the virtues from the emotions of the spectator'.[21] He could only understand the hold of the stage over the audience in absolutist terms, as the relationship of a superior over a subordinate, of a ruler over a subject, in which no freedom was allowed the latter to think for himself. For such a man, *Julius Caesar* was an abomination. The play did not follow the unities, nor did it possess a consistent, logical action that demonstrated the workings of reason and justified the legitimacy of any governmental authority. Above all, Shakespeare offended neoclassical decorum by placing admirable and heroic figures in circumstances that demeaned their status, 'the most foolish scenes of labourers and rabble' being set next to 'the greatest Roman heroes who speak of the most important affairs of state'.[22]

Gottsched's objections were answered by J. E. Schlegel, who, in comparing *Julius Caesar* with a play by Andreas Gryphius, achieved the crucial insight that Shakespeare could not be judged by the same criteria as the French neoclassicists as his priorities were different. Whereas in the French drama character was subordinated to action and moral purpose, in Shakespeare character predominated. His plays were 'more imitations of persons than imitations of a certain action'.[23] The play was given unity by the inner life of the characters and their relationships, not by the formal observation of the neoclassical unities. Schlegel also observed that Shakespeare created characters more from his own imagination than from historical documents. This gave his drama a human reality that was a welcome alternative to the wooden characters of Gryphius and, though he does not state it explicitly, of the contemporary German dramatists of Gottsched's school. Schlegel was not entirely independent of Gottsched's neoclassical tastes. He too deplored the mixture of high and low in *Julius Caesar* and found Shakespeare's language to be 'bombastic'. But his key observation on the importance of character in Shakespeare's plays was to have major repercussions in future dramatic criticism.

[21] Johann Christoph Gottsched, *Versuch einer critischen Dichtkunst, Ausgewählte Werke*, 11 vols. (Berlin and New York, 1973), vol. 6, pt. 2, p. 318.
[22] Gottsched, 'Anmerkungen über das 592 Stück des *Zuschauers*' (1742), in *Shakespeare-Rezeption. Die Diskussion um Shakespeare in Deutschland*, ed. Hansjürgen Blinn (Berlin, 1982), vol. 1, p. 62.
[23] Johann Elias Schlegel, 'Vergleichung Shakespears und Andreas Gryphs', *Ausgewählte Werke* (Weimar, 1963), p. 462.

Gottsched's influence over German literature declined as the Franco-phone culture of the courts lost its appeal for German writers, even though this culture continued as a powerful influence in Germany until well into the nineteenth century. Its pre-eminence was challenged by a rising middle class that used models from English and national German literature to give its own literature identity. Shakespeare was a pivotal figure in this change. An early stimulus to the rise of this culture was the publication in German translation between 1739 and 1743 of the complete run of Addison's *Spectator*, which included discussions of Shakespeare's genius and essays arguing that knowledge of the world was more important for a writer than skill at following the rules of neoclassical drama. Individual writers such as the Swiss Johann Bodmer cited English writers, including 'Saspar' (Shake-speare), to show that the imagination had a vital function in literary production.[24] The physician Albrecht von Haller conducted an extensive commentary on Shakespeare whom he regarded as 'a great and powerful exceptional figure in the history of poetry',[25] with deep knowledge of the human condition. He established an opposition between Shakespeare and Voltaire, favouring 'the natural audacity and greatness of the old Englishman against the polite and academic manners and oratory of Voltaire'. But only in the 1750s did Shakespeare become a subject for vigorous discussion, first in periodicals,[26] and then in the writings of those involved in the evolution of a German culture independent of the French-oriented courts.

Most prominent of these were the Berlin essayists, Lessing, Nicolai and Moses Mendelssohn, who edited a number of literary periodicals that did much to develop critical insights into contemporary literature.[27] One of the most famous of their articles, written by Lessing in 1759, rejected Gottsched's theatre by arguing that 'the great, the terrible, [and] the melancholic', all characteristics of the English drama, were more to German taste than 'the pretty, the tender, [and] the amorous', which were considered typical of the French.[28] In a later article, Lessing commented on how Shakespeare's characters speak nobly as neoclassical heroes do, while using the commonest of words as neoclassical heroes do not.[29] In

---

[24] Johann Jakob Bodmer, Preface to *Von dem Wunderbaren in der Poesie*, extracted in Pascal, *Shakespeare in Germany*, p. 37.

[25] Karl S. Guthke, 'Hallers Shakespeare-Bild', *Seminar*, 6, 2 (1970), 103.

[26] Several of the ideas of the major essayists of the later 1750s and 1760s were anticipated in lesser known, earlier periodicals. See Blinn, *Diskussion*, pp. 15–21.

[27] For a summary of the Shakespearean criticism of these three writers, see Eva J. Engel, 'Lessing, Christoph Friedrich Nicolai and Moses Mendelssohn: Advocates of Shakespeare', in *Lessing and the Enlightenment*, ed. Alexej Ugrinsky (Westport, Conn., 1986), pp. 25–34.

[28] Gotthold Ephraim Lessing, 'Literaturbriefe I. 17. Brief', in *Werke*, 8 vols. (Munich, 1973), vol. 5, p. 71.

[29] Lessing, *Werke*, vol. 5, p. 184.

Shakespeare, noble heroes do not appear as in neoclassical tragedy, in trappings that give them an aura of grandeur and invincibility.

These comments added a political dimension to the theme of character, which had originated in Schlegel's essay and had, to that point, been the over-riding concern in discussions of Shakespeare. Nicolai, for example, deplored the bad taste of the popular drama and the dryness of Gottsched's remedy for it, arguing that to solve both problems the German writer should study character in the real world and take Shakespeare as his model.[30] Shakespeare dealt with the reality of human experience in contrast to the idealised world of French drama. His insights into human nature were considered to be so penetrating that he gave to theatre an eminence that raised it above other humanistic disciplines. 'A Shakespeare', Mendelssohn wrote, 'has realised the causes, consequences and effects of jealousy in a splendid play [*Othello*?] better, more accurately and more completely than such material has been treated in all schools of worldly wisdom.'[31] Mendelssohn also praised Shakespeare's ability to exercise the imagination of his audience so they do not notice inconsistencies in plot and whether the unities are being followed or not.[32]

This line of critical thinking, characteristic of the German Enlightenment, came to fruition with the publication in 1769 of the *Hamburgische Dramaturgie* (*Hamburg Dramaturgy*), essays written by Lessing as a commentary on plays staged during the short-lived Hamburg national theatre project. As there were no plays by Shakespeare in the repertoire, he had no opportunity to write direct critical expositions on him, but he often used him as a foil, demonstrating how his play-world is more authentic and complete than that of neoclassical drama. He compares Voltaire's use of the ghost in *Semiramis* to the ghost in *Hamlet*, observing how Shakespeare carefully recreates all the conditions in which we normally expect ghosts to appear, so that while our reason tells us ghosts do not exist, its appearance strikes us as being quite natural. Voltaire, however, who wishes to avoid such popular associations, has his ghost appear among several people in broad daylight, which renders it laughable. A more arresting critical insight is Lessing's realisation that we are made afraid not so much by the circumstances as by Hamlet's reaction to the ghost. 'The ghost works on us', he wrote, 'more through [Hamlet] than by itself. The impression it makes on him passes on to us and the effect is too evident and strong for us

---

[30] Friedrich Nicolai, 'Briefe über den itzigen Zustand der schönen Wissenschaften in Deutschland', in Blinn, *Diskussion*, pp. 63–7.

[31] Moses Mendelssohn, from his review of Lowth's *De sacra poesi Hebraeorum; praelectiones academicae Oxonii habitae* (1757) in *Auseinandersetzung mit Shakespeare*, ed. Wolfgang Stellmacher (Berlin, 1976), p. 58.

[32] Moses Mendelssohn, 'Briefe, die neueste Litteratur betreffend', in Stellmacher, *Auseinandersetzung*, p. 59.

to doubt its supernatural origins.'[33] But Voltaire never learnt to speak to the audience through the character's experience, which Lessing sees as the essential line of communication between dramatist and spectator. In comparing studies of jealousy in Voltaire's *Orosman* and *Othello*, Lessing observes that Orosman commits a deed of jealousy but does not learn what jealousy is, as Voltaire is concerned solely with mechanics of plot. But *Othello* provides 'a complete manual of this dismal madness; in it we can learn everything that concerns it, awakens it and by which it may be avoided'.[34]

Shakespeare led Lessing to a view of theatre fundamentally different from Gottsched's. Gottsched could only see the stage as a stern mentor of its audience, Lessing perceived a more equal relationship. He did not deny the moral improvement theatre could achieve, but saw it as being effectuated by the spectator's attempt to understand the characters, his experience of the play being equivalent to his understanding of those characters' inner worlds. In this humane theatre, the spectator extended his knowledge of the world outside himself. Shakespeare more than any other dramatist could expand those horizons because his understanding of human nature was so comprehensive that one can feel compassion even for his blackest villains. In this way he appeared as a typical figure of the Enlightenment, for he widened the knowledge of all who knew his plays. Gottsched gave the spectator no freedom, but Shakespeare seemed to Lessing to do precisely that. Gottsched did not offer the audiences material that reflected their own lives; neither strictly speaking did Shakespeare, but his characterisation provided an important model to the German writers of domestic drama, whose plays depended strongly on character and among whom Lessing was the most distinguished. Furthermore, the eminence of Shakespeare in England, where he was regarded as the national dramatist, made him an exemplary figure for those seeking to create a German national drama, independent of aristocratic courts. In Shakespeare the interests of the rising middle class and German nationalism were united.[35]

Enthusiasm for Shakespeare was not, however, unqualified. Even the most sympathetic critics found shortcomings in his work, particularly when, by disturbing portrayals of character or breaches of decorum and good taste, it threatened to arouse disruptive emotions in the audience. The mixture of modes, first identified by Gottsched, upset even the most enthusiastic advocates such as Haller, who felt he had committed 'errors' in his predilection for 'strong images, bloody deaths and powerful emotions'.[36] Indeed, mid-eighteenth-century critics continually reproved

---

[33] Gotthold Ephraim Lessing, *Hamburgische Dramaturgie*, in *Werke*, vol. 4, p. 284.
[34] *Ibid.*, 4, p. 300.
[35] Eva Maria Inbar, 'Shakespeare-Rezeption im deutschen bürgerlichen Drama des 18. Jahrhunderts', *Germanische–Romanische Monatsschrift*, n.s. 30, 2 (1980), 133.
[36] Guthke, 'Hallers Shakespeare-Bild', p. 98.

Shakespeare for his love of violent action and emotions. They could only explain it away by arguing that he had had to appeal to audiences that had less cultivated tastes and were more barbaric than those of their own time.

No writer more typifies these mixed attitudes towards Shakespeare than the poet Christoph Martin Wieland. Wieland's first acquaintance with Shakespeare probably occurred in 1755 when he was studying in Zürich under Bodmer. Although Wieland soon freed himself from Bodmer's influence, the enthusiasm for Shakespeare he had inherited from him endured. This led him in 1757 to write a highly perceptive essay on the plays' peculiar quality, 'Theorie und Geschichte der Red-Kunst und Dicht-Kunst' ('Theory and History of Rhetoric and Poetry'). Wieland's essay had no impact at the time, for it was delivered solely to a small class of schoolboys he was teaching,[37] but it represents the formulation of ideas he was to repeat in later essays and suggests why he would embark on the first attempt to translate the plays into German. Wieland found Shakespeare's work distinguished by the depth of his knowledge of human behaviour. No one understood so well 'the small world' of 'the human heart'.[38] He prized Shakespeare too for his originality and his dependence solely upon 'nature'. 'Nature was the only source from which he created. His genius was his only muse and his poetry was ... in actuality inspiration.' However, Wieland did not see the plays as wild, asocial manifestations. By 'genius' he meant Shakespeare's ability to be true to nature while observing the laws of beauty: 'although in him everything is unalloyed nature, yet he knows how to beautify his characters in such a way that the resemblance does not do the slightest damage'. This moderation led Wieland to praise Shakespeare as a poet whose art both morally improves and elevates his audience. 'No one', Wieland wrote, 'has better known and better expressed moral beauty, sublimity, decency [and] kindness in sentiments and moral dealings than he.'

Such perceptions are important as a bridge between the tastes of the mid-eighteenth century and later decades. On the question of Shakespeare and the neoclassical unities, the wearisome bugbear of all conservative critics, Wieland was more original. He declared that Shakespeare could have observed the unities had he wished, but he did not care to. This insight led Wieland away from the generally held assumption that the stage must create as total an illusion of reality as possible. Instead, he argued that the artificiality of the stage should be accepted and the playwright be allowed freedom in his choice of place, his use of time, and his construction of the

---

[37] In fact its existence only became known in 1908. See Jeffrey B. Gardiner and Albert R. Schmitt, 'Christoph Martin Wieland: "Theorie und Geschichte der Red-Kunst und Dicht-Kunst. Anno 1757"'. An Early Defense of Shakespeare', *Lessing Yearbook* 5 (1973), 219–41.

[38] Christoph Martin Wieland, 'Theorie und Geschichte der Red-Kunst und Dicht-Kunst', in Blinn, *Diskussion*, p. 68.

action. The spectators, Wieland reasoned, would not be disturbed by this, for 'they can never forget that they are in the theatre, and even if the liveliness of the action does make them forget it for a few minutes, there are hundreds of small circumstances that remind them of it again'.[39]

Unfortunately Wieland did not pursue this line of thinking any further nor was he to do so in subsequent essays. If he had, he might have found an aesthetic to oppose the theory of the theatre as an illusionistic medium which dominated the thinking of his time and of the century to follow and was to have a fundamental influence on the way Shakespeare was staged. Instead, he retreated into common complaints about Shakespeare that threatened to contradict his positive statements. While he was happy about the playwright's treatment of place and time, he was less sanguine when it comes to freedom of genre or tone. He censured Shakespeare for 'mixing several comic scenes into his tragedies', taking him to task for 'all sorts of trifling *jeux d'esprits*, plays upon words and even vulgar jokes', evidence of a deplorable necessity to appeal to the 'ruling taste of the time and the lower portion of the parterre'.[40] This shows Wieland to have been aware of the work of art as a product of a certain time and place, but the distinctly moralistic bias of his remarks, characteristic of his time, tend to deprive his observations of significance. In the following year, he was to rationalise these reservations about Shakespeare in what has become his most frequently quoted comment on the subject: 'His beauties are for all nations and times, his mistakes are the mistakes of his time.'[41] Ultimately Wieland, like several of his contemporaries, was divided in his response to Shakespeare. He sensed in him a writer who challenged neoclassicism forcefully, but he was not prepared to assimilate fully the whole range of his *œuvre*.

Throughout his life in occasional essays and comments Wieland restated, often in more detail, the themes of the early 'Theorie' and occasionally showed that he could appreciate the mixed nature of Shakespeare's work. For example, he argued in favour of the coexistence of tragic and comic elements in the same character, as this is how people are in life.[42] He also showed himself capable of fine discrimination in discussing character. A detailed analysis of Lady Macbeth's mention of her father during the murder of Duncan indicates that Wieland was aware of the subtlety of Shakespeare's dramatic expression, for he made Lady Macbeth human and therefore as sympathetic to her audience as she is evil.[43] He also achieved an interesting insight into the creative process of the playwright. In one of his

[39] *Ibid.*, p. 69.   [40] *Ibid.*, p. 70.
[41] Wieland, 'An W. D. Sulzer', in Stellmacher, *Auseinandersetzung*, p. 64.
[42] Wieland, *Agathon*, extracted in Pascal, *Shakespeare in Germany*, p. 53.
[43] Wieland, 'Über eine Stelle in Shakespears *Macbeth*', in Blinn, *Diskussion*, pp. 145–7.

last major statements, he claimed Shakespeare's characters are unique because their creator possessed 'the gift to change himself into every character, to place himself in every situation and passion'.[44] In the same work, he continued to be enthusiastic about Shakespeare's spontaneous creation from the sources of nature and expanded on his refusal to follow the unities, drawing a rich parallel between theatre and architecture. 'Shakespeare's works', he wrote, 'contrast to regular tragedy . . . like Milan Cathedral or Westminster Abbey do to Greek temples or the façade of Strassburg Cathedral to the façade of the Louvre.'[45] The reference to the Gothic which follows this indicates that Wieland had been strongly influenced by the *Sturm und Drang* writers, who were more uncompromising in their admiration of Shakespeare.

SHAKESPEARE AND STURM UND DRANG

A full and unapologetic understanding of Shakespeare's plays first came in the 1770s with the *Sturm und Drang* writers, who idolised Shakespeare as a genius whose mighty creations provided a model that could free German drama and literature from the restraints of neoclassicism. More decisively than Lessing and his associates, *Sturm und Drang* wished to break with neoclassical values and with the social hierarchy those values enshrined. They prized Shakespeare above all other writers precisely because his plays seemed to defy neoclassical forms and violate tastes for whatever was French in literature and theatre. At the same time, his influence was not solely iconoclastic; it had a more lasting value in that *Sturm und Drang* writers were drawn to analyse the specific means by which the impact of the plays had been achieved. This resulted in a major body of Shakespearean criticism, representing the first phase in an outbreak of Shakespeare-worship in Germany that has rarely if ever been equalled elsewhere. Through the flood of writings that resulted, Shakespeare came to be assimilated as the 'third German classic writer' after Goethe and Schiller,[46] whose work has had as great an influence as that of the first two on subsequent German drama.[47]

One important work of English criticism prepared the ground for *Sturm und Drang*'s encounter with Shakespeare, Edward Young's celebrated essay *Conjectures on Original Composition*, which had been translated into German in 1760, only a year after its initial publication in England. Young's essay

[44] Wieland, 'Briefe an einen jungen Dichter', in Blinn, *Diskussion*, p. 159.

[45] Blinn, *Diskussion*, p. 160.

[46] Ulrich Suerbaum, 'Der deutsche Shakespeare', in *Festschrift Rudolf Stamm*, ed. Eduard Kolb and Jörg Hasler (Berne and Munich, 1969), p. 61.

[47] For a summary of this influence, see Horst Oppel, 'Shakespeare in Deutschland', *Englisch–deutsche Literaturbeziehungen*, 1 (1971), 98–125.

was not entirely original,[48] but he posited more clearly than other critics had done a fruitful distinction between two types of writer, the imitator who copies and the genius who creates from his boundless imagination. Young endowed this genius with seemingly mystical qualities; in possessing 'the power of accomplishing great things without the means generally reputed necessary to that end', the genius projects the illusion that he 'partake[s] of something divine'.[49] Shakespeare, a 'star of the first magnitude', exemplified such genius; his lack of learning and ignorance of conventional dramatic forms, Young claimed, were virtues for they allowed his instincts and imagination total freedom. Young's Shakespeare was attractive to the writers of *Sturm und Drang*, who were searching for a literature that did not repeat given forms.

Young's thought had a substantial influence over the most important critical statement made on Shakespeare in the late 1760s, *Briefe über Merkwürdigkeiten der Literatur* (*Letters on Notabilities in Literature*), written by Heinrich von Gerstenberg between 1766 and 1770. The twenty-six letters cover a broad range of foreign and German writers, but the five that discuss Shakespeare had the most impact. Like Young, Gerstenberg wrote that Shakespeare did not create from artificial models, but from nature – 'this darling genius of maternal nature',[50] he called him. Unlike Young, however, Gerstenberg saw *how* Shakespeare's 'genius' led him to original form and he defined that form. Shakespeare, he argued, was not properly appreciated because he was judged by critical principles that applied to Greek drama. The Greeks, he claimed, aimed to manipulate the passions, but Shakespeare was concerned instead to represent life in all its fullness. This means his plays are not conventional 'tragedies' and 'comedies', but are 'living pictures of moral nature'.[51]

Gerstenberg's phrase had historic resonance. First the idea of a play as picture challenged the neoclassical assumption that drama involves the rigorous and rational unfolding of an action that holds its audience by manipulating its responses. In contrast, Shakespeare's plays, having the amplitude of pictures, exercise a different influence. Gerstenberg explained this in a comparison of *Othello* with *The Revenge*, a tragedy by Young, who was not as successful a dramatist as he was a critic. Young, Gerstenberg explains, arouses feelings of jealousy in the audience by making them feel

---

[48] Several of his insights into Shakespeare, for example, were taken from Dryden, Pope and Addison, among other critics. See Alois Brandl, 'Edward Young: *On Original Composition*: Ein Beitrag zur Geschichte der Shakespeare-Kritik im achtzehnten Jahrhundert', *Shakespeare-Jahrbuch*, 39 (1903), 2–3.

[49] Edward Young, *Complete Works: Poetry and Prose*, ed. James Nichols (Hildesheim, 1968), p. 556.

[50] Heinrich Wilhelm von Gerstenberg, *Briefe über Merkwürdigkeiten der Literatur*, ed. Alexander von Weilen (Heilbronn, 1890), p. 121.

[51] *Ibid.*, p. 113.

they are being actively worked upon by the dramatic situation; Shake-speare, however, explores the phenomenon of jealousy, examining its operations in the individual and how the situation works upon him. The drama occurs outside the spectators and even though they are drawn into it, it is separate from them, and they remain aware of this in the same way that they are aware a picture is separate. The unity of the picture comes through the play's action. In *Richard II* and the Henry IV plays, for example, the action is the destruction of the King and everything in these apparently sprawling works relates to this. 'I see throughout', wrote Gerstenberg, 'a distinct whole that has beginning, middle and end, proportion, design, contrasting characters and contrasting groups.'[52] Each element throws light on other elements. Consequently, in *Henry IV Part 1*, Hal's wildness throws 'that much more splendid a light' on Hotspur's bravery, while Hal's final heroism is more striking in the light of his earlier debauchery. Gerstenberg sustains his description of the plays as pictures, regarding them as 'a pictorial unity in design and composition, to which all proportions have a correct relation, and which indicates an order'.[53] The meaning of the play can only be grasped once its form has been understood.

The second part of Gerstenberg's historic phrase, 'moral nature', meant that Shakespeare did not reproduce surface appearances of nature, but explored what has been called 'a higher artistic reality and truth'.[54] This highlights the motives of characters and places them in the context of a larger whole. Like J.E. Schlegel, Gerstenberg found the plays to be 'imitations of persons', not actions, and like Schlegel he paid bountiful tribute to Shakespeare's ability to see into the depths of human behaviour. This is complemented invaluably by his unparalleled mastery of language, which enabled him to reproduce exactly the characteristic speech of all classes and professions. Shakespeare's plays truly represent 'humanity! the world! everything!'[55]

Gerstenberg's analysis refined earlier critics' thinking on Shakespeare and was original in defining the specific form of the plays, independently of conventional theories of genre. What is most striking about the analysis is how it discovers in Shakespeare a larger whole that is less uniform and closer to life as it is lived than is the tightly enclosed world of neoclassical drama. So far, even the most sympathetic of critics had deplored Shake-speare's mixture of comic and pathetic. But Gerstenberg welcomed it as it was close to life and dramatically effective. In *King Lear* he found that the Fool aroused acute pity, in *Hamlet* he considered the grave-diggers'

---

[52] *Ibid.*, p. 161.   [53] *Ibid.*, p. 163.
[54] Karl S. Guthke, 'Richtungskonstanten in der deutschen Shakespeare-deutung des 18. Jahrhunderts', *Shakespeare-Jahrbuch*, 98 (1962), 71.
[55] Gerstenberg, *Briefe*, p. 112.

speeches to intensify, not impair, the tragic impact, while the witches in *Macbeth* filled him with horror, not ridicule. Gerstenberg thought himself into Shakespeare's world and discovered strengths where previous writers had found imperfections.

His understanding of Shakespeare was not flawless. For example, after having dismissed the idea of genre classification, he unaccountably reverted to it, and, without any sense of the speech's irony, used Polonius's classification of genres to pigeonhole rather inaccurately the complete canon by the categories of tragedy, history (including all the Roman plays), comedy, pastoral, pastoral–comical, and pastoral–historical (*Love's Labour's Lost*). Also the two plays he subjected to detailed analysis, *The Merry Wives of Windsor* and *The Comedy of Errors*, are the least suited of all to demonstrate the dramaturgy he had identified. Moreover, following another English critic, Lord Kames,[56] he showed an intolerance for Shakespeare's word-play. Even though he understood how widespread the practice of punning was at the time, he could only accept it in the 'worst and drollest parts' of the play.[57] So, while his general understanding of Shakespeare went beyond that of his contemporaries, in details Gerstenberg was still a man of his age.

Boundless enthusiasm for Shakespeare was a definitive feature of *Sturm und Drang*. This school, which made the first sustained attempt to find an identity for German literature, originated during the brief but momentous association of Goethe, Herder and other young writers in Strassburg during the early 1770s. For them, freedom of expression and action were over-riding priorities, so they idolised great men who seemed capable of acting without restraint.[58] Consequently the idea of Shakespeare as a genius, creating from a limitless imagination and disdaining imitation of conventional form, had a potent appeal to them.

Goethe first read Shakespeare's plays in extracts when he was a student in Leipzig in 1767, but only when he became acquainted with Herder, who encouraged him to read them in English, did he discover their full range.[59] They were soon the central reading of the group of writers who formed the core of *Sturm und Drang*. As Goethe recalled in his autobiography,

---

[56] Lord Kames (Henry Home) was best known for his popular *Elements of Criticism*, published in 1762 and translated into German between 1762 and 1766. Although Kames had a sound appreciation of Shakespeare's depiction of passion, his literal mind could not make sense of the elaborate metaphors. The influence of Kames on Gerstenberg's thinking seems to contradict that of Young.

[57] Gerstenberg, *Briefe*, pp. 126–7.

[58] See chapter 5 of Roy Pascal's *The German Sturm und Drang* (Manchester, 1953) for a full discussion of *Sturm und Drang*'s idea of 'the creative personality'.

[59] Albert Leitzmann, 'Dodds' *Beauties of Shakespeare* als Quelle für Goethe und Herder', *Shakespeare-Jahrbuch*, 55 (1919), 59.

> In our Strassburg society, Shakespeare, translated and in the original, in fragments and as a whole, in passages and extracts, worked his influence on us so that in the same way that men come to know the Bible, we came to know Shakespeare, imitating in our conversations the strengths and failings of his time, with which he had made us familiar, taking the greatest joy in his quibbles and competing with him through translating them with original audacity.[60]

Here, for the first time, were German writers and critics willing to accept the works as they are, finding stimulus even in their 'errors'. From their reading grew a vastly expanded vision of Shakespeare as 'genius' that was to have a widespread influence on German thought and was best expressed in three famous essays that resulted from those intense discussions of Shakespeare.

The earliest of these may have been Goethe's speech 'Zum Shakespeares-Tag' (On Shakespeare's Day'), though it was not published until 1854.[61] This intense articulation of *Sturm und Drang* bardolatry was delivered during a festivity in honour of Shakespeare at the Goethe family house in October 1771, modelled on similar festivities arranged by Garrick in Stratford in 1769. This was not an occasion for objective assessment, and the speech, as Friedrich Gundolf has pointed out, is more an expression of Goethe's own youthful dilemmas and ambitions than a piece of criticism.[62] But as the limitations and values Goethe considered Shakespeare to have freed him from are those of contemporary neoclassical and rococo literature, his comments can be taken as having national resonance and as being representative of what Shakespeare meant to *Sturm und Drang*.

The most striking aspect of Shakespeare's impact is the limitless energy Goethe considered he gave him. He recalls his first reading of Shakespeare as a significant moment of growth:

> The first page I read of him made me his own for the rest of my life, and as I finished the first play I stood like one who has been blind from birth being given the gift of sight by a miraculous hand. I understood, I felt in the liveliest way how my existence extended to infinity, everything was new to me, unknown, and the unaccustomed light hurt my eyes.[63]

This led Goethe to reject the unities as fetters on the imagination and to see French tragedies as nothing but self-parodies, 'as like each other as shoes'. He had neither the inclination nor, perhaps, the capacity to define how Shakespeare's plays differ from the French, but he conceived of them as a

---

[60] *Dichtung und Wahrheit*, *Goethes Werke*, ser. 1, vol. 28, pp. 74–5.

[61] Ernst Beutler, 'Goethe und Shakespeare', in *Goethes Rede zum Schäkespears Tag* (Weimar, 1938), p. 19.

[62] Friedrich Gundolf, *Shakespeare und der deutsche Geist*, 8th edn (Berlin, 1927), pp. 223–8.

[63] 'Zum Shakespeares-Tag', *Goethes Werke*, ser. 1, vol. 12, pp. 224–5.

linear aggregation of events, 'a beautiful peepshow in which the history of the world floats past on the invisible threads of time'. The only unity he saw was that each play centres around 'the secret point, that no philosopher has yet seen or determined, in which the individuality of our ego, the pretended freedom of our will, collides with the necessary course of the whole'.[64] While this view is limiting and inaccurate,[65] for Goethe it gave the plays a special importance.

Important, too, was Goethe's sense of the wholeness of Shakespeare's characters. He did not analyse any characters in detail or make the issue of characterisation prominent, but he identified characters with nature as if they had been created independently of any concern for the conventional theatre: 'Nature! Nature!' was his famous exclamation, 'no people so close to Nature as Shakespeare's!'. Here was the true appeal of Shakespeare for both Goethe and *Sturm und Drang*; 'Shakespeare's theatre gave them an exhibition of the whole of human nature, gave completeness in the description of life.'[66] The idea of Shakespeare as the creator of a whole world from his own imagination encouraged Goethe to compare him to Prometheus, which led him to a momentous conclusion. Lessing, Wieland and even Gerstenberg had tried to reconcile Shakespeare with the idea, shared with Gottsched, of theatre promoting the moral betterment of the audience. Goethe's Shakespeare, however, confounded the assumptions on which betterment can be achieved, as his plays demonstrate the inter-dependence, not the mutual exclusiveness of good and evil.

> What noble philosophers have said about the world is also true of Shakespeare's, that whatever we call evil is only the other side of good, which is necessary to its existence, and belongs to the whole.[67]

Shakespearean drama does not morally regulate the audience, but opens to them the multiplicity of the world, demonstrating the fallacy rather than the validity of accepted moral perceptions.[68] The ultimate implication of Goethe's speech is that Shakespeare's plays can further the audience's growth through expanding their understanding of the world but without insisting that such growth occur within a moral framework. They can free the audience to think independently of an inherited moral system. Not a trace of Gottschedian moralism can be discovered in Goethe's vision of Shakespeare-Prometheus.

[64] *Ibid.*, p. 226.   [65] Kurt Ermann, *Goethes Shakespeare-Bild* (Tübingen, 1983), p. 47.

[66] Walter F. Schirmer, 'Shakespeare und der junge Goethe', *Publications of the English Goethe Society*, 17 (1947), 36.

[67] *Goethes Werke*, ser. 1, vol. 12, p. 227.

[68] For a discussion of the influence of Spinoza on Goethe's thought in this regard see Ursula Wertheim, 'Philosophische und ästhetische Aspekte in Prosastücken Goethes über Shakespeare', *Goethe*, 26 (1964), 54–76.

Herder, some five years older than Goethe, had had more time to assimilate Shakespeare's work and view it more objectively. His knowledge of Shakespeare dated back to 1764 when he had studied *Hamlet* in the original. His interest in him arose mainly from his fascination with folk-poetry, the imagery of which he considered to be the original language of the human race. Shakespeare, as he read in Dr Johnson's edition of the plays and in the commentary of Joseph Warton, constructed his plays mainly from folk-songs and ballads, and he appealed to his countrymen because he worked from popular sources unique to England. Also from Percy's *Reliques*, published in Germany in 1771, and from Theobold, Herder acquired the idea that Shakespeare, like Homer, had been handed down through the generations and that the First Folio represented 'many scattered fragments culled from all kinds of sources'.[69]

Herder's version of the genesis and transmission of Shakespeare's works obviously was not accurate. Despite this, Gundolf was probably right when he wrote of Herder's great essay on Shakespeare that 'nothing more profound or comprehensive on Shakespeare's total poetic condition has been written'.[70] Certainly Herder elevated Shakespeare to a cultural importance unprecedented in German, possibly even in English critical thought. Published in 1773 in a collection that included his own essay on folk-poetry and Goethe's essay on Strassburg Minster, Herder's 'Shakespeare' was not an apologetics for his work and it vigorously rebutted all neoclassical objections. As these rebuttals arose from a thoroughly worked out theory of the origins of popular art, they were especially effective. They also provided a theoretical basis for the criticism of both Goethe and Gerstenberg, of which Herder must have been aware as he had considered sending a version of the essay to Gerstenberg for publication in the *Briefe*.[71]

Herder began by hailing Shakespeare as a titan, 'sitting high on a rocky summit! at his feet tempests, thunderstorms and the tumult of the sea; but his head in the rays of heaven'.[72] He hoped to set this mighty figure in a clearer light, by explaining the semi-divine nature of the true artist, whose ability to recreate the world in his own image is the fullest realisation of human potential and proof of his godlike qualities.[73] His vision of the artist was a mighty aggrandisement of Edward Young's.[74]

[69] Gillies, A. 'Herder's Essay on Shakespeare: *Das Herz der Untersuchung*', *Modern Language Review*, 32 (1937), 269.

[70] Gundolf, *Shakespeare und der deutsche Geist*, p. 211.

[71] Rudolf Haym, *Herder* (Berlin, 1958), pp. 457–8. The three different versions of the Shakespeare essay, only the last of which was published, are discussed by Hertha Isaacsen in *Der junge Herder und Shakespeare* (Berlin, 1930), pp. 23–40.

[72] Johann Gottfried Herder, 'Shakespeare', *Werke*, 2 vols. (Munich, n.d. [1953]), vol. 1, p. 875.

[73] Fritz Blättner, 'Das Shakespeare-Bild Herders', in *Vom Geist der Dichtung*, ed. Fritz Martini (Hamburg, 1949), pp. 56–60.

[74] Hans Wolffheim (ed.), *Die Entdeckung Shakespeares* (Hamburg, 1959), pp. 53–4.

But however mystical the vision of the artist, Herder understood the development of art as a materialistic process. His research had convinced him that it does not arise solely from individual imagination, but that it grows as a natural phenomenon from popular experience, with the artist's mind as catalyst. Art evolves biologically within a given society. As it is therefore subject to the laws of nature and of its particular situation, any arbitrary critical principles, such as the neoclassical unities, have no validity. Art from different societies and ages can be understood only by criteria peculiar to them.

Herder demonstrated this by distinguishing between ancient Greek and Shakespearean drama. The unities, he argued, were essential in the Greek theatre because it originated in the dithyrambic chorus. All development evolved by the natural law of unity of place dictated by the presence of the chorus.

> From this origin certain things become clear, that otherwise one has to misunderstand terribly, looking on them as dead rules. That *simplicity of the Greek fable*, that *sobriety of Greek manners*, that *sustained formality of expression, music, setting, unity of place and time* – all this lay . . . naturally and essentially, without trickery and sorcery, in the origin of Greek tragedy . . . All this was the husk in which the seed grew.[75]

Shakespearean drama had no less natural origins, growing as it did from an established theatrical culture of 'history and marionette plays'. But Elizabethan society was not as simple as the Greeks', as it was composed of 'multifarious classes, customs, convictions, peoples and dialects', so while the Greek dramatist by nature of his upbringing and environment was concerned to demonstrate the unity of the world, Shakespeare demonstrated its diversity. 'Therefore he formed classes and human beings, peoples and dialects, the king and fools, fools and the king into a magnificent whole!' While the Greeks focused on a single action to reflect their society, Shakespeare's action was less tightly patterned. As Shakespeare's society was closer to his own, Herder found his plays to be more relevant than those of the Greeks.[76]

Herder had a sound sense of dramatic form about which he is fairly specific. Gerstenberg had described a play by Shakespeare as a 'picture', a term Herder used too. Goethe had described it as a 'peepshow' in which events followed one upon the other as in history. Herder, with his view of history as a biological process, agreed but also found a pattern in the action. The plays were biological entities in which the dramatic action grows from the seed of the opening scene. Of *King Lear* he wrote,

---

[75] Herder, *Werke*, vol. 1, p. 877.
[76] All the above quotations are from Herder, *Werke*, vol. 1, pp. 884–5.

the first scene of [Lear's] appearance already bears within it all the seeds of his fate through to the harvest of the darkest future. See! the kind-hearted squanderer, the impetuous, merciless man, the childish father will soon be in the courtyards of his daughters – pleading, praying, begging, cursing, raving, blessing – ah God! and foreboding madness.[77]

Herder did not comment on the character of Lear alone but demonstrated how the diverse strands of the play relate thematically to the central plot. All 'accidental circumstances, motives, characters and situations', the most disparate scenes are essential to the play as they intensify the feeling of overwhelming fate dominating the action. Herder saw nothing that should be excluded as everything is a function of the life that is the play.

Herder's essay on Shakespeare was an epochal event as it effectively challenged the neoclassical assumption that one set of rules was valid for all art. Consequently Shakespeare's failure to adhere to neoclassical models was no failure at all. Furthermore, the essay provided historical justification for radical critical discussions such as Gerstenberg's. Then, as Shakespeare, the 'interpreter of nature in all her tongues', was seen to represent all phases of a diverse society, the coexistence of tragedy and comedy was accounted for. Just as importantly, Herder explained why the need to adhere to neoclassical principles, resented by *Sturm und Drang*, was so imprisoning. If art developed biologically, then it was only free when allowed to grow naturally.

Herder's essay took an uncompromising stance against the prevalence of French neoclassical forms in the still dominant though now waning court cultures. He granted French drama elegance, beauty and the capacity to enlighten its audience, and appreciated it as a natural expression of a rigorously hierarchical society, but as it was now separated from its roots, its action and characters 'lack spirit, life, nature [and] truth'.[78] In contrast Shakespeare's drama seemed natural and vigorous. Through writings such as Herder's, neoclassical drama came to be seen as symbolic of an increasingly friable aristocratic culture, while Shakespeare's plays, though of an older date, appeared to embody a democratic spirit and natural energy that was powerfully antagonistic to this culture. Although the neoclassical hold on Germany was never completely loosened, writings such as Herder's Shakespeare essay provided a vital challenge to it.[79]

The third important *Sturm und Drang* essay, 'Anmerkungen übers Theater' ('Observations on the Theatre'), was by Jakob Lenz, one of the group's most promising playwrights. The essay was published in 1774 as a

---

[77] *Ibid.*, p. 886.   [78] *Ibid.*, p. 882.
[79] For a vigorous analysis of Herder's writings on Shakespeare from the Marxist point of view, see Wolfgang Stellmacher, *Herders Shakespeare-Bild: Shakespeare-Rezeption im Sturm und Drang. Dynamisches Weltbild und bürgerliches Nationaldrama* (Berlin, 1978).

preface to Lenz's translation of *Love's Labour's Lost*, though Lenz claimed that he had written it in Strassburg two years before the publication of Herder's essay, suggesting perhaps that some of Herder's ideas originated with him.[80] Stylistically, he was so close to Goethe that an early reviewer mistook both his essay and translation for Goethe's work. But in contrast to Goethe's then-unpublished Shakespeare speech, Lenz's writing lacks emotional directness. It does not have the exhilarating range of Herder's vision either. Lenz was also more concerned with practical theatre matters[81] and looked to Shakespeare to provide him with a dramaturgical model different from current ones.[82]

Naturally Lenz shared ideas with Goethe and Herder, especially on genius, which he saw as a godlike quality, as the ability to penetrate to the essence of things. He also shared their hatred of the French drama, which led to the major point of his essay. The classical dramatist, by whom he understood ancient Greek and French tragic writers, was concerned solely with what Aristotle had identified as action, which Lenz labels 'the fate of humanity'. Shakespeare, he felt, was concerned with humanity alone. While the classical dramatist, in subjecting his characters to a plot that reveals forces determining their behaviour, arouses 'blind and servile fear' in his audience, Shakespeare explored the essential humanity of his characters. In particular he examined great figures of history who have freed themselves from determining forces. So insistent is Lenz on the importance of the hero's autonomy in drama that it almost invalidated his view of Shakespeare. After all few of his plays, especially *Love's Labour's Lost* to which the essay is a preface, actually realise this theme, and even *Coriolanus*, which Lenz partially translated, ends with a conspicuous demonstration of how the hero is determined by the external world. Such an all-consuming concern is neither the central point of Shakespeare nor of Lenz's own plays.[83]

Nevertheless, Lenz's essay was important, above all for his insistence that Shakespeare shows not the beautiful side of nature but human beings as they actually are. More than any other critic he prepared the way for a realistic theatre.[84] His essay argued that Shakespeare humanised heroism, as even his most exalted characters are human beings, without the trappings of neoclassicism to surround them in an aura of infallibility and invincibi-

---

[80] The issue is discussed by Eva Maria Inbar in *Shakespeare in Deutschland: Der Fall Lenz* (Tübingen, 1982), pp. 19–23.

[81] Hans-Gunther Schwarz, 'Lenz und Shakespeare', *Shakespeare-Jahrbuch* (Heidelberg, 1971), 86.

[82] Inbar, *Lenz*, p. 31.

[83] René Girard, *Lenz, 1751–1792: Genèse d'une dramaturgie du tragi-comique* (Paris, 1968), pp. 163–74.

[84] Schwarz, 'Lenz und Shakespeare', p. 87.

lity. More than any other *Sturm und Drang* writer, Lenz put the theme of Shakespeare as a master of characterisation to radical use.

> His speech is the speech of the bravest genius, uprooting earth and heaven, giving expression to the thoughts flooding from him. Equally conversant, equally strong in each human relationship, he raised a stage for the whole human race, where everyone stands, is amazed, is joyful, can find themselves, from the highest to the lowest. His kings and queens are as little restrained as the lowest rabble, feeling warm blood in their beating hearts, or giving vent to their bile in roguish jokes, for they too are human beneath the crinoline, know no vapours, do not die before our eyes in idle formulae, do not know the well-being of death.[85]

In one way, there is little difference between this and Gottsched's criticism, except that what Gottsched regarded as the greatest evil of Shakespeare's work is here seen by Lenz as its greatest strength.

SHAKESPEARE: 'THE RUINS OF A COLOSSUS'

The discussion of Shakespeare in *Wilhelm Meisters Lehrjahre* indicates that Goethe's views on Shakespeare underwent considerable tempering as he grew older. Wilhelm's first experience of Shakespeare is similar to that of his creator, but when it comes to staging him, he encounters problems, which reflect the wider problems of the German theatre. First, with most serious theatre in the hands of the aristocracy, it was difficult to find any substantial patron prepared to sponsor a performance. Frederick the Great possibly expressed the opinions of his class best when he dismissed the whole Shakespearean canon as 'laughable farces, worthy only of being played in the wilds of Canada'.[86] Secondly, although some realism – as distinct from the formal, rhetorical style of French acting – had evolved in the work of the leading actors of the 1770s, few were capable of realising the complex characters of Shakespeare. Thirdly, the response such characters elicited from the audience was disturbing as they seemed to ask for sympathy and understanding while they were not, in themselves, morally admirable beings, a phenomenon that challenged the widely-held belief in the theatre as a morally improving institution. Finally, Shakespeare challenged the physical limitations of theatre as it was then practised. Essentially, the theatre attempted to create the illusion of dramatic action as a world complete and to itself. This was not necessarily realistic but both scenery and style of performance gave the impression of the stage as a world separate from the audience. The technical means to do this were not sophisticated. Plays were given against a system of wings and backdrops

---

[85] Jakob Michael Reinhold Lenz, 'Anmerkungen übers Theater', in Blinn, *Diskussion*, p. 143.
[86] Friedrich II von Preussen, 'De la littérature allemande', in Blinn, *Diskussion*, p. 151.

that changed from scene to scene, but which could not be easily adapted to the frequent scene changes required by Shakespeare's sprawling dramas.

The physical dilemma presented by Shakespeare is clear from Herder's essay, which states most clearly the gap between Shakespeare as a cultural force and as a playwright for the contemporary theatre. Some commentators have found the essay to be informed by an acute sense of the needs of the theatre,[87] others feel it shows no sense of the theatrical, treating Shakespeare only as a lyric poet.[88] There are good reasons to favour the latter view. Herder accepted Shakespeare's need to change scene frequently as he needed to show a various world. As the play is also a biological whole, all scenes are crucial to the composition of the whole. All is organic and cannot be tampered with. 'Take from this plant its soil, sap and strength, and plant it in the air: take from these people their place, time and individual existence – you have taken breath and soul from them.'[89] But the very fact of performance in the contemporary theatre may take 'breath and soul' from the plays. In a key passage Herder claims that when he reads them he cannot imagine the theatre. 'For me, when I read [Shakespeare], stage, actors, wings disappear.' The world summoned up for him is too fluid and interconnected to be represented successfully on stage.

> His stage appears as a sea of events where wave thunders on wave. The appearances of nature advance and retreat, interweave, so disparate do they seem; they beget and destroy themselves, so as to bring to fulfilment the intention of the creator, who seems to have experienced all planes of drunkenness and disorder.[90]

Herder had little knowledge of the stage conditions for which Shakespeare's plays were written and therefore was unable to imagine a staging that might realise this more fluid action. Nevertheless, he recognised that Shakespeare's handling of time and space on the stage is different and more subtle than in the neoclassical theatre. Dramatic time and literal time, treated as nearly identical in neoclassical drama, are in fact different. For Herder, time on Shakespeare's stage reflects time as we experience it imaginatively, when length depends on our mood, emotion and interest in the events, so that a minute can seem like an hour and an hour a minute. Also, Herder pointed out, Shakespeare was not obliged to depict just one scene, but could use the stage to simulate the freedom of the mind, passing from one location to another with the greatest of ease, similar to the way in which the mind operates in a dream. But Herder could not suggest how such a stage could be achieved; technologically it was inconceivable. In the

---

[87] Isaacsen, *Der junge Herder und Shakespeare*, pp. 40–7.
[88] Wilhelm Dobbek, 'Herder und Shakespeare', *Shakespeare-Jahrbuch*, 91 (1955), 35.
[89] Herder, *Werke*, vol. I, p. 890.   [90] *Ibid.*, p. 885.

final paragraph, therefore, he was forced to concede that the adaptations of Garrick with their alterations and cuts were inevitable as Shakespeare's drama is entirely unsuited to live representation. In the theatre, it will appear little more than 'the ruins of a colossus, of pyramids, which each person gazes at in wonder and none understand'.[91]

Nevertheless, by the end of the eighteenth century, Shakespeare was being performed on the German stage, not in the original versions read by *Sturm und Drang* writers but in versions adapted to suit the moral and political functions of the court theatre, which remained the norm well into the nineteenth century. Therefore the plays had to be adapted so as to be in conformity with neoclassical principles, even though these principles were, as critics of Shakespeare realised, alien to them. But over the years, the theatre worked towards making the vision of Shakespeare initiated by the writings of *Sturm und Drang* into a reality on stage. Wilhelm Meister sensed that only 'a few cups from the great ocean of true nature' revealed to him by Shakespeare could be realised in the theatre. In Goethe's time, that was true, stage practice could not meet the imaginative challenges Shakespeare offered it, but the most compelling aspect of the history of his plays in the German theatre is that actors, directors, designers and translators were inspired to meet those challenges. In some cases they did so successfully.

[91] *Ibid.*, p. 895.

2

Seventeenth-century beginnings: the English Comedians

Eighteenth-century German criticism on Shakespeare is marked by its tone of discovery. Writers experience his plays as new. They open up expansive vistas, suggesting much that is unexplored in individual and social experience. Had those writers been fully conversant with the history of their own theatre, they may not have been quite so enthusiastic about Shakespeare and the potential impact of his plays on German literature and theatre. Some of his plays, in vastly simplified versions, had been current in the repertoires of wandering troupes of actors since the late sixteenth century, but these actors and the theatrical fare they offered were widely regarded as standing for all that had made the popular theatre an institution that impeded rather than advanced the development of theatre as a consequential force in German society. Even though some eighteenth-century critics sensed a connection between the Shakespeare they read and the *Haupt- und Staatsaktionen* of the popular theatre,[1] their purpose in championing Shakespeare was not to revitalise or elevate the traditional popular theatre, but to furnish a literary model that provided an alternative to the prevailing neoclassicism of the German courts. But, even though there is scant evidence of continuity between the drama of seventeenth-century wandering troupes and the critical and theatrical emergence of Shakespeare in the latter half of the eighteenth century, the treatment Shakespeare's plays received at the hands of the troupes is of interest. First, it furnishes a prime example of how social and theatrical conditions can lead to radical alterations in the text of a play. Secondly, despite the discontinuity, certain principles that can be detected in these early versions of Shakespeare will also be seen to be at work under a different and more sophisticated guise in later periods.

---

[1] Wieland, for example, in his 'Briefe an einen jungen Dichter. Dritter Brief', in Blinn, *Diskussion*, p. 159.

In contrast to England, Spain and Italy, theatre in Germany at the end of the sixteenth century was extremely underdeveloped. Whereas in countries with a mature theatre, there had been significant continuity between the festive performance of religious drama, the rise of wandering players and the foundation of permanent, professional theatres in the larger cities, in Germany such connections did not exist. As the mystery cycles declined in the early sixteenth century, no vigorous, widespread theatrical activity took their place. Pupils in the schools might occasionally perform plays, humanistic works, written under the influence of classical models, with a distinct moralistic bias.[2] There was also some popular drama of peasant origin, the *Fastnachtspiele*, brief pieces of domestic intrigue, performed during Shrovetide festivities by amateurs in private homes.[3] Also in some cities, guilds of Mastersingers were responsible for the occasional public theatrical presentation. Nuremberg, with Hans Sachs as a leading Master-singer, might even have developed into a centre for theatre, but his death in 1576, ironically in the year when the first professional theatres were opening in London and Madrid, indicated the end rather than the beginning of a phase of German theatre. After this, what little dramatic activity there was took place in private, was performed by amateurs and was solely festive in nature, given only on special occasions for religious or educational purposes.

One of the most important contributions made to the development of German theatre by the 'English Comedians', who first brought the plays of Shakespeare and other English dramatists to Germany, was to create an awareness of theatre as an activity in its own right, not just as a diversion at holiday festivities or as a means of religious instruction.[4] These English Comedians were initially troupes of actors who, due to the intense competition of the London theatre and restrictions on performance in the English provinces, travelled on the continent, especially central and eastern Europe, in an attempt to find fields more lucrative than England could offer. The first record of any definite performance dates from 1586, when a small group of actors, which had previously been with William Kempe at the court of the King of Denmark, provided entertainment at the court of the Elector of Saxony.[5] But a more significant date is 1592, for in that year the London actor Robert Browne arrived in Germany with a small troupe of players to provide entertainment for the court of Duke Heinrich Julius

[2] Hans Knudsen, *Deutsche Theatergeschichte* (Stuttgart, 1970), p. 108.
[3] Otto Mann, *Geschichte des deutschen Dramas* (Stuttgart, 1963), pp. 22–34.
[4] Anna Baesecke, *Das Schauspiel der englischen Komödianten in Deutschland* (Halle, 1935), pp. 1–22.
[5] *Shakespeare in Germany in the Sixteenth and Seventeenth Centuries*, ed. Albert Cohn (London and Berlin, 1865; rep. 1967), p. xxiii.

of Brunswick. Browne was to continue for the next thirty years as the leader of various troupes that had a major presence in the theatre of several German cities.[6] The number of such troupes increased in the early seventeenth century, so that shortly before the outbreak of the Thirty Years War in 1618, there were four or five well-established groups of English Comedians touring parts of Germany. By this time, the troupes also included several actors who were native speakers of German and a repertoire with many plays of German or non-English origin. When the opportunities for performance declined because of the war, some companies disbanded, most of the English actors retiring to London. When the London theatres closed in 1642, some actors returned to Germany. The last major troupe, led by Joris Joliphus (George Jolly), remained until 1660,[7] when they returned to London as the theatres reopened after the restoration of the monarchy. So substantial had the impact of these travelling actors been that until the eighteenth century several troupes of purely German actors continued to call themselves 'English Comedians'.[8]

The continuous presence of actors from England for over half a century suggests that the financial rewards to be found in Germany were not inconsiderable. In the absence of regular theatre, the English Comedians fulfilled a need. Nevertheless, for the actor with some pride in his profession, conditions under which he had to perform were usually trying and far from conducive to the presentation of plays in as stylistically accomplished a manner as could be seen in the London theatres.[9] For a start, as there were no permanent theatres in Germany as in London, the players had to put up with whatever quarters they could find – town squares, inn-yards, tennis-courts, fencing-schools – any space that would allow an audience to stand, preferably in vertical tiers, around three sides of a temporarily erected stage or in structures resembling a horse corral, which allowed the audience to stand on all sides (see plate 1). These haphazard conditions would have negatively influenced the performance in two ways. First, because the locale had not been specifically constructed for theatrical performances as most of the London theatres had been, the relationship between actor and audience was not at all close. So, unless the actor acted in

[6] See Emil Herz, *Englische Schauspieler und englisches Schauspiel zur Zeit Shakespeares in Deutschland* (Hamburg and Leipzig, 1903), pp. 7–24. Herz provides the standard chronology of all the known troupes of English comedians in Germany.

[7] R. J. Alexander, 'George Jolly [Joris Joliphus] der wandernde Player und Manager. Neues zu seiner Tätigkeit in Deutschland, 1648–1660', *Kleine Schriften der Gesellschaft für Theatergeschichte*, 29/30 (1978), 38–48.

[8] Gerhart Hoffmeister, 'The English Comedians in Germany', in *German Baroque Literature*, ed. Gerhart Hoffmeister (New York, 1983), p. 146.

[9] The most recent lengthy summary in English of the conditions under which the English Comedians performed can be found in the opening chapter of Jerzy Limon, *Gentlemen of a Company: English Players in Central and Eastern Europe, 1590–1660* (Cambridge, 1985).

1 English Comedians' performance conditions

a physically unambiguous and probably exaggerated manner, his performance was liable to be lost in indifferent space. Secondly, the spectacle that
was so notable a part of the London public theatre would be difficult to
reproduce under the rudimentary performance conditions prevailing in
Germany. Extended stays at an aristocratic court of a hospitable town
might have allowed troupes to construct stages better than the temporary
ones. For example, in 1613 John Spencer, one of the most celebrated
troupers in the early seventeenth century, erected in Regensburg a theatre
that included 'above the normal stage an upper stage that was thirty feet
high, supported by six pillars, over which was built a roof'.[10] But spacious
dimensions like these were denied to most players most of the time and
they had to make do with less elaborate structures, possibly just an open
fore-stage for generalised space and a rear-stage, enclosed on three sides by
curtains, used whenever the location of the action had to be particular-
ised.[11] Some provision may have been made for a balcony.

[10] Herz, *Englische Schauspieler*, p. 46.
[11] Roy Pascal, 'The Stage of the Englische Komödianten: Three Problems', *Modern Language Review*, 35, 3 (1940), 372–6.

The actor who wanted to earn a reasonable living had to travel constantly. As theatre for itself rather than as a festive event was an unfamiliar concept, municipal officials responsible for maintaining civic order and for guarding the moral welfare of their citizens were suspicious of the players who visited their towns. No play could be given without their permission and often, despite the most abject and flattering appeals from the players, such permission was denied. When it was granted, it was at the most for a week or two,[12] and, as if to deny the purely professional nature of the theatre, it would only be extended if the performances were associated with a fair or some other formal event in the community calendar.

The actors occasionally enjoyed aristocratic patronage, which allowed them to perform under more settled circumstances. Duke Heinrich Julius of Brunswick, a scholar of some note, probably offered extended hospitality to Browne early in his travels, as nine plays written by the Duke, all published in 1594, show the influence of the English drama.[13] A more substantial patron was Landgrave Moritz of Hessen-Cassel, who between 1593 and 1613 maintained troupes at his court in Cassel and in 1611 even built a capacious theatre, the Ottoneum – 'a beautiful theatre, specially constructed in the old Roman style, accommodating several thousands of people and all of them able to see'.[14] But aristocratic patronage could not guarantee continual employment, and, even before the Landgrave was forced to turn the actors off for financial reasons, they had to spend much of the year travelling. So, although Browne's troupe was periodically supported by the Landgrave, he had to tour to cities as far apart as Cologne, Munich and Prague. The only city he visited with any regularity was Frankfurt, where the spring and autumn fairs, attended by traders from all over the German-speaking world and further afield, gave him a broader and probably better-educated audience than ones he could attract elsewhere.[15]

Because of this constant travel, standards of performance could not be as high as they were in London. Given the appalling condition of roads, the troupes travelled light, carrying with them only the most rudimentary props and the most basic wardrobe. Court records show that when the players were resident they tried to acquire costumes as splendid as those of

---

[12] *Die Schauspiele der englischen Komödianten*, ed. Wilhelm Creizenach (Berlin and Stuttgart, n.d. [1889]), p. xv.

[13] Heinz Kindermann, *Theatergeschichte Europas*, 10 vols. (Salzburg, 1957–74), vol. 3, p. 353.

[14] Quoted in Hans Hartleb, *Deutschlands erster Theaterbau: Geschichte der englischen Komödianten unter Landgraf Moritz dem Gelehrten von Hessen-Cassel* (Berlin and Leipzig, 1936), p. 87. A description of the theatre in English can be found in Graham C. Adams, 'The Ottoneum: A Neglected Seventeenth-Century Theatre', *Shakespeare Studies*, 15 (1982), 243–68.

[15] Elizabeth Mentzel, *Geschichte der Schauspielkunst in Frankfurt am Main* (Frankfurt, 1882), p. 41.

the London theatre and props to create a magnificent spectacle,[16] but these were temporary acquisitions only. Travel would also influence the text of the plays performed. As copies of the plays were cumbersome to transport, they would have been kept to a minimum, so the actors would often give their roles from memories that were no doubt faulty. Frequently they would engage in improvisation.

For these reasons, when plays from the London theatre were performed by the English Comedians, both the action and the characters of the drama were simplified. But the most pressing cause for simplification must initially have been the language barrier between actors and audience. When the English Comedians first arrived, they were not regarded as actors in their own right, but as musicians and entertainers. The troupers that performed for the Elector of Saxony in 1586 were referred to as 'instrumentalists'[17] and were praised for their skill at music and acrobatics. The letters of recommendation that gave Browne access to Germany in 1592 also requested that his troupe be allowed to practise 'their profession by performing of music, feats of agility and games of comedies, tragedies and histories'.[18] The order of listing may not be insignificant. When Browne's troupe performed at the Frankfurt autumn fair, a German audience member had little to say about their acting but was enthusiastic about their music and acrobatics. 'They have such wonderful, good music', he wrote to his wife, 'and are so perfect at jumping and dancing that I have never yet heard nor seen their like.'[19] But his enthusiasm was not reciprocated by an English traveller, Fynes Moryson, who described them as 'despised Stage players come out of England into Germany ... having neither a complete number of Actours, nor any good Apparell, nor any ornament of the Stage'.[20] They attracted attention not by their mimetic abilities but because the audience was fascinated by 'theire gesture and Action'. As Browne's troupe could not perform in German, their initial success was limited, so to establish a bond of language between stage and audience, he employed a German-speaking clown who summarised the action and entertained by recounting or enacting comically obscene incidents. By the early seventeenth century, however, most English actors had a fair knowledge of German, and evidence suggests that English was fast disappearing as the primary stage language.[21] All the same, actors continued to appeal as much

[16] See Hartleb, *Deutschlands erster Theaterbau*, pp. 12–69 for details of the costumes and props of a company of English Comedians in permanent residence at a court.

[17] Cohn, *Shakespeare in Germany*, p. xxiii.   [18] *Ibid.*, p. xxix.

[19] Quoted in Willem Schrickx, 'English Actors at the Courts of Wolfenbüttel, Brussels and Graz during the Lifetime of Shakespeare', *Shakespeare Survey*, 33 (1980), 156.

[20] Quoted in Alois Brandl, 'Englische Komödianten in Frankfurt a.M.', *Shakespeare-Jahrbuch*, 40 (1904), 230.

[21] Herz (pp. 17–18) summarises the transition from English into German, which was well under way by the end of the sixteenth century.

by their acrobatics and music as by their powers as interpreters of character. Indeed, when Spencer's troupe was at the height of its success, with the unusually large number of twenty-four members, a significant number of them were musicians.[22] But even when the English Comedians acquired proficiency in German, they could not create, in German, play-texts that were as linguistically rich as the original English plays, as German in the early seventeenth century was too undeveloped a language to allow for a satisfactory translation of even the most verbally meagre of Elizabethan dramatists.

SHAKESPEAREAN MATERIAL

The English Comedians' repertoire consisted initially of plays from the London theatre for which Shakespeare wrote and acted. But when the Comedians came over to Germany they were not at all concerned to give a faithful representation of the plays as they might have been seen in London. In fact Shakespeare's plays were probably of less use to them than, for example, those of Marlowe or Kyd, as these incorporated sensational situations and gory events more consistently than Shakespeare's. In addition, Shakespeare's plots were more complex and involved more finely drawn characters. So, when his plays found their way into the German theatre, it was in a form very different from that known to us from the First Folio.

There were three ways in which Shakespearean material was incorporated into the German theatre. First, there were those plays written by German playwrights with plots bearing a similarity to Shakespeare's. Either the playwrights knew his work from performances given by the English Comedians or they used the same sources as Shakespeare did. The plays of the Duke of Brunswick show a knowledge of English drama in their use of sub-plot, while the humour of their clown figures resembles the humour of Thomas Sackville, the clown in Browne's troupe.[23] The *Comedia von der schönen Phaenicia* (*Comedy of Beautiful Phoenicia*)[24] by the prolific Jakob Ayrer might have been based on the Hero/Claudio plot in *Much Ado About Nothing* and its comic servant role is similar to Benedick's. Ayrer's *Comedia von der schönen Sidea* (*Comedy of Beautiful Sidea*)[25] has much in common with the Ferdinand/Miranda interest in *The Tempest*, only the later date of Shakespeare's play indicates the use of a common source or even Shakespeare's utilisation of Ayrer's material.[26] The anonymous *Trage-*

---

[22] Creizenach, *Schauspiele*, p. xiv.   [23] Herz, *Englische Schauspiele*, pp. 32–3.

[24] Extracts from the German text with corresponding English translation can be found in Cohn, *Shakespeare in Germany*, pp. 81–112.

[25] In German and English in Cohn, *Shakespeare in Germany*, pp. 5–76.

[26] Ayrer died in 1605, some thirteen years before the play was published in the collection *Orbis theatricum*. The play was probably produced in 1595 in Nuremberg. See Geoffrey Bullough,

dia von Julio und Hyppolita (*Tragedy of Julius and Hippolyta*) (1600)[27] bears such a resemblance to the sub-plot of *Two Gentlemen of Verona*, but with a tragic not a comic outcome, that it was probably written with knowledge of Shakespeare's original. But interesting as these are as examples of early German play-writing, there is no evidence they were used by the English Comedians.

The second way in which Shakespeare entered the German theatre is through plays that incorporated key episodes from his works into a dramatic action drawn from various sources. For example, it is not known for certain when *The Merchant of Venice* was first given in Germany. It may have been given by John Green's troupe in Passau in 1607 and at the court of the Archduke Ferdinand in Graz in 1608.[28] A *Jud von Venedig* (*Jew of Venice*) was given in Halle in 1611, while a notable series of performances by Green's troupe in Dresden in 1626 comprised several Shakespearean titles, including one *Comödia von Josepho Juden von Venedigk* (*Comedy of Joseph, Jew of Venice*).[29] There is nothing to suggest that any of these plays were *The Merchant of Venice* but a manuscript of a play by Christoph Blümel, *Das wohlgesprochene Urteil* (*The Well-Spoken Judgement*), dated between 1650 and 1660, could well be a later version of the play used on these occasions.[30] *Das wohlgesprochene Urteil*, which dramatises how a Prince of Cyprus woos and wins Anciletta, a young Venetian lady, conflates episodes from different plays and dramatic traditions. The opening act comes from Marlowe's *Jew of Malta*. Set in Cyprus, it details how the Jews are expelled for their ruthless economic exploitation of the populace. As with Marlowe's play, the tone is openly anti-semitic. The middle acts, in which the Prince travels to Venice, woos Anciletta, and goes deeply into debt by borrowing from a Jew who had been expelled from Cyprus, include episodes resembling moments in *The Merchant of Venice*. It is more likely, however, that they originated from other sources, especially from French comedy, which was becoming an important part of the German repertoire by the mid-seventeenth century, and from popular German and Italian farce. The only ascertainable 'Shakespearean' part of the play is the last act, which comprises the contest between the Prince and

Narrative and Dramatic Sources of Shakespeare, 8 vols. (London and New York, 1957–75), vol. 8, pp. 248–9 for a discussion of Ayrer's and Shakespeare's use of the material.

[27] In *Spieltexte der Wanderbühne*, 4 vols. (Berlin, 1970), vol. 1, ed. Manfred Brauneck. Available in English translation in Cohn, *Shakespeare in Germany*, pp. 118–55.

[28] This also could have been *The Jew of Malta*. See Orlene Murad, *The English Comedians at the Court in Graz, 1607–1608* (Salzburg, 1978), pp. 59–61.

[29] Ernst Leopold Stahl, *Shakespeare und das deutsche Theater* (Stuttgart, 1947), p. 12. Other plays possibly based on Shakespearean originals given in Dresden in 1626 were *Romeo and Juliet*, *Julius Caesar*, *Hamlet* and *King Lear*.

[30] The German text is available in *Die englischen Comoedianten zur Zeit Shakespeares in Österreich*, ed. Johannes Meissner (Vienna, 1884), pp. 131–89. It can be found in English translation in *Shakespeare in Germany, 1590–1700*, ed. Ernest Brennecke, (Chicago, 1964), pp. 112–89.

the Jew, who uses the pledge of the pound of flesh to exact revenge for being expelled from Cyprus. The dilemma is resolved by Anciletta, who, disguised as a lawyer, insists that no blood be shed while the flesh is cut and that exactly one pound be taken from the Prince's body. But with the exception of the phrase 'a second Daniel', uttered first by Joseph, then by the clown Pickelhering, nowhere does the text recall Shakespeare's language. Indeed, as with all of the English Comedians' plays, *Das wohlgesprochene Urteil* was delivered in relatively crude prose approximate to colloquial German rather than in language that recaptured the poetry of Shakespeare's blank verse. How the play had evolved is unknown, but Blümel and earlier adapters from which he might have worked would probably not have used any printed edition or prompt-copies but memories of a performance of the original play or of a performance adapted from the original. This was not a theatre that prized a play as the unique product of an individual creative mind or felt any necessity to preserve it in performance unchanged. Indeed, another play performed by the English Comedians, *Tugend- und Liebes-Streit* (*Conflict of Love and Virtue*),[31] has an action either borrowed from *Twelfth Night* or based on the same source, but placed in a dramatic framework identical to that of *Das wohlgesprochene Urteil*. In the comic scenes especially, there are passages that are almost identical. This indicates that the English Comedians felt free to combine different episodes from different plays if they felt it would make for good theatre.

ADAPTATIONS OF SHAKESPEARE

Not all of Shakespeare's plays found their way on to the German stage in quite so fragmented a fashion. Some were seen in versions clearly based on a fairly close knowledge of the original. Three of these adaptations have survived, providing the most immediate evidence of how Shakespeare's plays were first treated on the German stage.

In order to understand this treatment, it may be helpful first to compare one of Shakespeare's most famous speeches, Hamlet's advice to the Players, with its German counterpart in *Der bestrafte Brudermord* (*Fratricide Revenged*), an adaptation of *Hamlet*. The German Hamlet offers advice that differs radically from Shakespeare's. Shakespeare's Hamlet encourages the actors to be restrained in performance and, through the exercise of their 'discretion', learn how to 'suit the action to the word, the word to the action'. The actor's complete realisation of the character should be modified by a judicious tempering that ensures he 'o'erstep not the

---

[31] The German text is in Creizenach, *Schauspiele*, pp. 73–124, and an English translation in Brennecke, *Shakespeare in Germany*, pp. 197–245.

modesty of nature' (III: 2, 15–16).[32] The German Hamlet sees things very differently. For him the essence of performance lies in the Players' doing everything 'correctly'. He recalls a performance he once saw them give in Wittenberg.

> Ihr höret oft nicht gleich, was die Zuschauer urtheilen, denn da waren auch etliche, die hatten seidne Strümpfe und weisse Schuh an, aber auf dem Haupte hatten sie schwarze Hüte, die waren voll Federn, unten bald so voll als oben, die Plomaschen waren, ich glaube, sie musten anstatt der Schlaf-mützen damit in den Betten gelegen haben, das steht so schlimm, und ist leicht zu ändern. Auch könnt ihr wohl etlichen davon sagen, wenn sie eine königliche oder fürstliche Person agiren, dass sie doch nicht so sehr gucken, wenn sie ein Compliment gegen eine Dame machen, auch nicht so viel spanische Pfauentritte und solche Fechtermienen, denn ein Potentat lacht darüber, sein naturell ist das beste: der einen König agiret, muss sich einbilden, dass er in dem Spiel ein König sey, und ein Bauer auch wie ein Bauer.

> (You actors do not clearly understand how your audience judges you, for there were some of you who wore silk hose and white shoes, but on their [*sic*] heads they wore black hats with as many feathers drooping below as were left on top. I think they must have worn such plumage in bed instead of nightcaps. That is too bad, and may be so easily remedied. You might also tell some of them that when they act the part of a royal or noble person, they should not gawk when they compliment a lady, nor strut like Spanish peacocks. It is best to be entirely natural; whoever acts a king must imagine that he is a king in the play; and if a peasant, likewise as a peasant.)[33]

The contrast is striking. Shakespeare's Hamlet judges the authenticity of a performance by the completeness of the actor's characterisation and the restraint of his style, the German Hamlet by the suitability of the costumes and by how well the actor imitates the appearances of the social world. Even though he urges the actors to be 'natural', his conception of acting is superficial in contrast to Shakespeare's Hamlet. Furthermore, while Shake-speare's Hamlet speaks with springy rhythm and controls a sophisticated range of vocabulary embracing the language of both common discourse and aesthetics, the German Hamlet speaks prosaically in words that do little to distinguish him from other characters.

The German Hamlet also has different ideas about the function of theatre. When Shakespeare's Hamlet speaks of the purpose of performance,

---

[32] William Shakespeare, *Hamlet*, ed. Philip Edwards (Cambridge, 1985), p. 288. All further quotations and references to passages from Shakespeare's plays will be incorporated in the text. They have been taken from the latest edition of the plays published by Cambridge University Press.

[33] *Der bestrafte Brudermord*, in Creizenach, *Schauspiele*, p. 163. Translation from Brennecke, *Shakespeare in Germany*, p. 268.

he is judiciously imprecise. 'The purpose of playing', he says, '. . . is, to hold as 'twere, the mirror up to nature; to show virtue her own feature, scorn her own image, and the very age and body of the time his form and pressure' (III: 2, 17–20). For Hamlet, theatre should arouse the self-awareness of its audience, though he does not prescribe the consequences of this. The German Hamlet is more confident about the effect of theatre. It is a mirror, he says, 'denn man kan in einem Spiegel seine Flecken sehen' ('one can see one's own blemishes in a mirror').[34] After the play-scene he expands on how theatre makes audiences into good citizens. His words seem to anticipate Gottsched when he claims that actors 'breiten aus die Gerechtig-keit und löbliche Regierung der Fürsten, sie strafen die Laster und erheben die Tugenden, sie rühmen die Frommen, und weisen, wie die Tyranney gestraft wird' ('proclaim the justice and the worthy rule of our nobles; they denounce vices and extol virtues; they praise the virtuous, and show how tyranny may be punished').[35] Shakespeare's Hamlet sees drama as pri-marily the materialisation of inner experience, the German Hamlet as the imitation of the appearances of the external world. Shakespeare's Hamlet is prepared to allow the moral effect, if any, of the action to come about through the audience's contemplation of themselves; the German Hamlet sees the stage as a pulpit from which moral dicta are handed out. The difference might be taken as symbolic of the difference between Shake-speare's plays as seen in the Elizabethan theatre and on the stage of the English Comedians.

It is difficult, to be quite honest, to summon up great enthusiasm for the early German adaptations of Shakespeare. His plays hold the stage by the resonance and allusiveness of his language, the fecundity of his imagination in creating strikingly complete characters and the magnitude of his dramatic action, in which diverse social and private experiences are so combined as to make the plays symbolic of broad realms of the human condition. But such aspects are so entirely missing in the German adaptations that one tends to sympathise with the audience at William Poel's English language revival of *Der bestrafte Brudermord* in 1925, who found themselves snickering at the characters rather than feeling fear or sympathy with them.[36] And as these plays both in plot and language refer unmistakably to the originals, they often strike us as little more than gross travesties of these originals. Nevertheless, they are of historical interest, both as documents of their theatre and, more pertinently, because the moral purpose behind them, as articulated by Hamlet in *Der bestrafte Brudermord*, technically foreshadows the moral purpose behind the more accomplished versions of Shakespeare performed in later centuries.

[34] Creizenach, *Schauspiele*, p. 164.   [35] *Ibid.*, p. 167.
[36] *William Poel's Prompt-Book of Fratricide Punished*, ed. J. Isaacs (London, 1956), p. xiv.

The earliest of the adaptations that has survived is *Titus Andronicus*, included in the first collection of the English Comedians' plays to be published in Germany, in 1620.[37] Due to its bloodthirsty and sensational action, this early tragedy may well have been one of the most popular plays in the repertoire. It was supplanted by a classicised version in the middle of the seventeenth century, though a manuscript of 1699 shows that the text derived from Shakespeare was still performed at the end of the century.[38] Its publication predates the First Folio, so it must have been based on earlier versions of the Shakespeare play and possibly on an anonymous piece, *Titus and Vespasian*, performed in London in 1591.[39] *Romeo and Juliet* also appeared in a version based on Shakespeare's original play. There are records of it being given at Nördlingen in 1604, then at Dresden in 1626 and in 1646,[40] but it is impossible to determine the versions used on these occasions as the only extant manuscript, not published complete until the middle of the nineteenth century,[41] dates from the end of the seventeenth century. It is obviously based on the First Folio. There is an even greater gap between the first ascertainable performance of *Hamlet*, in Dresden in 1626, and the only known manuscript of *Der bestrafte Brudermord*, which dates from 1710, several decades after the last English comedians had left the country. Though the manuscript itself has not survived, a reliable version was published by the dramaturg H. A. O. Reichard in 1781 in his *Ollapotrida*.[42]

Der bestrafte Brudermord, which is only one-fifth the length of *Hamlet*, offers a fine example of how Shakespeare's plays were simplified structurally to suit German performance conditions. Act I of *Hamlet* has three plotlines: the visitation of the Ghost, Hamlet's disaffection with the court and himself, and Polonius and his family. Each plotline is introduced so as to reflect upon the others, in particular allowing the audience to recognise the connection between the Ghost and Hamlet's deep antipathy towards the court and all it stands for. In this way, Shakespeare's diverse plotting

---

[37] *Spieltexte der Wanderbühne* (see note 27) is a modern reprinting of this collection.
[38] Creizenach, *Schauspiele*, p. 12.
[39] Brennecke, *Shakespeare in Germany*, p. 14.
[40] Stahl, *Shakespeare und das deutsche Theater*, pp. 11–12.
[41] The version in Cohn, *Shakespeare in Germany*, pp. 309–406 is still the only complete version of the play available.
[42] The vexed question of the relationship between *Der bestrafte Brudermord* and the various versions of *Hamlet* is discussed in detail by Reinhold Freudenstein in *Der bestrafte Brudermord: Shakespeares Hamlet auf der Wanderbühne des 17. Jahrhunderts* (Hamburg, 1958). He reviews the thirty-five articles on the subject written between 1857 and 1958. Four of these claim it was based solely on the first quarto, four of them on both quartos, one of them on the First Folio, seven of them on the First Folio and the Ur-Hamlet, and nineteen of them on the Ur-Hamlet alone. Some authorities even believe *Der bestrafte Brudermord* may be a translation of the Ur-Hamlet. Freudenstein insists that whoever wrote it did not base his version on any one source, but used whatever elements he felt would please the audience.

acquires unity. But this technique requires the audience to have a capacious memory that can remember a plotline when they are not seeing it on stage. Such a memory the English Comedians could not, it would appear, rely on. In *Der bestrafte Brudermord* the action is simplified and made linear. One line of action at a time is pursued without interruption. All scenes with the Ghost on the battlements (I:1, I:4 and 5) occur consecutively, so that Hamlet knows of his father's murder before the court scene (I:2) takes place. He does not, however, act on his knowledge but remains even more silent than in Shakespeare. Act II comprises the scenes where the King and Corambus (Polonius) spy on Hamlet and Ophelia (III:1), followed at once by the arrival of the Players (II:2) and then by the play-scene (III:2). And so the play proceeds to the end, without any attempt to hold the audience's interest in one plotline while they are seeing another represented on stage. This means there is no tension; each event occurs not as a unit in a larger structure, but as a discrete incident in a series. To ensure unity, Shakespeare foreshadowed events, reminded one of past moments and continually pointed up thematic similarities between scenes, but the English Comedians eschewed such technical subtleties, allowing characters to come on stage unheralded and then to disappear with equal rapidity. The most obvious example is at the very end, when Hamlet, who lies dying, names 'Fortempras' the new King of Denmark. This character has not until this moment even been mentioned.

The refusal to employ tension as a structural principle is also demonstrated in the German version of *Romeo and Juliet*. The play opens with a scene not in Shakespeare, in which Montague and Capulet declare peace in the presence of the Prince. It begins, therefore, at a point where, in terms of the larger action, Shakespeare ends. As a result, the German play never gains the momentum Shakespeare's does. The hostility between the families is not endemic, but is of importance only as a factor that disrupts the lovers' lives. There is no external pressure on Romeo and Juliet that intensifies and endangers their love. Juliet's marriage to Paris, for example, is not used to apply pressure to her need to resolve her predicament. Shakespeare introduced the theme of the marriage in the second scene of the play (I:2), in a conversation between Paris and Capulet. Lady Capulet takes it up in the next scene (I:3) as she talks to Juliet and the Nurse, so that by the time the lovers meet at the ball, the audience knows very well how family politics will threaten Juliet's love for Romeo. In the German version, no mention is made of the marriage until after the balcony-scene, even though Paris has already been introduced. This omission is not haphazard. To introduce the possibility of a marriage to Paris would create a dramatically ambivalent situation, directly in opposition to the English Comedians' intent to create the utmost simplicity in dramatic conflict.

Therefore the marriage with Paris is introduced only when an inciting cause is needed for Romeo and Juliet to get married. Juliet, therefore, marries Romeo because she is afraid of marrying Paris, not because the urgency of her feelings drives her to it. Such simplified plotting does not depend upon vital energy and individual life within the characters.

The lack of energy and life is reflected too in the inadequate language of the adaptations. Whenever a character is called on to express what passes for urgent inner feeling, he or she does it not in fresh images which are startlingly apt descriptions of inner feeling, but in language drawn from the clichés of poetry. Take, for example, Juliet. Shakespeare introduces her very gradually. When she first appears with her mother and the Nurse (1:3), she hardly speaks; at the ball she briefly engages with Romeo in some dexterous word-play, but only in the balcony-scene does she express the wealth of her feelings. These scenes allow the audience to discover Juliet's emotional state progressively and to feel the rich poetry she speaks as a spontaneous expression of that state. But in the German adaptation, as soon as she appears she launches into a long speech contrasting the joys of spring with the melancholy of enforced solitude.

> O grosse Belustigung dieser Frühlings Zeit, wan man sich ergötzen kan in den lustbahren Gärten, felder vnd wälder ... wan der zephirus den blätterreichen Bawmen schmeichlet ... Aber sage Julieta wass frewde genüest du, weil ich wie eine Einsambe turteltaube eingesperrt, vnd alss eine gefangene leben muess indeme mich meiner Eltern Zucht aller frewd berauben?

> (Oh! how great is the enjoyment of this spring-time, when one may delight in the merry gardens, fields and woods ... when the zephyr dallies with the leafy tree ... But say, Juliet, what pleasure dost thou [*sic*] enjoy while I am pent up like a solitary turtle and forced to live like a prisoner, deprived of every enjoyment by parental control?)[43]

Some lines later she explains she is a girl of spotless and iron virtue. This Juliet is a type, the aristocratic young maiden as seen through the eyes of popular poetry and drama. Romeo fares no better. He initially woos Juliet beneath her balcony by having a page sing to the lute, casting the whole event in a framework of commonplace formality. He also begins the scene by speaking, against all sense, of 'der himmlischen schönheit der Julieta, deren ich mich schon langsam verplichtet habe' ('the heavenly beauty of Juliet, to whom I have long devoted myself'),[44] one of the frequent careless slips evident in the texts of the English Comedians. Not surprisingly, the following scene involves exchange of the tritest of vows. As a result, even though the lovers have more stage-time together in relationship to the

---

[43] Cohn, *Shakespeare in Germany*, pp. 316–18.   [44] *Ibid.*, pp. 340.

whole play than they do in the original, we discover far less about them as, quite frankly, there is nothing to discover. In their later scenes, they reach no warmer a footing than they do in the balcony-scene, and in the bedroom-scene before Romeo leaves for Mantua it is quite clear that they have not slept together. The formality of their final lines, alternative six-line stanzas in rhyming couplets, typifies the formality of their relationship. Through the lovers we do not come to understand, as we do in Shakespeare, the experience of sexual awakening; instead we merely encounter stereotypical ideas as to how aristocratic lovers express themselves. Like most of the plays performed by the English Comedians, the action has been removed from any experience which members of the audience might recognise as approximate to their own into a formulaically conceived social, historical or mythological world bearing little relationship to life as it is lived on any social stratum or in any geographical location.

Shakespeare's characters are forceful and attractive because of the fullness with which they are drawn and because they embody powerful contradictions. As eighteenth-century critics were to argue not unconvincingly, their presence alone can carry both the meaning and the justification of the drama. Shakespeare's *Titus Andronicus*, for example, would be little more than a farrago of gory incidents were it not for the character of Titus. In Shakespeare's opening act, Titus is an archetype, albeit a crude one, for the later tragic heroes. He is a heroic warrior who has spawned 'five and twenty valiant sons' (I:1, 79) and seen all but four die in battle. But the strength that brought him victory in the service of Rome is also self-destructive. This is displayed by his sacrifice of Tamora's son Alarbus, then by his murder of his own son Mutius, when Mutius was actually defending the interests of his sister, Titus's daughter. Because of this violent opening, in which staid political spectacle is invaded by bloody anarchy, the horrendous incidents that compose the play's action are understood to be partially a consequence of Titus's cruelty and impulsiveness. They have a cause beyond that of sheer malice in Titus's enemies, which saves them from being entirely meretricious. But the English Comedians, in striving for simplicity and lack of ambiguity, could not allow such a cause. In the severely cut opening scene, some 518 lines of Shakespearean verse being compressed into about 100 lines of German prose, Titus is nothing but an admirable, public-spirited man, who renounces the imperial crown out of concern for the community. The sacrifice of Alarbus and the murder of Mutius are cut so that the horrors subsequently visited on Titus and his family are without cause. Shakespeare's Rome is, as Titus says, 'a wilderness of tigers' (III:1, 54). To underscore this, even the most innocent of his characters, Lavinia, is partly the author of her fate, as her violation results from her and Bassanius's taunting of Tamora. In the German play, she is less brazen and just mildly upbraids Aetiopissa (the German equivalent to Tamora) before the terrible onslaught on herself and her husband begins.

Such simplifications and omissions make the conflict melodramatic, asking for a simple response from the audience, sympathy for the good, persecuted characters, antipathy towards the evil. This means that another of Shakespeare's characters, Aaron the Moor, is reduced in stature. In the original he is a thoroughgoing villain whose villainy attracts by its very ingenuity and by the courage with which it flies in the face of orthodoxy. In the German play, Aaron becomes the less subtly named Morian and he reveals himself less subtly too. Aaron's opening speech in Shakespeare (II:1, 1–25) is rich in classical allusions, his love for Tamora has a Promethean quality to it; in the German play, where the speech is, unusually, extended considerably, Morian confines himself to smutty tales about how he finds his way into the Queen's bedroom and incredible claims to earth-shattering prowess in battle. In this speech material has been borrowed from the later speeches of Shakespeare's Aaron, where, with distinct relish and to our covert amusement, he tells of how

> Oft I have digged up dead men from their graves
> And set them upright at their dear friends' doors
>
> (V:1, 135–6)

In the German play this is reduced to a mere statement of how he has committed 'tausendt vnd tausendt Schelmerey vnd Rauberey' ('thousands and thousands of rogueries and robberies').[45] The primitive conditions in which the play was performed also meant that no demonstration could be given of his spectacular villainy, so the ingenious trap by which Shakespeare's Aaron incriminates Quintus and Martius in the death of Bassinius is cut entirely. In fact, no reason is given for their arrest – it is suddenly announced as having happened. As a result, one neither feels a baffling admiration for Aaron's cleverness nor maintains a sense of the diabolical chain of events by which the Andronicus family is destroyed.

In *Titus Andronicus*, Shakespeare uses Rome as a metaphor for the self-destructiveness that arises once appetite and the desire for power have been allowed free rein. To underscore this, the final events, of Titus feeding Tamora her own sons, take place as Rome is being invaded by an army led by Titus's son Lucius (Vespasian in the German). This army is composed of Goths, as a final demonstration that neither familial, racial nor political loyalties mean anything in this world of unleashed impulse and unfettered ambition. In the German play, however, Rome is invaded by 'einen

45 *Spieltexte der Wanderbühne*, vol. 1, p. 467.

grossen tapperen vnd ausserlesenen versuchten Kriegesvolke' ('a great and valiant army of picked and experienced troops')[46] that for no particular reason has ravaged and plundered its way towards Rome, but will now restore order.

No attempt was made in the English Comedians' adaptations to use action as a metaphor for the human condition. In action and language they lack any sense of poetic expression.[47] The action includes only those incidents necessary to the progression of the story and all scenes in Shakespeare that retard the action but give insights into characters' motivations or provide metaphors for those characters' situations are cut. For example, in the German *Titus Andronicus*, those unnerving scenes that demonstrate the deterioration of Titus's sanity – the banquet where he upbraids Marcus for killing a fly (III:2) and the shooting of the arrows into the heavens (IV:3) – are omitted, as they hold up the action of the play. By the same rationale, *Der bestrafte Brudermord* is a bare skeleton of *Hamlet*. All Hamlet's soliloquies are cut, while the bedroom scene, although it includes all the events in Shakespeare, is in fact only a few lines long and ends with Hamlet moralistically berating his mother for her faithlessness: 'Pfui!' he says to her as he takes his farewell, 'schämt Euch, ich mag kein Wort mehr mit Euch reden!' ('Bah, shame on you. I no longer wish to speak with you!').[48] Its flat and unpoetic language is characteristic of the language used throughout these adaptations. Therefore when extracts of Shakespeare's verse are echoed in the prose dialogue, which they frequently are, they sound little more than banal paraphrase.

A most distinctive feature of Shakespeare's plays, and one that was to worry eighteenth-century critics, is the mixture of dramatic modes. The English Comedians did not reduce the plays to a uniform tone, especially as in the early days the clown was the main means by which they communicated with their audience. But, while they maintained the coexistence of the comic with the pathetic and tragic, it never had the point it does in Shakespeare. Shakespeare included comic characters in tragic plots, drew parallels between the serious and comic, and included verbal devices such as word-play in the speech of tragic characters. All this enabled his audience to see the action from an ironic point of view. This was not the purpose behind the juxtaposition of the comic and serious in the English Comedians' adaptations. The comic is there primarily to provide belly-laughs in an action that is otherwise unrelentingly serious or turgidly romantic. It exists despite, at times even in violation of, tragic action. *Titus Andronicus* is atypical as it has no clown figure, the action being unrelent-

[46] *Ibid.*, p. 506.
[47] *Das Schauspiel der Wanderbühne*, ed. Willi Flemming (Leipzig, 1931), p. 29.
[48] Creizenach, *Schauspiele*, p. 170.

ingly gloomy, but clowns appear in *Der bestrafte Brudermord* and *Romeo and Juliet*. In *Der bestrafte Brudermord*, the clown is Phantasmo, a foppish courtier, based on Osric, who appears unheralded in the middle of the third act. He has no satirical function as his Shakespearean counterpart does, but serves mainly to direct the laughter of the audience towards Ophelia, who suddenly develops a great passion for him when she goes mad. While Shakespeare introduced Ophelia's madness with disconcertingly obscene rhymes as an expression of her mental disorder, the German Ophelia becomes the butt of laughter through the exaggerated attempts of Phantasmo to escape her attentions. *Romeo and Juliet* contains a clown who was familiar to contemporary audiences as a generic type, Pickelherring, who had originated with the English Comedians earlier in the century.[49] The humour of the figure lay in the way he used his limited native intelligence to satisfy as frequently as possible his appetites for food and sex. He often spoke streams of obscenities distinguished mainly by the extra-ordinary variety with which they described a limited number of basic bodily functions. Pickelherring in *Romeo and Juliet* is not quite as versatile in this regard as he is in other plays,[50] as it is only his stomach, not his sexual appetite, that needs satisfying. But this very limitation displays how different the English Comedians' use of comedy was from Shakespeare's. In Shakespeare's *Romeo and Juliet*, it is precisely the Nurse's coarseness on sexual matters that provides the foil to the romantic love of Romeo and Juliet. In the German *Romeo and Juliet*, the Nurse survives as a garrulous figure, but Pickelherring carries the comedy in a way that detracts and distracts from the serious action of the play, rather than making it more pertinent. He cracks jokes while standing over the corpse of Tybalt and when he brings Juliet news of Romeo's banishment, consistently distracts attention from her own reaction to it by irrelevant jests.[51] He also interjects jokes as the Friar tries to reconcile Romeo to his banishment and as Juliet tries to persuade her father to put off the wedding with Paris. The result is not a dovetailing of the comic and serious, but a play that goes in two directions, as if the comedy is trying to deflect the attention of the audience away from the serious aspects of the action, possibly even denying their seriousness.

In short, the difference between Shakespeare's plays and the English Comedians' can be encapsulated in the difference between the advice given by the two respective Hamlets to the Players. Shakespeare's Hamlet speaks

---

[49] Willem Schrickx, ' "Pickelherring" and the English Actors in Germany', *Shakespeare Survey*, 36 (1983), 135–47.

[50] See in particular the Pickelherring in both *Das wohlgesprochene Urteil* and *Tugend- und Liebes-Streit*, where the quite unruly disorders of his bowels are a major and persistent topic of conversation.

[51] Cohn, *Shakespeare in Germany*, pp. 368–76.

of integrity in characterisation and stylistic control as the central energy of the performance, but the German Hamlet expects the Players to follow outward appearances, paying no attention to the character's inner life. While Shakespeare's Hamlet sees theatre as a means of arousing audiences to self-contemplation, no doubt through an action that requires considerable interpretative imagination, the only serious function the German Hamlet can see in theatre is that through it one can present the audience with a black and white morality that the action does nothing to question. While Shakespeare's plays involve characters in an action that encourages the audience to question the assumed rationality of humanity (*Titus Andronicus*), or asserts the primacy of individual experience over social imperatives (*Romeo and Juliet*), or questions both the political and metaphysical assumptions upon which the social order is founded (*Hamlet*), the German plays have no such ambition. Doubtless they were intended mainly to entertain, with the moralistic purpose Hamlet had defined as a secondary function; indeed it may well be that this moral statement was included more to justify the theatre in the eyes of the ever-suspicious authorities than to identify a purpose integral to the play. Consequently it is easy to dismiss the English Comedians and most historians of Shakespeare in Germany have done so.[52]

But, easy as it is to do, the work of the English Comedians can be too easily disparaged. Before they came to Germany the theatre was entirely undeveloped, and they did much to build the foundations of a profession that in the second half of the seventeenth century would be taken over entirely by German troupes under the leadership of German actor-managers. Furthermore, while acting in Germany during the late sixteenth century must have been impossibly stilted, with actors standing 'stiff like a stick reciting their learnt speeches',[53] the English actors introduced a liveliness of expression, a vividness in gesture and spontaneity in performance that drew enthusiastic audiences and did much to give life to a formerly lifeless art. This certainly did nothing to further the cause of Shakespeare in the German theatre, but it allowed for the creation of conditions that over a century later would give rise to a fully professional theatre. Among the various achievements of this theatre would be the evolution of a performance tradition in which Shakespeare's plays were given in versions more complete in poetry, characterisation and action than these earliest adaptations. Nevertheless, even these later adaptations had similarities to the adaptations of the seventeenth century.

[52] See for example the opening chapter of Gundolf's *Shakespeare und der deutsche Geist*.
[53] Flemming, *Schauspiel*, p. 31.

3

Shakespeare and the
mid-eighteenth-century theatre

THE NATIONAL THEATRE MOVEMENT AND THE DOMESTIC DRAMA

For the first half of the eighteenth century, professional actors in Germany worked under conditions scarcely better than those tolerated by the English Comedians. The only regular theatre over this period was at the courts of the various small states that comprised the confusingly diverse political patchwork of Germany. In these court theatres, the repertoire was confined mainly to Italian opera and French tragedy and comedy, performed in French by French actors. German actors still had to travel from town to town, often performing and living in the most squalid of circumstances. Early in the century, their repertoire was composed primarily of *Haupt- und Staatsaktionen*, plays that combined a sententious heroic action with obscene farce, which involved much improvisation. Such productions were a direct outgrowth from the days of the English Comedians.

The first consistent attempt to bridge the gap between the popular theatre and the 'high' culture of the court theatres was made by the acting troupe led by Caroline Neuber, who, under the tutelage of Gottsched, with limited success introduced on to the popular stage German versions of neoclassical tragedies written by him and playwrights of his persuasion. She also attempted, again not altogether successfully, to impose stylistic uniformity on tragedy and to introduce propriety into comedy by symbolically expelling from the stage Hanswurst, the generic low-comic figure who had been introduced by the English comedians. Despite her own and Gottsched's ambitions, however, Neuber was excluded from the court theatres. It was only after the mid-point of the century that the German theatre started moving slowly towards permanently bridging the gap between the court and popular cultures.

This change was a function of wider changes occurring within the social and political hierarchy of German life, which, in the latter half of the eighteenth century, was beginning its long transition from the rule of the aristocracy to that of the middle classes. This change was, it must be emphasised, gradual. Economic and political fragmentation and the lack of any major urban centres or of one capital city meant that Germany did not undergo either the continuous constitutional development of England or the turmoil that France experienced during the Revolution. While the German middle classes were undoubtedly stirred by some ambition for power, their status in most of the small states of which Germany was composed was relatively comfortable. As their economic well-being usually depended on the goodwill of the local aristocratic ruler, their resistance to the old absolutism tended to be passive, rather than active.[1] Not surprisingly, therefore, the drama that expressed the ambitions of this class would combine its values with a respect for the order that the old aristocratic dispensation stood for.

In the theatre, social changes were reflected in two major ways. First, the popular theatre, which by the middle of the century was attracting middle-class audiences, aspired to combine with the court theatres to form national theatres that would appeal to all social classes and not only to the aristocracy. Such a theatre would, according to J. E. Schlegel – as we have seen, the first major apologist for Shakespeare – not only entertain the audience but improve its morals and refine its taste. Indeed, he saw it as the central, formative institution of a society that prized moral rectitude and valued good taste, claiming, not perhaps too accurately, historical precedents for this.

> The good and courteous manners of the Athenians grew to the extent that the good taste of their theatre grew. The Romans started to become civil at the same time as they had a theatre after the model of the Greeks. People today are considered to be more refined to the same extent that their theatre is fine and more complete.[2]

Theatre, he argued, cultivates the taste of audiences so that they become more sensitive human beings and worthier citizens. During the 1750s and 1760s, calls for a national theatre on the model suggested by Schlegel could be heard with increasing frequency, though standing theatres, founded specifically to further this purpose and occupied by German acting troupes that needed no longer to travel to earn their living, were slow to be established. Even when the first national theatre was founded, in Hamburg in 1767, it lasted a scant two years. Not until 1776 did the first court theatre with a purely German company open, at Gotha under the direction of Konrad Ekhof. 1776 also saw the reconstitution of the Habsburg court

---

[1] Alan Menhennet, *Order and Freedom: Literature and Society in Germany from 1720 to 1805* (London, 1973), pp. 35–40.
[2] Johann Elias Schlegel, 'Gedanken zur Aufnahme des dänischen Theaters', *Ausgewählte Werke* (Weimar, 1963), p. 569.

theatre in Vienna, the Burgtheater, as a national theatre, while three years later, the Mannheim court theatre was also decreed a national theatre. Furthermore, during these years, under private auspices, Friedrich Ludwig Schröder established a standing theatre in Hamburg that, despite its liberal repertoire, also aimed primarily to improve the taste and manners of its audience.[3] Over the following decades, standing theatres came to be founded in all major German cities, most in the form of court theatres that now opened their doors to the general public.

The second way in which social change came to be reflected in the theatre was in the repertoire. By the middle of the century, both Gottschedian neoclassical tragedy and the rough-and-ready *Haupt- und Staatsaktionen* were fast disappearing, to be replaced by various forms of light entertainment, including the *Singspiel*, a comic play with songs and musical interludes. New too in the repertoire of the travelling troupes was the domestic drama, both comic and tragic, which was concerned not with the lives of historical or classical heroes, but with the everyday existence of the middle classes. Domestic drama, which fully realised the rational idealism of the Enlightenment, demonstrated the harmony and reasonability of the human condition and aimed to increase audience sympathy for their fellow human beings. In general, the domestic drama was sentimental in tone and moralistic in intent, advocating the virtues of sexual continence, diligence and loyalty to family. The first of these plays appeared in the 1750s in the form of translations of English playwrights such as Lillo and Moore, but through the efforts of native German playwrights, especially Lessing, the domestic drama increased in popularity over several decades, well after the troupes had settled into the standing theatres.[4] In fact, during the 1770s, the repertoires of both the newly-formed standing theatres and of those troupes that were still travelling suggest that there was a distinct difference, even antipathy, between the prominent literary movement of *Sturm und Drang* and the domestic drama. While *Sturm und Drang* writers had a substantial reading public, their plays enjoyed very little success in the theatre. For example, in 1776, the year that saw both the establishment of standing theatres with German repertoires and the first performance of several *Sturm und Drang* dramas, *Sturm und Drang* received only a minimal number of performances. A statistical analysis of the repertoires of the fourteen companies recorded in Reichard's *Theater-Kalendar* shows that while Lessing's comedy *Minna von Barnhelm* received twenty-eight performances and his tragedy *Emilia Galotti* twenty-one,

---

[3] Paul F. Hoffmann, *Friedrich Ludwig Schröder als Dramaturg und Regisseur* (Berlin, 1939), p. 2.
[4] Translations of Moore's *The Gambler* and Lillo's *The London Merchant* were first performed in 1754 and 1755 respectively, while Lessing's *Miss Sara Sampson*, the first and one of the most popular of all German domestic dramas, was first performed in 1755.

Goethe's *Götz von Berlichingen*, the most celebrated play of *Sturm und Drang*, which had created a great stir when published in 1774, received a scant three performances and Klinger's *Die Zwillinge* (*The Twins*), a major work of *Sturm und Drang*, only seven.[5]

Such statistics would suggest that the German theatre was still little prepared to stage the works of Shakespeare, the icon of *Sturm und Drang*. A major obstacle to their acceptance on stage was the relatively narrow range of dramatic material that audiences were prepared to accept, combined with a persistent taste for the styles and forms of French theatre. Although the opening of the national theatres occurred at the expense of the French companies in the court theatres, the middle-class audience expressed its new-found theatrical freedom not by embracing the aesthetics of *Sturm und Drang*, but by co-opting the Francophone tastes of the aristocracy into their own drama. The most popular play at the independent Hamburg national theatre between 1767 and 1769 was *Minna von Barnhelm*, but after that the most frequently performed works were the comedies of Molière, Marivaux, Destouches and La Chaussée, followed by the domestic drama of Beaumarchais and Diderot. Shakespeare was not performed once.[6]

Had Shakespeare's plays been performed unaltered during the 1760s and 1770s, they would have strongly offended audiences' tastes. For a play to succeed at this time, it had to be set in an environment that approximated to the everyday experience of the audience. Shakespeare's plays, with their unfamiliar historical or fantastic settings, would not appeal to such constricted tastes. Audiences also favoured a restrained realism in dialogue, which meant that the lyrical and descriptive passages containing much of Shakespeare's greatest poetry would not be considered suitable for theatrical representation. By retarding the action such passages were, to the thinking of the time, *de facto* undramatic. Audiences also expected dramatic action to be easily comprehensible and complete; it should also demonstrate the workings of a rational order. Shakespeare, however, offended the conventions of eighteenth-century dramaturgy. Often his plays did not dramatise the whole story, they left too much of the action to the imagination of the audience. His inconsistencies in plotting and brash toleration of anachronism would have been considered unpardonable deficiencies, while the mixture of comic and pathetic elements would have jarred audiences' sensitivities, as they, like all but the writers of *Sturm und Drang*, preferred the unity of tone associated with the French drama. It goes

---

[5] Karl S. Guthke, 'Repertoire: Deutsches Theaterleben im Jahre 1776', in *Literarisches Leben im achtzehnten Jahrhundert in Deutschland und in der Schweiz* (Berne and Munich, 1975), p. 293. Some popular comedies and *Singspiele* were performed more frequently than Lessing's plays.
[6] Sybille Maurer-Schmoock, *Deutsches Theater im 18. Jahrhundert* (Tübingen, 1983), pp. 130–1. *Minna von Barnhelm* was given sixteen times, Diderot's *Der Hausvater* (*Le Père de famille*) twelve times and Beaumarchais's *Eugénie* ten times.

without saying that his coarse humour and obscenity were inadmissible in performance. Additionally, audiences preferred playwrights to observe the neoclassical unities, which Shakespeare emphatically did not.

But perhaps the main objection to Shakespeare on stage at this time would have been centred around the discomforting outlook implied by his plays. Mid-eighteenth-century audiences were accustomed to sympathise with the characters they saw on stage and took pleasure in having the conflicts they experienced resolved rationally. Plays should conclude not with a display of man as the victim of irrational forces, but with an ending that demonstrates the operation of a 'poetic justice that guarantees the moral view'.[7] Accordingly, audiences preferred the mild situations and touching humanity of the domestic drama, not the violent action and refulgent personalities of unadapted Shakespeare.

> People wanted to feel compassion not violent emotion, [see] pictures of families, not elemental human tragedy, order and comprehension, not the rousing and bewildering creation of a poetic world, the well-tried, everyday types of the sentimental middle-class drama, not the daringly outlined, superhuman and almost inhuman characters of the Englishman.[8]

The vision *Sturm und Drang* had of Shakespeare was totally antithetical to prevailing theatrical tastes. *Sturm und Drang* regarded him as a visionary with access to the irrational centre of human conduct and understanding of man as a natural being. His plays demonstrated neither the working of a moralistic 'poetic justice', nor did they argue for social cohesion in the way that the domestic drama did. *Sturm und Drang* prized Shakespeare's characters because they shattered the narrow limits of dramatic action as circumscribed by contemporary taste. Indeed, for them the plays validated the values of the individual rather than those of society.[9] Given such a view, Shakespeare's drama could be regarded as potentially subversive of social order and therefore directly opposed to the purpose of theatre in the eighteenth century.

Despite these obstacles, Shakespeare could not be entirely ignored. While *Sturm und Drang* enthusiasm for Shakespeare was not immediately reciprocated in the theatre, that enthusiasm had been in part the outcome of a popular interest in Shakespeare that had been growing among the German reading public during the 1760s. This growth of interest may, indeed, be partially associated with the vogue for domestic drama, as, despite their exotic settings, certain of Shakespeare's plays such as *Romeo*

---

[7] Karl S. Guthke, 'Shakespeare im Urteil der deutschen Theaterkritik des 18. Jahrhunderts', *Shakespeare Jahrbuch* (Heidelberg, 1967), 52.
[8] Guthke, 'Kritik', p. 45.   [9] Gundolf, *Shakespeare und der deutsche Geist*, pp. 252–79.

and Juliet and *Othello* were regarded as forerunners of the genre.[10] During the 1770s, the theatre began to respond to the reading public's interest in Shakespeare, and, as the decade progressed, attempts were made to reconcile that interest with the practice of the theatre. Hence, when Shakespeare's plays eventually found their way on to the German stage, they were given in adaptations designed specifically to appeal to audiences raised on the domestic drama.

WIELAND'S TRANSLATION OF SHAKESPEARE

The widespread interest in Shakespeare among the reading public of the 1760s was due to the highly popular translations of several of his plays by the poet Christoph Martin Wieland. These translations were overdue. Much of the early critical discussion of Shakespeare had been conducted by writers who had a very limited knowledge of his work. Even Lessing, Shakespeare's keenest advocate before *Sturm und Drang*, probably knew only a handful of the plays.[11] Most critics had to judge Shakespeare by reputation or by the few translations available, which were far from adequate. The first complete translation of any Shakespeare play, of *Julius Caesar* in 1741, had been made not by a man of letters at all, but by the Prussian ambassador to England, C. W. von Borck, who had so little confidence in the quality of the play that he claimed he had translated it out of idleness.[12] His translation gave no idea of the variety of Shakespeare's language, for it was in alexandrines, the metrical form then used in all neoclassical tragedy. It was also applied indiscriminately, both where Shakespeare used blank verse and where he used prose.[13] Some scenes from *Richard III* were published in a Leipzig periodical in 1755,[14] and three years later a translation of Garrick's adaptation of *Romeo and Juliet* was published in Basel. This was the most substantial achievement in Shakespearean translation to that point, written as it was in fairly creditable blank verse.[15]

[10] Roger Bauer, 'Die europäische Shakespeare-Rezeption im 18. Jahrhundert', *Shakespeare-Jahrbuch* (Heidelberg, 1985), 154–5.

[11] These were probably *Othello, Hamlet, Richard III, Romeo and Juliet* and *King Lear*. See E. M. Batley, 'Rational and Irrational Elements in Lessing's Shakespeare Criticism', *Germanic Review*, 45 (1970), 7.

[12] Caspar Wilhelm von Borck, 'Versuch einer gebundenen Uebersetzung des Trauer-Spiels von dem Tode des Julius Caesar', in Blinn, *Diskussion*, p. 40. This was the translation that initiated the first major debate about Shakespeare between Gottsched and J. E. Schlegel.

[13] See the edition in Joachim Müller, *Shakespeare und ein deutscher Anfang* (Berlin, 1977).

[14] In *Neue Erweiterungen der Erkenntnis und des Vergnügens* (Frankfurt and Leipzig). The scenes are reprinted in Rudolf Genée, *Geschichte der Shakespeare'schen Dramen in Deutschland* (Leipzig, 1870), pp. 456–71.

[15] The translation was by Simon Grynaeus, published in a three-volume anthology that included several other English plays. See Simon Grynaeus, *Die erste deutsche Romeo-Übersetzung*, ed. Ernst Heinrich Mensel (Northampton, Mass., 1933) for a discussion of the translation and the complete text.

Only in 1762 did Wieland begin his famous translation, which was initially intended to be of the complete plays.

It would be difficult to overstate the importance of Wieland's translation in the introduction of Shakespeare into Germany. In the eighteenth century, most foreign plays were published, as *Richard III* had been, in passages linked by plot summary, not as a complete text, so the very conception behind Wieland's work, a complete translation of foreign texts, was novel. So too was his claim that he made no attempt to make the plays more beautiful than they are.[16] The very publication and Wieland's ambitions reflected the importance Shakespeare was rapidly acquiring among German readers. So too did the public reception. Published between 1762 and 1766, the twenty-two plays he managed to translate were probably more widely read than any other published drama in Germany.[17] Although there were those who were quick to correct, improve and expand his work, especially Johann Joachim Eschenburg, who published a revised translation of all the plays in 1775, until the famous Schlegel/Tieck edition began to appear at the end of the century, Wieland's translations remained the edition of Shakespeare the public read and the one on which theatre people based their stage versions.

Despite this popularity, the initial critical reaction was not entirely favourable, primarily because Wieland failed to meet the expectations either of conservative critical opinion or of those critics who knew and appreciated Shakespeare in English. For example, the playwright Christian Felix Weisse, who was representative of conservative opinion, questioned the wisdom of complete translations, fearing that the 'German Shake-speares' they would spawn would return the theatre to its crude origins. They 'will awaken the buried Hanswursts, sing grave songs, become raving kings, present tempests and storms with witches dances in calfo-nium, and have death knells rung loudly by the grave'.[18] On the other hand, critics who had a close knowledge of Shakespeare, such as Heinrich von Gerstenberg, faulted Wieland for his failure to recapture in German the quality of the original English, upbraiding him for his 'mistakes in tone, the stiffness of form, the foolish reprimands of the footnotes and the failure to understand Shakespeare's humour'.[19] It may well have been this dual

[16] Christoph Martin Wieland, *Gesammelte Schriften*, ed. Ernst Stadler, 10 vols. (Berlin, 1911), section 2, vol. 3, p. 566.
[17] The plays were issued as follows: 1762, vol. 1, *A Midsummer Night's Dream* and *King Lear*; 1763, vol. 2, *As You Like It, Measure for Measure* and *The Tempest*; vol. 3, *The Merchant of Venice, Timon of Athens* and *King John*; 1764, vol. 4, *Julius Caesar, Antony and Cleopatra* and *The Comedy of Errors*; vol. 5, *Richard II, Henry IV Part 1*, and *Henry IV Part 2*; 1765, vol. 6, *Much Ado About Nothing, Macbeth* and *Two Gentlemen of Verona*; 1766, vol. 7, *Romeo and Juliet, Othello* and *Twelfth Night*; vol. 8, *Hamlet* and *The Winter's Tale*.
[18] Quoted in Ernst Stadler, *Wielands Shakespeare* (Strassburg, 1910), p. 78.
[19] Quoted Stadler, *Wielands Shakespeare*, p. 82.

hostility that led Wieland to give up the 'Herculean labour' of translating all the plays, though even before the first volume was published, there were signs he was beginning to tire from the extended, disciplined effort required for successful translation.

Critical cavils notwithstanding, the translations were widely popular and eventually gained critical respect. Lessing considered them to be 'a book that cannot be recommended enough among us',[20] while Goethe preferred to read them for their 'great naturalness',[21] even after the appearance of the Schlegel translations. No doubt he recalled that, in his *Sturm und Drang* period, even though he read some Shakespeare in English, he also relied considerably on Wieland's translations. So, while the negative critical reaction might have been caused by Wieland's failing to please either literary conservatives or radical critics, by the same token he could also appeal to conservative and radical readers because, like his criticism, the translations incorporated both the enthusiasm and the reservations of mid-eighteenth-century opinion on Shakespeare. On the one hand, Wieland realised that Shakespeare challenged the prevalence of neoclassicism and mild domestic drama, because his plays embodied a vision of the total experience of human nature far beyond that of any contemporary writer.[22] On the other hand, he was not prepared to assimilate fully the range of Shakespeare's *œuvre* and the variety of dramatic expression necessitated by the totality of his vision. This limitation was reflected in his translation. Gundolf has described it as the work of an eighteenth-century 'poet of sensibility', who dismissed Shakespeare's crudities and irregularities because they offended his delicate feelings: 'It was not his reason that rebelled, but his nerves.'[23] Gundolf saw Wieland as an 'impressionist' with no sense of form, who delighted in playing with appearances, taking 'Shakespeare's work as a sum of details, play by play, scene by scene, speech by speech, verse by verse – impromptus whose spiritual centre he never searched for'. More recent critics have articulately defended Wieland's work,[24] so that now it is easier to appreciate it as a product of its time, even though it could never be regarded as a lastingly adequate version of Shakespeare's plays.

Although the translations initially made their impact on the reading rather than the theatre-going public, they were not written in total ignorance of the theatre. As a young man, Wieland had been associated

[20] Lessing, *Werke*, vol. 4, p. 301.
[21] *Goethes Gespräche*, 5 vols. (Zurich and Stuttgart, 1969), vol. 2, p. 766.
[22] 'Brief an Zimmermann. 24. April 1758', in Stellmacher, *Auseinandersetzung*, p. 64.
[23] Gundolf, *Shakespeare und der deutsche Geist*, p. 175.
[24] See especially Urs Helmensdorfer, 'Wielands deutscher Shakespeare', in *Der deutsche Shakespeare*, ed. Reinhold Grimm *et al.* (Basel, Hamburg and Vienna, 1965), pp. 59–74, and Kenneth E. Larson, 'Wieland's Shakespeare: A Reappraisal', *Lessing Yearbook*, 16 (1984), 229–49.

with an amateur theatre group in his home town of Biberach in Swabia, which had been active since the seventeenth century, staging plays usually at the traditional times of Christmas and Shrovetide. It is certain that neither the actors' skills nor the physical production were particularly distinguished, nor did the Biberach performances have any impact on larger developments in the German theatre. Nevertheless, as early as 1761, Wieland was responsible for staging in Biberach what was almost certainly the first production of any Shakespeare play in Germany under his name, *The Tempest*. Later productions of Shakespeare were staged after Wieland had left Biberach. Virtually nothing is known of them except the cast lists, which are extensive, suggesting that the plays were given in fairly complete versions. Productions included *Antony and Cleopatra* in 1769, a play not to be seen in the professional theatre until the nineteenth century, *Macbeth* in 1771, *Hamlet* in 1773, *Othello* and *Romeo and Juliet* in 1774, *As You Like It* in 1775, which would not be seen elsewhere for over a century, *Two Gentlemen of Verona* in 1782 and *King Lear* in 1797.[25] In all cases, the Wieland translations of Shakespeare were probably used.

All of Wieland's translations with the exception of the first, *A Midsummer Night's Dream*, are in prose. This was not out of caprice but because Wieland believed that for Shakespeare form was nothing and content all, so the meaning was all that needed to be communicated.[26] He also had problems coming to terms with Shakespeare's language. As German in the middle of the eighteenth century was still more limited in vocabulary and syntactical variety than Elizabethan English had been, it was difficult to find verbal parallels to Shakespeare's rich English. Wieland must frequently have found himself oppressed by this inadequacy, for he accuses Shakespeare of using language that is 'hard, inflexible, turgid and twisted'.[27] At the same time, one suspects such shortcomings may have had personal causes. His translation of *A Midsummer Night's Dream* shows that he had an acute appreciation of Shakespeare's verse, while in the later translations several prose passages have an authentic Shakespearean ring to them, which suggests that Wieland might have had the capacity to produce translations that some of his negative critics would have appreciated had he not been hindered by lack of energy and an imperfect knowledge of English. Such passages are followed by long sections of literal translation that are lacking in rhythm and life. Disconcertingly, there is no means of detecting why some passages are translated literally and others are given a more poetic

---

[25] Little is known of this theatre. Stahl provides a summary of its work with regard to Shakespeare (*Shakespeare und das deutsche Theater*, pp. 50–7). Further information can be found in L. F. Ofterdinger, 'Geschichte des Theaters in Biberach', *Württemburgische Vierteljahrschrift für Landesgeschichte*, 6 (1883). The translation Wieland used for the production of *The Tempest* is lost.

[26] Stadler, *Wielands Shakespeare*, p. 25.   [27] Wieland, *Gesammelte Schriften*, 2, 3, p. 566.

rendering. As a result, variety appears to be inconsistency and, along with the frequent mistranslations, misunderstandings, omissions and the notorious footnotes, it mars the overall achievement of the translations.

The translations' strengths and weakness are apparent in the version of *Macbeth*, published in 1765, a year before Wieland gave the project up uncompleted. This translation is of particular interest as it was one of the first to be staged in the theatre in Biberach. As the production was a popular success, the text may have had some qualities that appealed to Wieland's contemporaries.

For eighteenth-century audiences, Macbeth would have been a figure difficult to assimilate as in him are mixed traits that cannot be rationally associated. He is an amalgam of heroism, weakness and thorough evil. Audience response to him is confusing, as one is invited to abhor the man while sympathising with him, a response familiar perhaps to seventeenth- or twentieth-century audiences, but alien to those of the eighteenth, who generally expected to respond in a simpler way to dramatic characters. Wieland copes with this by playing down Macbeth's villainous side. He is primarily a man 'full of the milk of human kindness' and thoroughly distressed by 'the promptings of nature'. He does not have the size and barbarity of Shakespeare's hero. In the Sergeant's description of the battle against the Norwegian-led rebels, Macbeth is simply a brave soldier in Duncan's cause. The language lacks Shakespeare's brutality, 'disdaining fortune' becomes 'mit edler Verachtung des Glücks' ('with noble disdain of good fortune'), 'valour's minion' becomes 'Liebling der Tapferkeit' ('darling of valour'), while the graphic 'unseam'd him from the nave to the chaps' becomes the less strong 'er ihn von Wirbel bis zum Kinn aufgespaltet' ('he split him from the crown to the chin').[28] As Wieland's prose lacks the momentum of blank verse, one does not feel caught up in the dangerous excitement of Macbeth's heroics. More importantly, he missed those places where Shakespeare draws parallels between Macbeth and the rebels he is fighting. For example, in translating Ross's report on the fight with Cawdor, Wieland avoided mentioning 'self-comparisons'. Later, when Ross tells Macbeth how Duncan received the news of his heroism, all reference to 'what thyself didst make strange images of death' was omitted. The foreshadowing of the murder of Duncan in the language is absent; so therefore is much of the compulsion that draws Macbeth to commit it.

If the heroism of Wieland's Macbeth is not double-edged, neither are other salient features of his character. The prose deprives him of the stature which verse can give dramatic character. In particular, Wieland disliked Shakespeare's use of rhyme as he considered it more suited to comedy, but

[28] *Ibid.*, p. 73.

this means that the grim humour of Macbeth's comments on Duncan's death-knell and the need for Banquo's soul to find heaven or hell is missing and the comments appear irrelevant. Throughout metaphors are either paraphrased or simplified, so that highly expressive lines like Macbeth's

> this my hand will rather
> The multitudinous seas incarnadine,
> Making the green-one red (II:2, 61-3)

become, lamely, 'eh würde diese meine Hand deine unermessliche See zu Purpur machen' ('this my hand would rather make your [Neptune's] immeasurable sea purple').[29] While a vestige of the original meaning is there, the tortured syntax that so aptly captures Macbeth's torment and his powerful imagination has gone. Also, whenever Wieland feels bound to give a painstakingly literal explanation of Shakespeare's images and allusions, his characters become insufferably prosaic. So Lady Macbeth, in comparing her husband to 'the poor cat i' the adage', has to explain exactly what the adage is, and the concise 'letting I dare not wait upon I would' becomes 'die gerne Fische fienge, wenn sie nur die Füsse nicht nass machen musste' ('would gladly catch fish, if only she did not have to get her feet wet').[30] At such moments, the intimacy and humanity for which Shakespeare was valued appears to emerge as a domesticity far in spirit from the original.

It would be easy to multiply instances of the inadequacy of Wieland's translation, but it is not wholly a failure. Gundolf claims Wieland had no sense of Shakespeare's language as 'the expression and form of spiritual experience',[31] which may be true, but in contrast to the stiff alexandrines that had passed for elevated tragic utterance in Borck's translation of *Julius Caesar*, Wieland's idiomatic prose is often fresh and vital. For example, the dialogue between Macbeth and his wife immediately after the murder is tense and atmospheric. More impressive are some passages where the prose borders on poetry. For example Wieland's rendering of 'Come, seeling night' accurately captures the foreboding of the original.[32] For the first time in German, a high tragic experience is communicated to the audience in language approximating to that of everyday life.

No discussion of Wieland's translations can avoid the question of the footnotes. It was customary for translations to be accompanied by footnotes explaining obscure philological points, historical allusions and other information the reader might not necessarily know. Wieland used his footnotes for such a purpose, taking several of them from English editors, but he also used them to make several aesthetic judgements. While these

---

[29] *Ibid.*, p. 90.   [30] *Ibid.*, p. 85.   [31] Gundolf, *Shakespeare und der deutsche Geist*, p. 173.
[32] Wieland, *Gesammelte Schriften*, 2, 3, p. 101.

have traditionally been taken as indicative of the limitations of his appreciation of Shakespeare, they also served the valuable function of distancing, and therefore making more acceptable to the general reader, material that otherwise might have been met with impatience, even disgust.[33] They do not burden the translations – indeed, whole acts have no footnotes at all – but when they come they can be obtrusive, especially when clustered together after several pages without them. They may suggest that at particular phases in the translation, Wieland grew aggravated with his material and therefore imply that the variability in the translations' quality was due to his changing moods.

The commonest use of the footnote is to comment on Shakespeare's word-play. Often the pun is explained, and, if it is humorous, it is rebuked, for Wieland, in common with most critics of his day, disliked such wit. Nicholas Rowe had dismissed it as 'the common vice of the age [Shakespeare] lived in',[34] Wieland called it 'frosty humour'. As the translations progressed, his complaints became more frequent, until eventually he cut whole stretches of dialogue, even whole scenes. He became especially irate with word-play that involved sexual innuendo or appeals to the proverbially low taste of the Elizabethan audience. So, for example, he dismissed Toby Belch and Andrew Aguecheek as 'a pair of idle, dissolute, drunken rascals, whose stale jokes, word-play and absurd notions could only amuse an English theatre and then only friends of depraved taste and the mob'.[35] Also he thought the Falstaff scenes appeal only to an Englishman 'who has a good portion of punch in his head'.[36] Wieland so cut the plays in which these characters appear that the final translations are more in the form in which most translations were published, in extracts.

At times it is difficult to understand why Wieland objects to Shakespeare's vulgarity. Salarino's innocent line in the opening scene of *The Merchant of Venice*, 'I know Antonio is sad to think upon his merchandise', calls forth a veritable diatribe against the lapses in taste that are a specific feature of this play.[37] But Wieland can allow obscenities to pass him by without comment. In *Measure for Measure* mention of Pompey's bum is omitted, but the overdoing of Mistress Overdone is included and goes unremarked.[38] Interestingly enough, the most striking breaches of decorum like the Porter's scene in *Macbeth* are not commented upon; in fact, in this specific case, the translation is both literal and effective. There is

---

[33] See Eva Maria Inbar, 'Zur Funktion der Fussnoten in Wielands Shakespeare-Übersetzung', *Literaturwissenschaftliches Jahrbuch der Görres Gesellschaft*, 21 (1980), 57–73.

[34] Nicholas Rowe, 'Life of Shakespeare', *The Plays of William Shakespeare*, ed. George Steevens (London, 1774), p. xvi.

[35] Wieland, *Gesammelte Schriften*, 2, 3, p. 361.   [36] *Ibid.*, 2, 2, p. 511.   [37] *Ibid.*, p. 3.

[38] Though the line is mistranslated as 'Overdone was the last', not 'by the last'. Wieland, *Gesammelte Schriften*, 2, 1, p. 258.

also no excessive comment on Shakespeare's most sexual play, *Othello*. Only Emilia's coarseness causes a cutting remark. This suggests that sex alone did not offend Wieland; rather he found it difficult to accept the mixture of the poetic with the earthly, the refined with the coarsely sensual. Both *The Merchant of Venice* and *Romeo and Juliet* offended him greatly for this reason.

CHRISTIAN FELIX WEISSE

Wieland's translation of *Romeo and Juliet* was performed in Biberach in December 1774. It did not, however, find a wider audience, possibly because there was already a highly popular version of the play written by the very man who had questioned the wisdom of a complete translation of Shakespeare, Christian Felix Weisse. By profession a collector of taxes in Leipzig, as a young man Weisse had been a close friend of Lessing. His facility with his pen encouraged him to write plays, several of which found their way into the regular repertoire. Weisse's most successful work was in the *Singspiel*, but he is best known to history as author of two of the most widely-performed adaptations of Shakespearean material in the whole of the eighteenth century, *Richard III* (1759) and *Romeo und Julie* (1767). Although these plays would not stand revival today, they are of interest as their popularity suggests they typify much that appealed to contemporary taste. *Richard III* was probably written with no knowledge of Shakespeare's play,[39] so it is of tangential interest in the history of Shakespearean performance. But *Romeo und Julie* is another matter entirely, as Weisse refashioned the play with full knowledge of Shakespeare's work and, however limited it appears in contrast to Shakespeare's tragedy, this so-called 'improved' original still has some life of its own. First performed in Leipzig in April 1767 by Gottfried Koch's troupe, it quickly found its way into the repertoires of most of the travelling actors and was probably in its time the most successful tragedy yet written for the German stage.[40]

Weisse knew Garrick's adaptation of *Romeo and Juliet*, and he acknowledged Garrick's influence over his thinking on the play. Garrick, while not altering Shakespeare's action, had cut or modified several of the elaborate metaphors, word-plays and rhymes on the grounds that such 'Jingle and Quibble . . . were always thought the great objection to reviving [the play].'[41] Weisse agreed, adding that Shakespeare had

---

[39] Weisse claimed he only read Shakespeare's play after completing his own. See Christian Felix Weisse, *Richard der Dritte*, ed. Daniel Jacoby and August Sauer (Berlin, 1904; reprinted Nendeln, 1968), p. 7.

[40] Stahl, *Shakespeare und das deutsche Theater*, p. 61.

[41] *The Plays of David Garrick*, 7 vols. (Carbondale and Edwardsville, 1980–2), vol. 3, ed. Harry William Pedicord and Frederick Louis Bergmann, p. 77.

overburdened his play with several trivial and superfluous things that are unnecessary to the action. In several places his wit so overflows that it lapses into childishness . . . The frequent rhymes he mixes in weaken the veracity of the natural conversation, so indispensable to dramatic dialogue, especially when the setting and action are taken from domestic life.[42]

Above everything else Weisse, who subtitled *Romeo und Julie* 'a bourgeois tragedy', was concerned to capture the reality of domestic life with which his audience was familiar. While he restricted the action to Verona, he exploited none of the setting's poetic potential, locating his action firmly in the Capulet household, rewriting it in idiomatic prose and recasting it in the closed form of the domestic drama. The reduced dimensions of his play-world are also reflected in the *dramatis personae*, which he cut from Shakespeare's thirty-one characters to eight: Romeo, Julie, Herr von Capellet, Frau von Capellet, Montecchio (Montague), Laura (Julie's confidante), Benvoglio (a doctor) and Pietro (Romeo's servant). As Montecchio only appears in the last scene,[43] Romeo only in Acts I and V and Pietro just incidentally, the majority of the action is carried by five characters.

Neatness and clarity are the essence of this adaptation. For a start, like most writers of domestic drama, Weisse observed the unities. The opening line of the play, delivered by Julie, who is waiting for Romeo in her room, is 'the clock has already struck twelve', and in the last act Pietro says it is half-past eleven when the dying Romeo asks him for the time.[44] The twenty-four hours of the action include most of Shakespeare's events from the lovers' night together to the end. The ball, the balcony-scene and Tybalt's death are all recounted in an expository conversation between Julie and Laura as the play opens. This gives Weisse the opportunity to clarify Shakespeare's problematical time-scheme and make the chronology of events more orderly. The ball where Romeo and Julie met took place two months ago, the death of Tybalt one month ago and the secret wedding of the lovers some time in the past too. Romeo has to leave only because his hiding-place has been discovered. Also, as the month of mourning Tybalt's death is now past, Julie can marry Paris, a fact that Weisse has Herr von Capellet emphasise so strongly that he seems to be reproving Shakespeare for his carelessness in not observing the decorum of mourning. Like the well-made plays of the nineteenth century, which it foreshadows, *Romeo und Julie* dramatises the catastrophe of a long series of events. Unity of place is less rigidly observed than that of time. Acts I

---

[42] Christian Felix Weisse, *Romeo und Julie*, in *Die Aufnahme Shakespeares auf der Bühne der Aufklärung in den sechziger und siebziger Jahren*, ed. Fritz Brüggemann (Leipzig, n.d. [1937]), p. 256.
[43] His role was cut in later editions of the play.   [44] Weisse, *Romeo*, pp. 237 and 297.

through IV are set in Julie's room, but Act V is shifted to the churchyard, not, one suspects, from necessity, as it would have been quite possible, even convenient, to play it in Julie's room, but because the gloomy surroundings had popular appeal.

Suspense is Weisse's main constructive principle, with everything depending on whether the secret of the marriage will be discovered. All of Acts II and III centre around whether Julie will successfully resist her parents' demand that she marry Paris. Great care is also taken to establish the credibility of her apparent death. Benvoglio, who arranges it all, carefully outlines the time each phase of her burial will take, painstakingly explaining the plague laws, which require instant burial.[45] After she has drunk the draught, suspense continues through her mother wishing to stay with her while she sleeps. After she is 'dead', there is even a danger she will not be buried as her father wants to keep her 'corpse' in the house, a proceeding he is only dissuaded from by the vision of his daughter's unquiet spirit not being laid to rest.[46] The misunderstanding by which Romeo thinks Julie is really dead is more simple and credible than in Shakespeare.

What is most striking in Weisse's plotting is his care to make all events as probable as he could. Critics had faulted Shakespeare for improbability and Weisse corrected this. Each detail had to be justified. For example, while there are no pressing reasons why Shakespeare's Juliet does not flee with Romeo, there are for Weisse's. Julie pleads with Romeo to let her go with him, but he resists her on the grounds that running away is not suitable for a lady of her rank, then by the more convincing argument that if she goes with him, they will be hunted down, brought back to Verona, and parted for ever.[47] Later in the play, Weisse was careful to have Benvoglio explain why he has the sleeping-draught with him, and, at the end of Act IV, to make sure that Julie can credibly arise from her coffin, had him instruct Laura not to screw down the coffin, as he may wish to examine her to discover the cause of her illness.[18] The purpose of such clarity becomes apparent in Act V when Julie, on waking to see Romeo dying, loads him with questions. This is not for the audience to find out what has happened, for they know; rather it is for them to be convinced the characters themselves know. The probable world Weisse creates on stage is a complete entity, logical, enclosed, independent and inviolable. It is a play-world totally different from that of the Elizabethan theatre or the English comedians. It is a creation of the illusionistic stage.

Weisse's themes resemble Shakespeare's though they are articulated differently. Both plays focus on how young love is destroyed by an

---

[45] *Ibid.*, p. 275.   [46] *Ibid.*, p. 289.   [47] *Ibid.*, p. 245.   [48] *Ibid.*, pp. 274 and 290–1.

indifferent world, both concentrate on conflict between generations. But for Weisse, the feud between the Montecchios and Capellets is a secondary concern. As a domestic dramatist, he is more interested in relationships within the family, in this case that between parent and child. So strong is this concern that when Romeo returns he almost seems an irrelevant figure. Capellet and his wife have a far more dominant presence. They are both figures familiar from the domestic drama. Capellet is the overbearing father, who sees himself as representing 'the healthy reason of man' against 'this giddy, whining, cowardly sex'[49] of women. His extended paroxysms of grief over Julie's 'dead' body might seem to be inconsistent with his tyrannical nature, but they do not come as a surprise or seem false, due to Weisse's care to place him constantly in a context where he is seen ironically. This is achieved by his being seen through the eyes of the women characters. Frau von Capellet, unlike Shakespeare's unpleasant virago, stands for the humane values that appealed to audiences of the day. She is torn between sympathy for her daughter and the obligation to obey her husband. Her ambiguous position means she sees the world other than in the black and white values of her husband. For example, she suggests Tybalt was probably the architect of his own fate and, even though she is ignorant of Julie's marriage, agrees that Romeo is not a villain. She even speculates that he might have been punished enough. 'If Romeo has a conscience,' she observes to Julie, 'then he is already sufficiently punished.'[50] Through her, that sympathy, which is an important constituent of the domestic drama, is felt as a more potent force than Capellet's wanton raving.

The lovers are not Shakespeare's impulsive adolescents. Romeo is a sober young man, sensitive to Julie's love, capable of tears as he parts from her, but careful and responsible above all else. His grief does not blot out the rest of the world. When he dispatches Pietro with letters before he dies, he makes it clear his affairs are well arranged. Indeed, so orderly is his death that one is tempted to question its necessity. Julie is a more complex, even problematic creation, and her presence gives the play interest. She is more than just the young, enthusiastic lover who never doubts the strength of her feelings for Romeo. From the opening scene on, she is obsessed with death, so that the sleeping-draught holds a peculiar fascination for her. She puzzles her family. Her month-long mourning for Tybalt strikes them not as an oddity but as normal behaviour for her, suggesting that the girl is hysterical. This gives her role, by far the largest in the play, an individual dimension and makes it a genuine challenge for the actress, who must decide whether her constant lamentations are purely intended to put off her

---

[49] *Ibid.*, p. 269.   [50] *Ibid.*, p. 259.

marriage to Paris or whether they are an expression of her personality. If they are the latter, then the hysteria they indicate makes a credible character out of traits that otherwise would seem contradictory, in particular her pitifully abject behaviour to her father and her potential heroism that will brave any torment to be united with her lover. Weisse's Julie is possibly closer to Ibsen than she is to Shakespeare, but she is a fine example of how Shakespearean material could enrich later playwrights' conceptions of character.

In spirit, Weisse's *Romeo und Julie* is far from Shakespeare. It has none of his poetry; in fact, Weisse often seems to be parodying it. For example, when Romeo and Julie part, like their Shakespearean counterparts they are confused as to whether a nightingale or lark is singing, but this confusion is communicated in a dialogue that, in contrast to Shakespeare, strikes us as being of withering banality:

> ROMEO: Hörst du draussen die Lerche, den Vorboten des Morgens! Ich muss fort, ich muss fort Julie!
> JULIE: Nein, nein, Romeo, es ist die Nachtigall und nicht die Lerche! du darfst nicht fort!
> ROMEO: O wär' es so! aber siehst du nicht die Dämmerung schon über jene Hügel herübersteigen?
> JULIE: Nein, Romeo, glaube mir, es ist der Mond, der zu meinem Troste am Himmel verzögert.

> (ROMEO: Do you hear the lark out there, the messenger of morning? I must be gone. I must be gone, Julie! JULIE: No, no, Romeo, it is the nightingale and not the lark! You need not go! ROMEO: If only it were! but do you not see the dawn already crossing the hills? JULIE: No, Romeo, believe me, it is the moon that delays in the sky for my comfort).[51]

But it is banal primarily because we are reminded of the richness of its source. When Weisse does not recall the language of the original, his dialogue can be tense and convincing. By the same token, the small world of the Capellet household, intolerably restrictive in contrast to Shakespeare's Verona, works on its own terms. Furthermore, the conflict between daughter and parents is quite exciting, and in its day the final meeting of the lovers was able to draw copious tears from its audiences. In 1767, no play attributed to Shakespeare had yet been seen on the public stage. For all its limitations, Weisse's reinterpretation of *Romeo and Juliet* to suit contemporary tastes was an important step toward the eventual acceptance of Shakespeare in the German theatre.

---

[51] *Ibid.*, p. 248.

MACBETH IN THE POPULAR THEATRE OF VIENNA

By the early 1770s, a few more Shakespeare plays had been adapted to fit the form and milieu of the domestic drama.[52] But though the domestic drama was the primary dramatic mode of the 1760s and 1770s, it was not the sole one. In Vienna, for example, the popular theatre still encompassed a repertoire that was recognisably an offshoot from the drama of the English Comedians, appealing to a broad cross-section of audiences which retained a delight in spectacle, in sensational theatrical effects and in the mixture of the comic with the heroic and pathetic. Since the early eighteenth century, All Souls' Day had been celebrated in Vienna by a performance of Tirso de Molina's Don Juan play, *The Stone Guest*, but it had been banned in 1769 as it was considered to offend against good taste. The gap was filled by the actor Stephanie the Younger, best known as the later librettist for Mozart's *Die Entführung aus dem Serail* (*The Abduction from the Seraglio*), who adapted *Macbeth* for the occasion, incorporating into the action events that recall moments from Molina's play. This metamorphosis of the tragedy, among the most notorious of all Shakespearean adaptations, might well be regarded as an anomaly of theatre history, were it not for the moderately widespread popular and even critical acclaim it earned during the 1770s, not only in Vienna but even in some German cities.

After its first performance in November 1772, a critic found Stephanie's version to be a considerable improvement over the original as it recast Shakespeare's material into a 'regular' play in which an improbable action was made probable.[53] It is difficult to accede to this judgement, even when the play is viewed in the light of its time. For a start, while Stephanie pursued the conventional purpose of improving morals, he demonstrated an antithetical intent in his wish to satisfy the Viennese audience's love for sensational events and astonishing spectacle. His desire to bring the play into conformity with the mainstream of German drama is evident first in his attempt to compress the action into the limit of the unities. The play does not cover the whole of Macbeth's seventeen-year reign, only the last forty-eight hours or so of his life, which comprises Malcolm's invasion of Scotland and Macbeth's defeat. Into this is crammed the murder of Banquo, the appearance of his ghost at the banquet, the Malcolm–Macduff meeting and the sleep-walking scene. Stephanie had problems sticking to

---

[52] In addition to Weisse's two Shakespearean plays, Genée lists the following adaptations: 1768, *Marcus Brutus* by Bodmer; 1769, *Othello* by C. H. Schmid; 1770, *Das Schnupfstuch oder der Mohr von Venedig*, *Othello* by 'J. H. S'.; 1771, *Die lustigen Abentheuer an der Wienn* by Pelzel (*Merry Wives*); and 1772, *Cymbeline* by Johann Sulzer (pp. 217–27).

[53] See Erich Schumacher, *Macbeth auf der deutschen Bühne* (Emsdetten, 1938), pp. 28–38 for a performance history and a summary of the mixed critical reception Stephanie's play received.

the unity of place, but all the action takes place roughly in and around Macbeth's castle.

Stephanie's characters are also the one-dimensional ciphers intrinsic to the most rudimentary moralistic drama. Like the puppets of the English Comedians' plays, they have no inner life. Macbeth, nothing but a bloody killer, raves like a stock tyrant. Stephanie tried to recapture the ambivalence with which Shakespeare invested Lady Macbeth, but in fact he merely created a woman who inexplicably professes violent attachment to her husband's victims one minute, only to urge him to destroy them the next. The ending has a crudely impressive theatricality as Stephanie drives home his point about the self-destructiveness of power by having a delirious Lady Macbeth stab her husband to death, but all the credibility of this climax has been nullified by the cause of her madness. This had suddenly struck her as she heard the statue of Duncan, like Molina's Commendatore, prophesying revenge for crimes committed against him, a piece of sensationalism that works against the creation of a dramatic environment in which the action can have a morally effective impact.

Stephanie had little understanding of how Shakespeare used poetry to explore character. His prose text includes frequent borrowings from Wieland's translation – in fact the sleepwalking scene is given almost *verbatim*[54] – but none of these extracts provides access to the emotional life of the characters, as they do in Shakespeare; they are used either to give the normally commonplace dialogue a certain grandiloquence or to make a moralistic statement. Just before his wife stabs him, Macbeth reflects on his condition in a speech recalling lines from 'Tomorrow and tomorrow . . .':

> Nun, dann Tod! Komme doch, saume nicht, ich erwarte dich mit Verlangen. Was bist du? Bist du so schreckhaft? – Nein, mir bist du es nicht; ich sehe dich an wie ein Diener von Schauspielern, du nimmst mir mein Kleid ab, damit es morgen ein andrer tragen könne; mein Spiel ist aus. Ich habe die Rolle eines Konigs gespielt. Gut oder schlecht? Das lasse ich der Nachwelt über, genug, ich war König wie einer, der dazu geboren worden.

> (Now death! Come, do not delay, I await you with longing. What are you? Are you so terrible? – No, to me you are not; I see you as a servant of actors, you take my clothes off me, so that tomorrow another can wear them; my acting is finished. I have played the role of a king. Good or bad? That I leave to posterity, enough that I was king like one born to it.)[55]

---

[54] There are also some echoes of Wieland's Shakespeare in the banquet scene and in the scene between Malcolm and Macduff. After Macduff has heard of the death of his wife and children, he engages in banter with a surviving child that is taken directly from the Lady Macduff scene, a clear example of Stephanie's failure to judge the specific tone of a scene.

[55] Stephanie der Jüngere, *Macbeth*, in Brüggemann, *Aufklärung*, p. 161.

Such is the general standard of utterance in this play.

Stephanie appeals to contemporary sentimental taste by expanding the role of Fleance and introducing a new character, one Gonerill, the eldest daughter of Macduff. These figures, who bear not the slightest resemblance to their Shakespearean originals, are in love with each other, Both are paragons of virtue. Fleance is the active agent of revenge for his father's murder, while Gonerill, who begins the play as Lady Macbeth's confidante, lends the action pathos as she seems to be unceasingly in the process of separating from or being united with her father and her lover. Such transactions require all the paraphernalia of intrigue. Letters are exchanged and intercepted and disguises adopted, one of which involves an appearance by Gonerill in man's clothing, guaranteed no doubt to arouse less than virtuous feelings among the male members of the audience.

What is perhaps most notable in Stephanie's adaptation is his treatment of the supernatural elements, which were possibly the main reason why he chose *Macbeth* for the All Souls' Day performance. The witches never appear. Their prophecy is referred to by Macbeth as having occurred seventeen years earlier and he talks of seeing in a dream the eight kings descended from Banquo. The visible manifestations of the supernatural are more of the order of the ghost in Voltaire's *Semiramis*, as described by Lessing in the *Hamburgische Dramaturgie*. The play begins with a horrendous storm, borrowed from *King Lear*, which is understood at once to be a judgement from heaven, because the last such storm occurred seventeen years before, the night Duncan was murdered. Duncan's ghost appears to Macbeth and Banquo at the point where Shakespeare used the witches. It also turns up as the statue that drives Lady Macbeth mad and, at the end, to place a laurel wreath on Malcolm's head while the palace is being consumed by flames, another touch borrowed from the Don Juan story. If all this seems somewhat mechanical, so too does the appearance of Banquo's ghost, which, like the *Semiramis* ghost, is seen by all, to whom he shows his wounds and then points the finger of accusation at Macbeth. While Shakespeare never fully explained the status of supernatural appearances, treating them more as manifestations of characters' psychic states than as evidence of divine power, there is no mystery about them for Stephanie. They represent an absolute divine order, an enclosed, tightly-structured metaphysical universe that can be accounted for through entirely rational principles and that communicates clearly the message that overthrowing the divine order is wrong and tyranny self-destructive.

In this travesty of Shakespeare's tragic world, there is one positive feature, the character of Curan, whose name has been borrowed from *King Lear* but whose role approximates to Seton's. He is a direct descendant of Hanswurst, the Clown who originated with the English Comedians and who could still be seen on the popular Viennese stage. His jokes are often reminiscent of the Fool's in *Lear* and may well have been borrowed from that play, though they are greatly simplified. Nevertheless the character is effective as, in contrast to the clowns of the English Comedians, his comic commentary is closely interwoven with the action and allows for a potentially ironic viewpoint. In particular, his aphorisms on fashionable clothes, which imply that power is mutable, are particularly effective when delivered just before the appearance of Banquo's ghost. Through Curan, Shakespeare's tragi-comic mode, so suspected by most eighteenth-century critics, is briefly restored.

Macbeth was eventually withdrawn from the Viennese repertoire at Stephanie's request. As a founding member of the Burgtheater when it was newly constituted as a national theatre in 1776, he rejected his work as unworthy of such a theatre due to its 'ghostly apparitions, exaggerated characters and . . . its bad taste'.[56] Nevertheless it was occasionally seen in other Viennese theatres and in theatres in Germany. But, by the late 1770s, as critics and audiences had the opportunity to see plays closer to Wieland's version of Shakespeare, adaptations such as Stephanie's *Macbeth* began to disappear from the stage. Its last recorded performance was at the Theater auf der Wieden in 1796.[57]

Inadequate as Stephanie's and indeed Weisse's rewritings of Shakespeare were, they materialised contemporary understanding of Shakespeare. They are not to be dismissed absolutely, for limited and even grotesque as they might be, they still prepared audiences for the time when Shakespeare's plays would be seen in versions closer to the original.

[56] Stahl, *Shakespeare und das deutsche Theater*, p. 77.
[57] Stellmacher, *Auseinandersetzung*, p. 33.

4

Shakespeare introduced: Schröder's *Hamlet* and other adaptations

THE VOGUE FOR HAMLET

Few if any events in the introduction of Shakespeare to the German theatre were more important than the production of *Hamlet* given by the Ackermann company in Hamburg in September 1776. The performance was greeted with an unusually unanimous response from the public. As a local newspaper reported,

> Individual opinion about acting and plays are usually very different but at the three successive performances of *Hamlet* in Hamburg, in each case the numerous audience in the playhouse was so attentive, so transported, that it seemed as if there were only *one* person present, only *one* pair of eyes, only *one* pair of hands, because the stillness was so universal, the silence so numbed, [there was] wonder, weeping, and applause ...[1]

Public enthusiasm did not abate. *Hamlet* was given with uncommon regularity over the next several seasons and was quickly taken up by almost every standing theatre and wandering troupe in Germany. By the end of the decade the whole country had been gripped by a veritable 'Hamlet-fever', so that the dramaturg Johann Friedrich Schink could write in 1781,

> Where in Germany is a troupe of actors ... that has not performed *Hamlet*? Royal cities and tiny market towns, splendid halls and wooden booths echo with his name, and men and boys, virtuosi and reading teachers, First Heroes and letter-carriers, struggle over him and flaunt their immortality.[2]

This sudden mania for Shakespeare's tragedy had many causes. The quality of the play may have first become apparent through the quality of the Ackermann company's performance. During the 1750s and 1760s, as a troupe of wandering players under the leadership of Konrad Ackermann, it had introduced several of the most important foreign and German

---

[1] From the *Hamburger-Adress-Nachrichtung*, as quoted in Alexander von Weilen, *Hamlet auf der deutschen Bühne bis zur Gegenwart* (Berlin, 1908), p. 37.
[2] Johann Friedrich Schink, *Dramaturgische Fragmente*, vol. 1 (4 vols., Graz, 1781), p. 153.

domestic dramas into the repertoire. In the 1770s, the troupe became resident in Hamburg, where under the direction of Ackermann's stepson, Friedrich Ludwig Schröder, the repertoire was expanded to include the plays of *Sturm und Drang* and Shakespeare. Under both Ackermann and Schröder, the company had developed a realistic style of acting ideally suited to these dramatic innovations. The wider popularity enjoyed by *Hamlet* may also be attributed to the extraordinary vogue enjoyed by Goethe's novel *Die Leiden des jungen Werthers* (*The Sorrows of Young Werther*), as the heroes of both works were considered to have much in common.[3] Indeed, the rise of interest in Shakespeare as a whole during the late 1770s has often been seen as an integral part of public interest in *Sturm und Drang*.[4]

One must be careful, however, in assuming too close an identity between the vogue for *Hamlet* and *Sturm und Drang*. Although Schröder was noted for his interest in the movement, he owed his success as a theatre manager to his uncanny ability to gauge public taste. As his theatre depended solely on the box-office and not on royal subvention for its survival, he had to please his audiences as well as challenge them. This meant that when he did produce the plays of *Sturm und Drang*, he adapted them to remain within the decorum of the domestic drama. For example, in 1774 he scaled down Goethe's famous 'Shakespearean' drama *Götz von Berlichingen* so that it could be performed without difficulty within the confines of the illusionistic stage.[5] To ensure a hearing for Shakespeare, he had to do the same to *Hamlet*, reconciling his need to please public taste with his desire to retain as much as possible of the original play's spirit so that it struck audiences as a remarkable work.

In fact, the Hamburg performance of *Hamlet* was not the first in Germany. Schröder had been inspired to put it on by an inadequate performance he had seen of it in Prague in August 1776. This was in a version by Franz Heufeld, that had first been performed in Vienna in January 1773. Heufeld's *Hamlet* was itself an adaptation of Wieland's translation, severely edited to suit the exigencies of the eighteenth-century stage. Nothing could illustrate more fully the process of adaptation Shakespeare's plays had to go through in order to gain a footing in the German theatre than the transformations *Hamlet* underwent, from Wieland's translation through to Schröder's final version of the play.

[3] Gundolf, *Shakespeare und der deutsche Geist*, pp. 244–5.
[4] Kindermann, *Theatergeschichte Europas*, vol. 4, pp. 249–53.
[5] Dieter Hoffmeier, *Ästhetische und methodische Grundlagen der Schauspielkunst F. L. Schröders* (Dresden, 1955), p. 59.

HAMLET: FROM WIELAND TO SCHRÖDER

Wieland's prose translation of *Hamlet* demonstrates his familiar limitations as both a translator of and commentator on Shakespeare. His German has little of the vigour and peculiarity of the original. It is more generalised, easier to understand, more prosaic and genteel than Shakespeare's English. Difficult metaphors are simplified, paraphrased or just cut, while the Elizabethan predilection for playing on words, especially notable in the role of Hamlet, earns Wieland's constant reproof. Much of Hamlet's humour disappears, especially when it borders on the obscene. Wieland did not translate the whole play either. He summarised Hamlet's account of the pirate's raid, the scene with Osric and the arrival of Fortinbras, out of the conviction that such passages did little to further the plot. He would also have liked to have cut the gravediggers' scene, but felt it should be retained so that his readers could gain some idea of it.[6] These cuts and myriad alterations in phrasing create an incomplete picture both of the play and of its central character, who becomes in Wieland's eyes an inactive melancholic, filled with an indifference towards his own life,

> which leaves to causal chance the great design of revenge on which his soul has grown, and which does not consider it worth the effort to make a plan or to take precautions, so that he himself is not implicated by his enemy.[7]

Heufeld's adaptation of the play, based on Wieland's translation, was first produced at the Habsburg Court Theatre in January 1773. Given the general suspicion in court circles of plays that violated the conventions of French dramaturgy, *Hamlet*'s presence in the Viennese theatre's repertoire is puzzling. Perhaps it was tolerated because at that time there was a greater middle-class component in the audience than at most court theatres,[8] but in actuality Heufeld's version had little in it to offend the royal authorities, for in adapting the play he rigorously observed the neoclassical unities and shifted the focus away from political and metaphysical issues to domestic ones. A cursory glance at his *dramatis personae* illustrates this. The cast is drastically reduced to accord with the narrow field of action characteristic of domestic drama, thirteen characters from *Hamlet*'s thirty being cut, including Laertes, Rosencrantz, Osric, the gravediggers and Fortinbras. The characters' names are germanised to make Shakespeare's quasi-classical environment more familiar to the audience, Claudius being referred to merely as 'the King', Polonius as Oldenholm and Horatio as Gustav.

To cater to the taste for relatively brief plays, Heufeld's version was

[6] Wieland, *Gesammelte Schriften*, 2, 3, p. 480.   [7] *Ibid.*, p. 486.
[8] Emil Haeussermann, *Das Wiener Burgtheater* (Vienna, Munich and Zurich, 1975), pp. 14–15. Interestingly enough, the first work staged at the Habsburg court theatre when it opened in 1742 was Carcani's opera *Ambleto*, based on material from the Hamlet story.

approximately half the length of Wieland's translation.[9] As the action had to be compressed into the unities, drastic modifications were necessary. In effect, only those events up to and including the scene in Gertrude's bedroom were dramatised, Shakespeare's final two acts being forced into about ten minutes of playing time. Even then, so that all events could be fitted into a twenty-four hour time-span, substantial cuts had to be made in the earlier acts. Ophelia and Oldenholm appear as speaking characters only at the start of Act III (Shakespeare II:2), when Ophelia tells of her encounter with the 'mad' Hamlet. Throughout, Oldenholm and Ophelia remain peripheral to the main action. Other scenes not bearing directly on the action are also cut, most notably those with Fortinbras. Most of the conversations between Hamlet and the First Player have gone, as have the Hecuba speeches. But the play before the King is given complete and in alexandrines, which suggests Heufeld was aware of the function of Shakespeare's archaic rhyming verse; Wieland had insensitively dismissed it as 'rhymes of untranslatable badness'.[10]

After the bedroom scene, Heufeld's action is bewilderingly swift, the search for Oldenholm's body, Ophelia's mad-scenes, Laertes's return, Hamlet's journey to England, the graveyard scenes, the duel and the appearance of Fortinbras all being excised. The action is confined to Gertrude's bedroom until the end. She tells the King that Hamlet has killed Oldenholm, whereupon he determines to send Hamlet to England. After a brief conversation between Gustav and Hamlet, in which Hamlet determines to kill the King, the King, Gertrude and Guildenstern return to drink to Hamlet's departure, without the presence of poison in the drinks being divulged to the audience. Gertrude drinks from the poisoned chalice and Hamlet murders the King. As she dies, Gertrude confesses her guilt and complicity in the murder of her first husband and Hamlet survives to rule Denmark.

Heufeld's adaptation is limited in scope. While Shakespeare wrote a resonant political tragedy, Heufeld produced domestic intrigue, which involves nothing more than characters' personal concerns. Setting the final act in Gertrude's bedroom seems peculiarly apposite, as none beyond the characters themselves are represented as being affected by the events. Wieland's already sparse prose is radically pruned. No attempt has been made to capture Shakespeare's luxuriant verse and expansive metaphors, while characters do not deliver general maxims and meditations on their condition, as these slow down the dramatic momentum. Although his excisions are not as drastic as in the seventeenth-century *Der bestrafte*

---

[9] Heufeld's version is approximately 1,900 prose lines and would take about two hours to perform.
[10] Wieland, *Gesammelte Schriften*, 2, 3, p. 447.

Brudermord, Heufeld showed a similar concern to have the play proceed as fast as possible. So, in the opening scene, the speech on Christmas Eve is cut, while Horatio's description of the dawn,

> But look, the morn in russet mantle clad,
> Walks o'er the dew of yon high eastern hill.

(I:I, 166–7)

becomes in the mouth of Gustav a prosaic 'Aber seht, der Morgen bricht an' ('But see, dawn is breaking').[11] Although Hamlet's soliloquies are retained, in severely cut form, all other general observations, such as Rosencrantz's 'the cease of majesty' speech, have disappeared. Although Rosencrantz has been cut, his lines survive in Guildenstern's mouth whenever they further the action. All comedy is scrupulously avoided. Oldenholm is, therefore, nothing more than an intriguer. So, for example, the ninety lines that Shakespeare uses to have Polonius show Hamlet's letter to the King (II:2) are shorn to the minimum required to communicate the idea that Hamlet is out of his senses.

Not surprisingly, Hamlet's character is radically altered. He is no longer deeply torn by doubts about himself or the world, nor is he the noble weakling Goethe envisaged in *Wilhelm Meisters Lehrjahre*. Instead he has just enough questions about the legitimacy of what he is to do to maintain suspense, though it is quite clear he will act when the circumstances are right. Heufeld, like all late eighteenth-century adapters of Shakespeare, followed the demands of theatrical convention rather than the interests of contemporary Shakespearean criticism. He subordinated character to action rather than emphasised character at the expense of action. As a result, he had Hamlet soliloquise only when it is necessary for exposition or to clarify the plot. Hamlet's meditations on the darker aspects of human experience, such as the 'vicious mole of nature' speech, were also cut. Heufeld's Hamlet is no vigorous satirist, especially as he has no opportunities to banter with Oldenholm. Furthermore, as Guildenstern is no longer a distasteful representative of an absolutist court, but an innocuous and well-meaning young man, Hamlet's exchanges with him have none of Shakespeare's pointed wit. The most violent outbreak of self-loathing, 'Oh what a rogue and peasant slave am I', is gutted; instead, after a few words of self-reproof for his dilatoriness, Hamlet proceeds confidently to plan how to trap the King. In Act v, before the final confrontation, Heufeld inserted a few lines from 'How all occasions do inform against me', but by prefacing them with the interpolation, 'Nein Gustav, keinen Augenblick länger! Ha, diese unedle Säumseligkeit!' ('No, Gustav, not a moment longer! Ha, this

---

11 *Der erste deutsche Bühnen-Hamlet: Die Bearbeitungen Heufelds und Schröders*, ed. Alexander von Weilen (Vienna, 1914), p. 7.

ignoble tardiness!')[12] he has Hamlet speak Shakespeare's words in a sense totally opposite to that of the original. At the end, he is the young ruler whose virtue and perseverance has been rewarded for preserving the moral order. In summation, Heufeld's Hamlet is an uncomplicated young man of action.

Heufeld was not an unskilled playwright and he knew how to exploit the pathos of death to the full. He realized too that audiences are generally more interested if they can find someone to pity. As Hamlet was an unsuitable object for this, Heufeld altered fundamentally Shakespeare's attitude towards Gertrude. As decorum and censorship would allow no display of sexuality, all references to Gertrude's physical appetites were cut. Instead, she progressively appears as the helpless victim of family strife. Her exact knowledge of her first husband's death is left vague for most of the action, though there are hints that a sense of guilt causes her acute anguish. As she dies, she reveals she has known all along of the murder. Hamlet then swiftly dispatches the King, so that the sole focus can be on Gertrude's agonizing death, which appears to be suitable punishment for her infidelity. In a moment supremely satisfying to an audience bred on sentimental domestic drama, as she dies, her magnanimous son forgives her.

Heufeld's *Hamlet* was a respectable success in Vienna, though generally lacklustre acting and Josef Lange's monotonous Hamlet did little to help it. Heufeld was praised for his skilful adaptation and for his 'critical discernment', as 'he has omitted the irregularity and episodic scenes of the original, so far as not to spoil the whole, and has thereby concentrated the action'.[13] Indeed, his version was preferred to Shakespeare's because contemporaries thought he had successfully caught the ambience and moral tone of the domestic drama while adhering to the dramaturgy of French tragedy.

Schröder was impressed when he saw the play in Prague. 'I felt the powerful effect', he wrote, 'which, under other circumstances, this play must make and decided on my return [to Hamburg] to bring it on stage as quickly as possible.'[14] As he put it on only a month after seeing it, he must have used Heufeld's version; his name did not appear on the playbills as adapter.[15] The success of *Hamlet* in Hamburg was not, therefore, due to novelties in the script. Even though Hamburg was a commercial city open to English influences, with a non-royalist government, audiences still

[12] Heufeld, p. 54.

[13] Quoted in Wilhelm Widmann, *Hamlets Bühnenlaufbahn (1601–1877)* (Leipzig, 1931), p. 50.

[14] Quoted by von Weilen, *Hamlet auf der deutschen Bühne*, p. 22.

[15] It should, however, be noted that Schröder's one contemporary biographer claims his adaptation was his own, with only the play-scene taken from Heufeld's version. See F. L. W. Meyer, *Friedrich Ludwig Schröder*, 2 vols. (Hamburg, 1819), vol. 1, p. 290. However, Schröder's later published versions are so obviously based on Heufeld that Meyer's claim has been discounted.

2 D. Chodowiecki, Johann Franz Hieronymus Brockmann as Hamlet

favoured French theatre, as Lessing had bitterly observed at the end of the abortive national theatre project in 1769.[16] For this reason, the success of *Hamlet* in Hamburg may well have been due more to the quality of the acting than to the script. Certainly, for the first night Schröder had cast at fullest strength, with Johann Brockmann as Hamlet, Johann Reinecke as the King, Dorothea Ackermann as Ophelia, and himself as the Ghost. Despite the reduced Heufeld version, these were actors capable of creating personalities from their one-dimensional characters. Brockmann, in particular, won great acclaim for his arresting interpretation of the central role.

Brockmann's Hamlet (see Plate 2) came at an important juncture in the development of German acting. Both the adroit art of improvisation and the bombastic style that had been employed in the performance of French tragedy were now virtually extinct. In their place was a stylistic vacuum. The realism of Konrad Ekhof, the senior actor of the 1770s, was widely copied, but his grave stage presence aroused calm admiration rather than excitement. The German theatre was in need of more energetic yet precise acting. Initially it had to look for this in foreign models, and it found one readily available in David Garrick.

Hamlet was a role which the Germans closely associated with Garrick. Earlier in 1776, a Hamburg periodical published Lichtenberg's famous letters on Garrick, which included detailed descriptions of his Hamlet.[17] Lichtenberg was impressed by Garrick's ability to give psychologically realistic portrayals with an uncommonly light touch and by his quick transitions. It might well have struck the German theatre-goer that Garrick was using the skills of the old improvisational theatre to realise the psychologically accurate characterisation required by the new domestic drama and, theoretically, by Shakespeare. From the first Hamburg performance on, Brockmann's Hamlet was frequently compared with Garrick's, not always to Brockmann's advantage. One newspaper felt he did not fully understand the part, as he failed to distinguish between when Hamlet is mad, or pretends to be mad, and when he is not.[18] Given the limitations of Heufeld's text, this judgement is not entirely fair and may indicate that the reviewer knew the original. However, the writer also commented that those who had seen Garrick as Hamlet felt that Brockmann would equal the English actor as his comprehension of the role grew. He was not monotonous like Lange, but flexible and various. Like Garrick, he represented mixed emotions that were not easily identifiable as they were composed of contradictory elements. While Brockmann could

[16] Lessing, *Werke*, vol. 4, pp. 698–9.
[17] See 'Briefe aus England', in *Lichtenbergs Werke* (Berlin and Weimar, p. 1978), pp. 212–14 and 218–20. An English translation of selected passages from these letters can be found in G. C. Lichtenberg, 'Impressions of Garrick', trans. John Nowell, *History Today*, 22 (1972), 161–8.
[18] The *Adress-Comptoir-Nachrichten*, quoted by von Weilen. *Hamlet auf der deutschen Bühne*, p. 39.

not express strong passion, he had, as Schröder's biographer noted, mastered 'all the softer features and transitions of humanity'. In particular, he realised

> the caresses that corrupted the heart [through his] face, which succeeded in expressing without exaggeration half ridicule and half submission, the pride, which in its courtesy still remained pride, the cloud of melancholy, which made way for joy: [these] have never been more happily expressed than [by Brockmann].[19]

Sometimes the subtlety of his nuances could become too distracting, as Moses Mendelssohn commented after seeing his celebrated appearances in Berlin in the winter of 1777–8. He wrote that he indulged in 'too lively movement and too many imitative gestures ... The Englishman [Garrick] may perhaps have *done* less and yet have *accomplished* more.'[20] Nevertheless, Brockmann's lightness and emotional subtlety appealed to audiences. He showed Hamlet in a softened light, underscoring the affinities of Heufeld's text with the domestic drama. In summary, this performance raised Brockmann to the level of 'the first actor in his *Fach* in Germany'. Schröder, however, was unhappy with Brockmann's Hamlet, calling it 'very often affected'.[21]

Schröder's dissatisfaction with Brockmann may have been because he knew how far he was from Shakespeare's original figure. Schröder, who read English, had been familiar with Shakespeare for years, and, unlike his fictional analogue Serlo in *Wilhelm Meisters Lehrjahre*, had a comprehensive understanding of the plays. No doubt he was also dissatisfied with Heufeld's work, wishing to reconcile his knowledge of the English original with what was permissible and physically possible in his own theatre. He did not, therefore, stay with Heufeld but set out to adapt the play himself. In so doing, he took the first steps in the long process of bridging the gap between theory and practice in the performance of Shakespeare in the German theatre.

Schröder wrote, staged and published two adaptations of *Hamlet*. The first, which he referred to disparagingly as 'scamped together',[22] was performed in November 1776 and published in 1777. In it, three elements of the original were restored.[23] First, Laertes reappeared, suggesting that Schröder appreciated the function of sub-plot in the structure of English drama. He still insisted, however, on keeping this sub-plot within the limits

---

[19] Meyer, *Schröder*, vol. 1, pp. 260–1.
[20] Quoted by Widmann, *Hamlets Bühnenlaufbahn*, pp. 98–9.
[21] Quoted by von Weilen, *Hamlet auf der deutschen Bühne*, pp. 39 and 52.
[22] *Schröder und Gotter*, ed. Berthold Litzmann (Hamburg and Leipzig, 1887), p. 45.
[23] I have used the version of the play published in Friedrich Ludwig Schröder, *Dramatische Werke*, ed. Eduard von Bulow, 4 vols. (Berlin, 1831), vol. 4.

of the unities and the law of probability by having Laertes return to the court through his ship being blown back into harbour by contrary winds the moment it has left. Secondly, Ophelia's mad-scenes were reinstated, which introduces a disquieting note and places Hamlet in a relatively negative light. Thirdly, the gravediggers' scene was introduced, with only obscure allusions cut. It does not end, however, with Hamlet confronting Laertes over Ophelia's grave, as the seemingly blasphemous implications would not have met with audience approval.

Not only did he add scenes, Schröder restored important passages of dialogue. Heufeld had cut the Ghost moving under the stage, but Schröder restored it, thus augmenting considerably the uncanny atmosphere. More significant were his additions to Hamlet's character. The puns on Brutus were reinstated, as was the conversation about the recorders and the shape of the cloud. Hamlet, as a result, is witty again. He is also more impassioned towards his mother. Heufeld had softened Hamlet's vehement attack upon his mother, but Schröder brought it closer to the original.

If Schröder's additions demonstrate a greater appreciation of Shakespeare than Heufeld's, his cuts show a more stringent sense of economy. He was even more concerned to maintain the aura of domestic drama, cutting the few references to preparations for war included by Heufeld. Surprisingly, he omitted Ophelia's account of Hamlet's 'madness' even though he restored the scene where Oldenholm advises her how to behave towards him. He cut too the arrival of the players, which makes Heufeld's already swift action advance even more swiftly. What little obscene talk Heufeld left in, Schröder excised, and he made Ophelia's mad-scene more decorous by far than Shakespeare's. Schröder made one interesting alteration in the order of scenes, by placing the prayer-scene between the nunnery and the play-scenes. The strategy has its point. Shakespeare placed the prayer-scene after the play-scene to heighten the atmosphere of guilt within the royal family, but Schröder was concerned, as Shakespeare was not, with the rationality of Hamlet's conduct, so he placed it where it made Hamlet's delay acceptable, at a point where he has no concrete evidence of the King's guilt. The image of Hamlet as a determined young man is not, therefore, weakened. The end of the play follows Heufeld, though with more incidents, including the mad-scenes and the gravediggers. At the end, Hamlet's journey to England is about to occur, with everyone, including Laertes, assembling in the hall to drink farewell to him. The catastrophe is as in Heufeld.

Brockmann would have played this augmented version of the play in Hamburg and during his celebrated visit to Berlin in the winter of 1777–8. In 1778, he left the Ackermann company to join the Burgtheater in Vienna, whereupon Schröder, who had so far played only the Ghost and the first gravedigger, took over the lead himself. When he did, he revised the text again, using both the English original and the new Eschenburg edition. His final version of *Hamlet*, published in 1778,[24] is the most successful of the three stage versions, though it was the version of November 1776 that was to be the standard adaptation used throughout Germany until the early nineteenth century.

In Schröder's final *Hamlet*, there was one major change in structure. To accommodate the gravediggers' scene, the 1777 version had been in six acts. These were reduced to five and the gravediggers omitted, perhaps because of unfavourable public response. Other structural changes were minor. The most significant changes were in characterisation, as Schröder began to explore the depths of character for which Shakespeare had been critically lauded, but which had not so far been demonstrated in texts for performance. Hamlet is more complete. The 'vicious mole of nature' speech is partially restored, so as to introduce a contemplative and misanthropic side to his character. His irreverence and wildness are intensified. Schröder included Hamlet's comparison of his uncle's reputation to that of the Players, and when he discovers the King's guilt after the play, he speaks in rhyming verse to express his jubilance. Schröder prefaced Hamlet quizzing Oldenholm on the shape of the cloud with comments on hats from Shakespeare's Osric scene. For the first time, 'How all occasions do inform against me' appears almost complete, though it is still used, as in Heufeld, to express Hamlet's confidence in action, this being underlined by an interpolated aside. As Hamlet leaves the King after being questioned about Oldenholm's body, he comments,

> Ich sehe einen Cherub, der sie sieht. (Zu GUSTAV), Auf Gustav, lass uns auf Mittel denken, die Rache meines ermordeten Vaters zu beschleunigen. (Zum KÖNIG) Lebt wohl, liebe Mutter.

> (I see a cherub that sees them. (To GUSTAV) Come, Gustav, let us think about means to hasten the revenge of my murdered father. (To KING) Goodbye, dear mother.)[25]

Hence, the final murder is still more an act of will than in Shakespeare. In the 1778 version, the King and Oldenholm were also more fully delineated: the King is a more actively malign figure, indicating Schröder's emancipation from having to portray royalty sympathetically, while Oldenholm is closer to the original fussy but callous Polonius. Schröder's characterisation is not as complete as Shakespeare's, but he filled his stage with more striking individuals than Heufeld had done.

---

[24] I have used the version of the play included in Brüggemann, *Aufklärung*.
[25] Schröder/Brüggemann, p. 222.

Schröder's interpretation of the role of Hamlet was historically important, because while his text was still bound by French dramaturgical conventions and the milieu of the domestic drama, as an actor he more completely embodied the spirit of *Sturm und Drang*. This became clear through the contrast between him and Brockmann. There are few detailed accounts of their performances. Meyer discusses both in his biography of Schröder; the Viennese actor J. H. F. Müller wrote about one of Brockmann's first appearances;[26] while Johann Schink wrote in detail of Brockmann's guest appearances in Berlin. Meyer claims Schink never saw Schröder in the role,[27] but an anonymous review of guest performances Schröder gave in Berlin so closely reflects Schink's ideas and resembles his style that it has been attributed to him.[28] There are also some brief reports in the daily press and occasional letters.

Schröder was a harsh actor with an impressive, even intimidating, stage presence. He did not, like Brockmann, ask for the audience's sympathy, neither was he as solemn as his great predecessor Ekhof. While he was as skilled as Brockmann in representing transitions and mixed states of mind, he could also embody unalloyed emotions without falsifying them or sounding shrill. Many felt his Hamlet, in which bitterness and cynicism were highlighted, to be entirely different from Brockmann's more malleable and pleasing prince.

From the account that has been attributed to Schink, the difference between the two is clear. Initially he felt Brockmann's Hamlet to be 'a true work of genius', but he quickly qualified his enthusiasm by complaining it was not complete. Schink considered Hamlet to be irredeemably separate from society, not by any rational decision, but because he is possessed by 'the deepest, depressing melancholy'.[29] Neither the Heufeld nor the Schröder texts encourage this view and the inconsistencies that Schink identified may be traced to this. For Schink, Hamlet's first appearance was crucial, as it is only here, before he knows of the Ghost, that his 'pure' character is apparent. Brockmann was close to Wilhelm Meister's Hamlet, a noble young man, too sensitive to respond to the situation he finds himself in. Pain at an incomprehensible inner struggle dominated his character in the opening scene, expressing itself in a sudden outburst of scorn against the King and his mother. Then he withdrew into melancholy. His first monologue was given close to tears, but skilled as he was at transitions, Brockmann turned from tears to laughter as Gustav and the watch entered. Schröder was more the embittered outsider. On his first

[26] J. H. F. Müller, *Abschied von der k.k. Hof- und National-Schaubühne* (Vienna, 1802), pp. 109–11.

[27] Meyer, *Schröder*, vol. 1, p. 308.

[28] Berthold Litzmann, *Friedrich Ludwig Schröder*, 2 vols. (Hamburg and Leipzig, 1890 and 1894), vol. 2, p. 255.

[29] Schink, *Dramaturgische Fragmente*, vol. 1, p. 162.

3 B. Göz, Friedrich Ludwig Schröder as Hamlet

appearance, he was acerbic, his first monologue an expression of boiling anger. Schröder's passion was coldly constrained, for he was already antagonistic to the King and his mother, using anger as a weapon in that conflict. The monologue 'O that this too too solid flesh would melt' he delivered urgently, the changes in his tone of voice representing conflicting impulses within him. So while in the text Schröder maintained a positive, rational Hamlet, in performance he was a less confident figure. He was strong, but not always sure of the sources from which that strength sprang.

Schink had had problems with Brockmann's representation of Hamlet's first meeting with the Ghost. Like most critics of the time, he valued the actor's ability to give as complete an illusion as possible of real behaviour.[30] Garrick's treatment of this scene, as reported by Lichtenberg, was regarded in Germany as a touchstone of realistic acting. So accurate and effective were the details by which Garrick realised Hamlet's fear that Lichtenberg found that 'even before he began to speak I shuddered repeatedly'. But horror was not an emotion Brockmann could communicate. Schink did not blame him for this: 'the contemporary theatre', he wrote, 'does not have sufficient greatness nor depth to make such an apparition deceptive and effective enough'.[31] He praised details of his performance but complained that it lacked psychological truth, as when he bent forwards to look at the Ghost, instead of backwards as Garrick had done. Schink's doubts were aggravated by Brockmann's conduct towards Gustav and the watch, for he alternated between moodiness and whimsicality with no apparent consistency. But Schröder (see Plate 3) responded to the Ghost as Schink wished. He was less articulate than Garrick, as he had to face mounting evidence in the objective world for his subjective anger. While Brockmann was fearful of the Ghost, Schröder had Hamlet master his fear so as to attend closely to what it said. This led him through pity to determination to renewed anger that finally transformed itself into a violent disgust at the world. With Gustav and the watch, Schröder behaved quietly, putting the Ghost to rest in an atmosphere of peace.

Brockmann's acting was a series of striking moments without what we would now call an easily discernible through-line. Schink felt his best moments were in the second half of the play, when his skill at slipping from one mood to another, at catching half-realised emotions that leave the audience uncertain of the character's true mental state, were better exercised. But Schink felt that Brockmann did not realise that while Hamlet makes a fool of others, he should never seem a fool himself. Brockmann was too much the court jester. Schröder avoided this by showing Hamlet to be a man of strong emotions. His madness was clearly a

---

[30] See Guthke, 'Kritik', pp. 55–8.
[31] Quoted in von Weilen, *Hamlet auf der deutschen Bühne*, p. 43.

disguise through which he could bring about his revenge. Schröder used the soliloquy 'What a masterpiece is man' to recall the loss of a perfect father, while Brockmann delivered it as if he were ridiculing the world. Schröder wrestled with the idea of suicide in 'To Be or Not to Be', but Brockmann used it to express Hamlet's inactivity and depression. In the nunnery-scene, Schröder made it clear that Hamlet loves Ophelia passionately, while Brockmann played the fool with her. In summary, Brockmann excelled at moments requiring a lightly ironic attitude towards the world, mingled with servility and self-pity, while Schröder revealed the unruly emotions of the character.

Meyer claimed that Brockmann, after reading the critique attributed to Schink and seeing Schröder act Hamlet in Vienna in 1780, decided to sacrifice his mannerisms and to bring his interpretation closer to Schröder's.[32] If he did, this was a pity, as the contrast between Brockmann and Schröder awoke a sense of the actor as interpretative artist, an awareness only possible when plays with characters as rich as Shakespeare's were introduced into the repertoire. Brockmann's acting was associated with Garrick's, but unlike Garrick he used the role to demonstrate technique, while the sentimentalist aura of his acting found favour with the audience. Schröder neither overtly displayed his actorial talents nor asked for audience approval. As a Mannheim critic wrote of him in 1780,

> He is never out of his role, this is transformed entirely in his mind, as food changes into blood . . . it is all his own, even that which he receives from art, even the thoughts and words of the poet.[33]

Schröder's acting represented a major step towards the evolution of a realistic theatre not imbued with the mild decorum of eighteenth-century manners. Also, through Schröder the interest expressed by mid-eighteenth-century critics in Shakespeare's characters first received theatrical realisation. He made the character of as much interest as the action.

SCHRÖDER AND SHAKESPEARE

Schröder's contribution towards the cause of Shakespeare in the German theatre was not limited to *Hamlet*. During the great years of his Hamburg directorship, between 1776 and 1780, he was also responsible for staging *Othello* in 1776, *The Merchant of Venice*, *The Comedy of Errors* and *Measure for Measure* in 1777, *King Lear*, *Richard II* and a single-evening version of *Henry IV* in 1778, and *Macbeth* in 1779. Few of these occasions represented the first performances of the play in Germany, but some of the adaptations were skilful enough in establishing a compromise between contemporary

---

[32] Meyer, *Schröder*, vol. 1, p. 308.   [33] Quoted Guthke, 'Kritik', p. 59.

4 Ferdinand Kobell, Friedrich Ludwig Schröder as Lear, 1778

taste and Shakespeare to do much to help lodge the plays in the regular German repertoire. Furthermore, Schröder, who included Shylock, Lear, Falstaff and Macbeth among his greatest roles, did much to amplify public and professional awareness of the range and scope the plays offered the actor.

Some of Schröder's adaptations were more radical than his *Hamlet*, while others were less so, demonstrating a capacity to allow a distinctively Shakespearean tone to be heard on the German stage. A good example of this latter category is the adaptation of *King Lear*, which, like the 1776 *Hamlet*, was to become the standard version used until well into the nineteenth century.

King Lear was not a play that had fared especially well in the eighteenth century. In England, it was given only in the Nahum Tate version, which reduced the tragedy to melodrama and made as much of an invented love interest between Edgar and Cordelia as it did of the fate of Gloucester and Lear. Schröder's *King Lear* is far closer to Shakespeare's. Its popularity, initially in Hamburg and then throughout Germany, attests to the gradual emancipation of the German theatre from the predominance of French dramaturgy, allowing for the inclusion of less uniform dramatic modes. However, the play is not entirely unadapted. For a start, the opening scene, in which the kingdom is divided, is cut, primarily because it was considered that audiences would not find it sufficiently credible as it was irrational.[34] Clearly, Schröder made no attempt to realise on stage Herder's concept of the play as an organic structure in which everything grows from the opening scene. Instead, all the necessary plot information is communicated in an expository conversation between Kent and Gloucester. Naturally, this upsets the balance of the play. Goneril and Regan cannot be the formidable hypocrites they are in Shakespeare, as there can be no contrast between their professions of love and the reality of its absence. Cordelia suffers too as she only appears at the very end of Act IV, and so cannot serve as the antithesis to her sisters. The moving power of her reconciliation with her father is also reduced, as when she appears she is a totally new character, not a redeeming ideal of innocence from the past.

The altered beginning thoroughly influenced Schröder's reading of the role (see plate 4). He first appeared as a leader in charge of an unruly band of knights, so he had less opportunity to represent the pathos of an old man whose mental powers are in decline. As with his Hamlet, anger seems to have been the predominant mood of the first half of his performance, an anger that manifested itself like a powerful disease.

> Fiery red the colour of his face, his eyes lightening, each muscle twitching feverishly, his lips quivering convulsively; his words the sounds of thunder, his hands stretched out, as if they wished to tear down the fulfilment of his curse from heaven; the whole carriage of his body, the expression of the tense condition of his soul.[35]

In contrast, the latter part of the role was notable for the delicacy with which Schröder delineated the gradations of reconciliation and rebirth of trust in Cordelia. While the part offered the range to be expected of a great Shakespearean play, both the omission of the opening scene and cuts during the scenes on the heath, especially the 'trial-scene' with poor Tom, meant that Schröder did not plumb the depths of Lear's madness. As Ludwig Tieck remarked, in a rare unfavourable comment on him, he had to work at the development of the madness,[36] as if it were not naturally part of the character. Possibly as a reflection of his unease with the irrational depths of the part, Schröder rewrote the ending. His Lear dies, but quite accountably of a heart attack, when he thinks that Cordelia has been killed, unlike Shakespeare's Lear who succumbs as a victim of the forces of universal irrationality. Cordelia, meanwhile, who has done nothing to deserve death, recovers after Lear has died and finishes the play mourning for him.

While the depiction of Lear's madness may not have been entirely

---

[34] I have used the version of *King Lear* found in Schröder, *Hamburgisches Theater* (Hamburg, 1785), vol. 4.
[35] Quoted Litzmann, *Schröder*, vol. 2, p. 246.
[36] Ludwig Tieck, extracted in *Deutsche Schauspielkunst*, ed. Monty Jacobs (Leipzig, 1913).

adequate, Schröder did introduce a characteristically Shakespearean tone to the play, remarkable for its time. This is the contrast between the drama of Lear's downfall and the sharp, often cruel humour of the Fool. Furthermore, while Edgar's speeches as poor Tom were severely pruned, no doubt to cater to the audience's sense of decency, he does hide his identity under the cover of madness and extreme indigence. As a result, majesty, that in conventional heroic tragedy was elevated above the dirt of common life, is here seen in direct contact with it, seen indeed through the eyes of the least privileged, if not the least articulate, stratum of society. In this way, the isolation in which Gottsched claimed eminent dramatic heroes should exist was challenged, as was the uniformity of dramatic mode such an isolation implied. So despite the limitations in the range of the central role, Schröder's *King Lear* might have been as large a step as his performance of Hamlet was towards the realisation on stage of the *Sturm und Drang* vision of Shakespeare.

This can hardly be said of another of Schröder's adaptations, his *Measure for Measure*, staged in 1777. After a mild success with the Hamburg public, who supported it for six performances, it was dropped from the repertoire, not to appear in Germany again, at least as a recognisably Shakespearean play, until well into the nineteenth century.[37] Given the generally squeamish attitude of late eighteenth-century audiences to any material that was in the slightest degree specific about sexual matters (all references to intercourse and the mutual attraction of Edmund and the sisters in *Lear* had been rigorously excised), Schröder's choice of *Measure for Measure* is peculiar and has never been satisfactorily explained.[38] Nevertheless, it is of interest in that Schröder not unsuccessfully reworked unpalatable material to make it less offensive to his audience. While his *Measure for Measure* was not, therefore, of historic importance, it provides a further example of his principles of adaptation.

In contrast to both *Hamlet* and *King Lear*, Schröder thoroughly rearranged the incidents of the original play.[39] His fundamental purpose was to make the situation clearer, to tighten the structure of the play and to compress the action into a time-span of twenty-four hours, a restriction that does it little harm. Furthermore, this rearrangement removes any ambivalence about the aims and motives of the Duke. In the opening scene, the Duke explains that, in company with a Brother Peter, he has been roaming the streets of his city (Vienna is never mentioned) in order to spy out injustices. In particular, he wishes to test the integrity of his cousin

---

[37] *Measure for Measure* was, in fact, best known to generations of German theatre-goers in an almost unrecognisable adaptation, entitled *Gerechtigkeit und Rache* (*Justice and Revenge*), by the minor playwright W. H. Brömel.

[38] Litzmann is at a loss to know why Schröder adapted it; see *Schröder*, vol. 2, p. 231.

[39] I have used the edition found in Schröder, *Maass für Maass* (Schwerin and Wismar, 1790).

Angelo, whose maltreatment of Mariana he knows all about. In contrast to Shakespeare's Duke, he articulates his motives clearly and does not reveal piecemeal to the audience his knowledge about his subjects, so as to call in question the integrity of his mission and to throw his own actions into a morally dubious light. Indeed, in an interpolated passage, he explains clearly everything he intends to do. He is, unambiguously, a ruler who wishes to improve the moral fibre of his subjects. This becomes the leading motif of most of the first act, a considerable amount of which is devoted to a conversation between the Duke and Lucio, constructed from all the conversations Shakespeare has them engage in throughout the play. Hence, by the end of the act, the moral distinction between the Duke and the most venal of his subjects is clearly drawn. After having served to define the probity of the Duke, Lucio disappears from the play, only to reappear in the final act to be punished for his lies.

There are two principles that guided the adaptation of the main body of the play. First, Schröder made no attempt to represent on stage the low life of the city. This means that much of the colour and energy of the original has gone. Pompey and Mistress Overdone are cut and some of their lines given to Froth. Escalus's interrogation of Froth and Elbow is included, but simplified. Its intention is to castigate sexual license, as distinct from Shakespeare's purpose, which, one might argue, is more to demonstrate the impossibility of discovering the truth when faced with the stupidity and corruption of humanity.

Schröder also recast his characters so that at no point is one uncertain as to their motives. These are frequently rationalised. For example, Shakespeare represented Mariana's willingness to become reconciled to Angelo as primarily a manifestation of thwarted desire and the irrationality of love; Schröder, however, at the start of Act IV interpolates a long passage giving all manner of reasons why she wishes still to be reconciled. The specifically sexual nature of her feelings is denied; instead she becomes shrouded with pathos. Though Claudio experiences the same bitter doubts that he does in Shakespeare, he becomes reconciled both to death and to his sister before the final unravelling of the plot. As he thinks he is approaching death, he also adopts a moralistic stance, which is alien to that of his Shakespearean counterpart. Isabella and Angelo remain perhaps the least changed, though the language of Angelo's desire for Isabella is generalised. At the end of the play, Schröder also avoided throwing the Duke's motives into a questionable light, by having him invite Isabella to visit his court to choose a suitable mate from among his courtiers, not by proposing marriage himself. Nothing is allowed to modify the moral certitude of this world.

In the last decades of the eighteenth century, Schröder remained the dominant figure in the introduction of Shakespeare to the German theatre.

His adaptations of *Hamlet* and *King Lear* were widely used until well into the nineteenth century. Between 1781 and 1785, he was a member of the Vienna Burgtheater, where he performed several of the roles he had first acted in Hamburg. He also toured in Germany, so that his forceful, realistic acting was widely seen and admired. Other actors, most notably Johann Reinecke, who began his career with Schröder in Hamburg, and David Borchers, an 'intuitive' character actor, achieved considerable recognition in their Shakespearean roles, but Schröder remained the dominant figure, even though his second directorship in Hamburg between 1785 and 1799 was less distinguished as far as Shakespeare was concerned, the only new production of any of his plays being *Much Ado About Nothing*.

Hamburg was far from being the only city where Shakespeare was performed; indeed, other cities had the distinction of giving the first German performances of some of the most important plays. Prague, for example, where Schröder first saw Heufeld's *Hamlet*, staged the German premières of *Richard II* in 1777 and *Timon of Athens* in 1778,[40] while the national theatre in Mannheim was responsible for the first German production of *Julius Caesar*. *Othello* and *Macbeth*, both in Schröder's repertoire but not particularly successful, were seen in notable performances by Döbbelin's company in Berlin and elsewhere. These tragedies, along with *Hamlet* and *King Lear*, were fairly regular offerings of the travelling troupes of players, who were still in the 1780s an important component of German theatrical life.

Still, in no way did Shakespeare suddenly conquer the German theatre. Of all the plays that were attributed directly to him and not to a modern adapter, only *Hamlet* was performed as frequently as the popular dramas of Kotzebue and Iffland or the more substantial plays of the young Schiller. Performance statistics from the court theatre at Mannheim, which was constituted a national theatre in 1779, are telling. Over the twenty-four years between 1779 and 1803, for which a detailed repertoire is available, there were upwards of 3,500 evenings of drama and opera at the theatre.[41] Of these evenings only 112 included a performance of a play by Shakespeare, and fifty-three, or almost one-half, of these performances were of adaptations so entirely free that they bear only the scantest resemblance to the original.[42] In fact only fifty-nine evenings, or approximately two-and-a-half evenings a year, were devoted to a play by Shakespeare. Twenty-seven of these evenings were taken up by *Hamlet*, eleven by *King Lear*, and

40　Stahl, *Shakespeare und das deutsche Theater*, pp. 126–8.
41　A complete listing is available in *Archiv und Bibliothek des Grossh. Hof- und Nationaltheaters in Mannheim: 1779–1839*, ed. Friedrich Walter, 2 vols. (Leipzig, 1899), vol. 2, pp. 259–418.
42　J. G. Schink's *Die bezähmte Widerbellerin oder Gassner der Zweite* (based on *The Taming of the Shrew*), Brömel's *Gerechtigkeit und Rache*, and Beck's *Der Quälgeister* (based on *Much Ado About Nothing*).

ten by *Julius Caesar*, the only Shakespearean play that Mannheim managed to introduce permanently to the German repertoire.[43] So, while Shakespeare had arrived on the German stage by the end of the eighteenth century, his plays had more of a toehold than a foothold in the repertoire. Moreover, the difference between those plays and the originals as read and idolised by *Sturm und Drang* was extreme.

[43] The Mannheim production of *Timon of Athens* received only two performances and *Coriolanus* one.

5

Shakespeare at the Weimar court theatre

When the Duke of Weimar appointed Goethe intendant of his court theatre in 1791, the time for Shakespeare's plays to be seen on a German stage in unadapted form might have seemed to be at hand. Goethe had not, as yet, published *Wilhelm Meisters Lehrjahre* and so his opinions about Shakespeare would publicly have appeared to be those of his young manhood. As we have seen, as a young man Goethe had been among the most vocal of those *Sturm und Drang* enthusiasts who saw in Shakespeare's plays the potential to vitalise a theatre permeated by what they conceived to be a spiritless drama constructed on French models. When Goethe appointed the dramatist Friedrich Schiller as his co-director in 1796, the possibility of unadapted Shakespeare being staged might have seemed even closer. As a young man, Schiller too had written forcefully on Shakespeare, praising his plays for a naturalness lacking in conventional drama. In an early essay, he had especially commended Shakespeare's ability to describe 'the passions and secret movements of the heart in the *specific expressions* of the persons',[1] in contrast to the generalised language and abstract characterisation of French tragedy. Furthermore, his celebrated first play *Die Räuber (The Robbers)* was permeated with Shakespearean motifs.

But neither Goethe's nor Schiller's confidence in the viability of Shakespeare's plays in the theatre had remained unshaken. Over the years Schiller too had had reservations about Shakespeare, akin to those later expressed by Goethe in *Wilhelm Meisters Lehrjahre*. In another early essay,[2] he found Shakespeare's powers of characterisation to be disturbing when used to depict the darker side of human experience. Several of his less salutary characters, he argued, are so accurately created that they are like case-histories of diseased patients. Representing them on stage might, therefore, affect the health of the actor, who could be infected by the role,

---

[1] Friedrich Schiller, 'Die Räuber. [Unterdrückte] Vorrede [1781]', Blinn, *Diskussion*, p. 154.

[2] 'Über den Zusammenhang der tierischen Natur des Menschen mit seiner geistigen', Schiller, *Werke*, Nationalausgabe, 47 vols. (Weimar, 1943–), vol. 20, p. 61.

and then of the spectator, who by visceral sympathy might feel the symptoms of the disease embodied by the actor. Also, while Schiller's early plays owed much to Shakespeare in characterisation and plot structure, as he matured as a playwright he found the dramatic voice most congenial to him through models taken as much from the classical as from the Elizabethan drama.[3] And then, although his early drama had several features in common with the *Sturm und Drang* writers of the previous decade, his view of theatre's social function was actually closer to that of the Enlightenment than *Sturm und Drang*. He was far from adopting the narrow Gottschedian perception of the stage as a moral tutor, but he did see its essential purpose to be the improvement of the audience by awakening within them an awareness of the eternal laws that bind human existence and by encouraging fortitude, compassion and civilised conduct.[4] In particular, Schiller did not value theatre primarily for its appeal to the imagination, nor for the sympathy audiences could feel for individual characters. He recognised the private pleasure of being a spectator, but prized the theatre chiefly as a civic institution that moulds society.[5]

Goethe also explored the potential of theatre as a cohesive social force, not only in *Wilhelm Meisters Lehrjahre* but in his occasional writings. As director of the Weimar court theatre, he tried to define a social function for theatrical performance. Prologues and epilogues which he wrote for specific occasions celebrate the bond between actors and audience, one which engenders 'pure morals' and 'higher *Bildung*'.[6] In particular, like Schiller, he understood how the sympathetic power of representation could work on audiences in a quasi-biological manner. This force of theatre, however, he tried to put to positive ends, as if the stage were the doctor, not the patient. If it were presented properly, he felt, theatre could create healthy minds and bodies and help heal those that are not.

> Dies aber zeig' ich euch vertraulich, dass wir
> Ganz eigentlich dem treuen Artz zur Seite stehn:
> Denn Geist und Körper innig sind ja verwandt:
> Ist jener froh, gleich fühlt sich dieser frei und wohl,
> Und manches Übel flüchtet vor der Heiterkeit.
> Hier also, meine Freunde, hier an diesen Platz
> Hat uns der Arzt zu seinem Beistand herbestellt
> Dass wer am Morgen badend seine Kur begann,
> Sie Abends end'ge schauend hier nach Herzenslust.

---

[3] The specific issue of Shakespeare's influence on Schiller as a dramatist is the main theme of Paul Steck, *Schiller und Shakespeare: Idee und Wirklichkeit* (Frankfurt, Berne and Las Vegas, 1977).
[4] Schiller, 'Was kann eine gute stehende Schaubühne eigentlich wirken?', *Werke*, vol. 20, pp. 97–100.
[5] *Ibid.*, p. 95.
[6] See for example 'Epilog: Gesprochen den 11. Juni 1792', in *Goethes Werke*, 1st ser., vol. 13, pp. 161–2. See 'Was wir bringen', in *Goethes Werke*, 1st ser., vol. 13, p. 73.

(But in good faith I will show you that actually we stand by the true doctor's side. Mind and body are inwardly related; if that one is happy, this one feels free and well, and much evil flies before cheerfulness. Therefore, my friends, the doctor has sent for us to stand by him here, so that whoever began bathing for his cure this morning, ends here in the evening, gazing to his heart's content.)[7]

Goethe's wish to use theatre to sustain social health became a dominant concern in his later years as a director. As he explained to Eckermann in his old age, 'everything morbid, weak, whining and sentimental, was once and for all excluded, as was everything terrible, gruesome and offensive to good morals; I was afraid to corrupt actors and audience with it'.[8]

Though Goethe's and Schiller's views of theatre were never expressed in opposition to Shakespeare, there was little room in the repertoire of the Weimar theatre for his plays as they had thought of them when they were younger. If theatre were to guarantee the health of society, then the deleterious aspects of Shakespeare's works should be avoided; the darker elements of experience, consistently exposed in the tragedies, could not easily be part of their positive theatre. After his *Sturm und Drang* period, Goethe, like Schiller, moved undeviatingly towards a theatre that was neoclassical in spirit, in which clarity of form and unity of action were pre-eminent considerations. He lost his enthusiasm for 'nature' and formlessness. In his own plays, this progression can be seen in the contrast between the 'Shakespearean' plays of his early years, *Götz von Berlichingen* (1773) and *Egmont* (1775–87), and the classical works of his middle years, the verse rendition of *Iphigenie auf Tauris* (1787) and *Torquato Tasso* (1790).

As far as acting was concerned, Goethe did not greatly value the raw naturalism associated with Shakespeare. In an essay of 1788,[9] he wrote of the actor not as an imitator of reality but as one who deliberately practises artifice. The audience's pleasure at a theatrical representation does not come, he claimed, from their assuming that what they see on stage is an approximation to everyday life, but from a 'self-willed illusion', in which they delight knowingly in the artificiality of the stage-event created for them. As a practitioner, Goethe exploited this artificiality. In tragedy, he had his actors develop into models of noble bearing, with decorous movement and flawless vocal delivery as prescribed in the famous 'Rules for Actors'.[10] The formality of the actor's bearing removed both himself

[7] 'Prolog: Halle, den 6. August 1811', in *Goethes Werke*, 1st ser., vol. 13, pp. 175–6.
[8] Johann Peter Eckermann, *Gespräche mit Goethe in den letzten Jahren seines Leben, 1823–1832*, 2 vols. (Leipzig, n.d.), vol. 2, p. 135.
[9] 'Frauenrollen auf dem römischen Theater durch Männer gespielt' ('Women's Roles played by Men in the Roman Theatre'), *Goethes Werke*, 1st ser., vol. 47, pp. 269–74.
[10] *Goethes Werke*, 1st ser. vol. 40, pp. 139–68. A full translation of the 'Rules' can be found in Marvin Carlson, *Goethe and the Weimar Theatre* (Ithaca and London, 1979), pp. 309–18.

and his audience from the more corrosive aspects of the character represented. Goethe's aesthetic writings suggested a further distancing from Shakespeare's plays. In them, he described art not as the exhibition of the real but as the creation of the beautiful. A key condition of beauty is total harmony that agrees with itself and not with natural phenomena. From the 'consistency of the work of art' arises inner truth. The successful work of art creates 'a small world for itself, in which everything proceeds by certain laws which will be felt in their own manner'.[11] Only the uneducated, Goethe claimed, require art and nature to be the same. By such reasoning, the grounds that legitimated his early enthusiasm for Shakespeare had entirely disappeared.

Schiller shared several of Goethe's ideas as to the nature and purpose of art, as is clear from the intense correspondence they undertook during the early years of their joint work in the Weimar theatre. Schiller agreed that art and reality should be divorced. 'Poetical representation', he wrote, 'can never coincide with reality, for the very reason that it is absolutely true.'[12] Any 'common imitation of nature', any attempt to reproduce the surface appearance of life, would hide this 'truth'. Instead the poet should use physical things only as 'symbolical expedients' that draw the spectator to see the truth behind the surface, realised through a world of the poet's own creating. This meant that Goethe and Schiller were markedly ambivalent about the very phenomenon of performance. On the one hand they respected the power of the actor to move the spectator, on the other they found actorial skills to have little use on their own. Schiller argued that to realise the 'symbolical' nature of drama properly, objects and actions should be 'indicated' rather than 'represented' on stage, as if too arresting a spectacle destroys rather than aids the playwright in his purpose.[13] Goethe also suspected any work 'that is fully visible to one's eyes', as 'that which is superfluous' tends to be 'more noticeable' than an action which passes 'before the eyes of the mind'.[14] Faced with the necessity of representation, Goethe suggested action on stage should be half-realised, as it is in 'antique bas-reliefs'. He also wished genre to be strictly controlled, so that no modal inconsistency discomposed the audience in their 'self-willed illusion'. Anything disrupting the rhythms of the play's world must be avoided. He came to dislike any play that was generically impure or mixed 'the pure conditions of art' with 'the desires of spectators and listeners who wish to find everything perfectly apparent'.[15]

Essentially, neither Goethe nor Schiller wished actors to be artists in their

[11] 'Über Wahrheit und Wahrscheinlichkeit der Kunstwerke', *Goethes Werke*, 1st ser., vol. 47, pp. 261–2.
[12] Schiller, *Werke*, vol. 29, p. 56.   [13] *Ibid.*, p. 179.
[14] *Goethes Werke*, 4th ser., 50 vols. (Weimar, 1887–1912), vol. 12, p. 85.
[15] *Goethes Werke*, 4th ser. vol. 12, p. 282.

own right; they were to be solely the means of binding spectators to the play, which could then exercise a hold over them that was little short of despotic. So much is clear from Schiller's commentary on Goethe's essay on the difference between epic and dramatic poetry. In it, he defined dramatic poetry partially by its effect on the audience, which must be held prisoner by the dramatic action.[16] Whereas epic poetry, he claimed, comprehends several events and even encompasses whole lives, tragedy is intense, and its action properly involves 'merely ... single extraordinary moments in human life'.[17] This difference in scope implies a different relationship between the poem or performance and the reader or spectator. Schiller explained that when reading epic poetry '*I* move around the object' as a free agent, whereas in watching drama 'I' surrender 'my' freedom to observe, think or imagine in order to follow the 'foreign power' of the poet's imagination.[18] This represented the development of an earlier idea that

> the tragic poet ... robs us of our freedom of mind, and as he directs and concentrates our powers in a single direction, he greatly simplifies his business and puts himself at an advantage while putting us at a dis-advantage.[19]

Schiller's concept of the poet as autocrat was justified by the end which tragedy serves, which is the awakening within the audience of 'a distinct consciousness of a teleological connection between things, of a sublime order, of a beneficent will'.[20]

The classical theatre of Weimar and unaltered Shakespeare were irreconcilable. Shakespeare created characters with a unique vitality, while Goethe and Schiller were uneasy about the effects of that vitality on their audience. Shakespeare revealed the multiplicity of life, while Weimar classicism furthered an art that envisioned an ideal unity and harmony. Shakespeare's works were generically mixed, while Goethe and Schiller wished for generic purity. Shakespeare, whose work frequently veered more towards the epic than the dramatic, allowed the spectator freedom in responding to the stage, while Goethe and Schiller wished to deny that freedom. Above all, the unaltered Shakespeare stood for whatever was unorthodox in theatre; certainly his plays did not seem to promote social harmony. In contrast, Goethe and Schiller as theatrical practitioners came to identify themselves with that specific function and in a specifically political context. The relationship between the stage and audience in the Weimar court theatre paralleled the benevolent but despotic relationship between ruler

---

[16] Schiller, *Werke*, vol. 29, p. 176.   [17] *Ibid.*, p. 265.   [18] *Ibid.*, p. 176.
[19] *Ibid.*, p. 66.
[20] 'Ueber die tragische Kunst', Schiller, *Werke*, vol. 20, p. 157.

and ruled in the Duchy of Weimar. In spirit, the teeming world of Shakespeare was far from that well-structured order. Never was the unsuitability of Shakespeare to the purpose of the German court theatre in the late eighteenth and early nineteenth centuries more clearly revealed.

But curiously, while there was antipathy between Shakespeare and the spirit of Weimar, his plays were not completely absent from the repertoire of the theatre. First, they could hardly be avoided as they were an essential component of the world drama that Goethe and Schiller wished to see reflected in the theatre's repertoire.[21] But more importantly, despite their reservations over Shakespeare, in crucial respects neither Goethe nor Schiller had lost their devotion to him. However irregular his work or unwieldy his plays in a theatre where the neoclassical unities and decorum were cultivated, no one could deny the man's vast creative energy. Schiller consistently praised Shakespeare for his unique penetration of the human mind, claiming that he developed rich tragic characters not just for the sake of authenticating action through motive, but to bring 'whole human beings and human lives on to the stage'.[22] Furthermore, as only the great poets can, Shakespeare explained the greatness of the world through the smallness of the work of art, the 'harmony of the small' leading spectators to understand the 'harmony of the great'.[23] Goethe was less explicit over his admiration for Shakespeare, but as Gundolf has argued, the English dramatist was a creative reservoir for him from which he constantly refreshed himself, so that while his ideas as a stage director and theorist may have varied, his intensely subjective appreciation of Shakespeare never really changed from that voiced in his address of 1771.[24] Throughout his life, Goethe paid tribute to Shakespeare's influence on his personal development, in his final months describing him to Eckermann as one of the supreme creative spirits of the human race.[25] Simply put, however disturbing or irregular the plays, there was too much in Shakespeare to lose. A point of reconciliation had to be found between him and the Weimar court theatre.

Eventually, nine of Shakespeare's plays were staged at Weimar during the twenty-six years of Goethe's intendancy.[26] The first was, strangely, *King John*, produced in November 1791, chosen possibly because the role of Prince Arthur was ideal for Goethe's favourite actress Christiane Neumann. *Hamlet* in Schröder's second version was given in January 1792,

[21] On repertoire, see Willi Flemming, *Goethe und das Theater seiner Zeit* (Stuttgart, 1968), pp. 218–37.
[22] 'Über Egmont: Trauerspiel von Goethe', Schiller, *Werke*, vol. 22, p. 200.
[23] 'Ueber das gegenwartige teutsche Theater', Schiller, *Werke*, vol. 20, p. 83.
[24] Gundolf, *Shakespeare und der deutsche Geist*, pp. 222–50.
[25] Eckermann, *Gespräche*, vol. 2, p. 360.
[26] Werner Deetjen, 'Shakespeare-Aufführungen unter Goethes Leitung', *Shakespeare-Jahrbuch*, 68 (1932), 10–35.

to be followed by *Henry IV* in April of the same year. Of these early productions, only *Hamlet* had any degree of success. Schröder's *King Lear* was given in 1796, then in 1800 came the most famous of all the Weimar Shakespeare productions, Schiller's adaptation of *Macbeth*. This was followed by a production of *Julius Caesar* in Schlegel's verse translation, which was impressively staged by Goethe but, due to the relatively small public the theatre could call upon, was given only three times, which meant that Schlegel himself was unable to see it.[27] *Othello* in Voss's translation was given in 1805 and *Hamlet* in Schlegel's translation in 1809. In 1812 Goethe produced his controversial adaptation of *Romeo and Juliet*, and in the same year the only Shakespearean comedy given at Weimar, *The Merchant of Venice*, was staged, mainly so that August Iffland as guest actor could give his interpretation of Shylock.[28]

MACBETH

Of the nine productions of Shakespeare staged at Weimar, perhaps the most thoroughgoing attempt to reach a point of reconciliation between Shakespeare and the ethos of the court theatre was the production of *Macbeth* in May 1800. Despite his inadequate English, Schiller was responsible for translating *Macbeth*, while Goethe arranged the scenario and the structure.[29] On the playbill, the production was advertised simply as 'a tragedy in five acts, newly adapted from Shakespeare'. In one regard, Shakespeare's original fulfils the demands of Weimar classicism, for in contrast to *Hamlet* and *King Lear* the action is concentrated and given unity through the constantly felt presence of Macbeth. This was probably why Goethe considered that *Macbeth* of all Shakespeare's plays was most suited to the demands of the stage.[30] But he also felt it suffered from a 'superabundance of content', which threatened to break the confines of form. He may have been thinking of the unsettling influence Macbeth can exercise on the audience, as the character is untempered by any redeeming vision. His terrifying destruction of order has no idealistic goal, as has, for example, the chaos caused by Schiller's Wallenstein.[31] Goethe was also uneasy at the witches' and the porter's scenes, grotesque and comic episodes that violated the general tone of high tragedy.

---

[27] *Ibid.*, pp. 24–5.   [28] See chapter 7, pp. 133–5.
[29] Heinrich Huesmann, *Shakespeare-Inszenierungen unter Goethe in Weimar* (Vienna, 1968), p. 114. The translation has, however, always been ascribed to Schiller and appears in some versions of his complete works. He used both the Wieland and Eschenburg translations as well as the English text.
[30] Eckermann, *Gespräche*, vol. 1, p. 171.
[31] Hans Heinrich Borcherdt, 'Schiller's Bühnenbearbeitungen Shakespearescher Werke', *Shakespeare-Jahrbuch*, 91 (1955), 61.

5 Goethe's sketch of the Witches in *Macbeth*, a Weimar production,
May 1800

The changes made to these scenes in the Weimar version of *Macbeth* illustrate most succinctly the distance between Shakespeare's tragic world and that of Goethe and Schiller. While Shakespeare's hags are nightmarish, folkloric figures, half-human, half-supernatural, the more disquieting because they are indeterminable, the Weimar witches are statuesque, like the norns of Nordic mythology or the Roman sibyls, impressive, impassive foretellers of the future (see plate 5). Banquo refers to them as

so grau von Haaren,
So riesenhaft und schrecklich anzusehen.

(so grey of hair / So gigantic and terrible to look upon.)[32]

in contrast to Shakespeare's Banquo, who finds them 'so wither'd and so wild in their attire' (I: 3, 40). In the 1800 production, they were played by veiled men, elevated on cothurni and wearing classical drapes. In later performances, the witches were beautiful young girls, who, though more appealing and human, were no more unsettling. The Weimar witches have a function distinctly different from Shakespeare's. Whether Shakespeare's witches can foretell the future is dubious; their main purpose is to release the demonic powers in Macbeth's character. The Weimar witches, however, explain clearly why they are there. In the first scene, considerably

---

[32] Schiller, *Werke*, vol. 13, p. 80.

expanded from Shakespeare's original, they say their purpose is 'ins Verderben führen den edeln Helden' ('to tempt the noble hero'). They 'streuen in die Brust die böse Saat' ('sow the evil seed') in whomever is 'tapfer, gerecht und gut' ('valiant, upright and good'),[33] which they consider Macbeth to be. They hate him because he is fortunate. The opening to Shakespeare's Act I, scene 4 is also rewritten. The first witch does not speak of the sailor's wife, but tells a fable of how she forced a poor but happy fisherman to suicide by awakening his latent greed. However perverse the forces of fate represented by the witches, they are logical beings, whose antipathy towards humanity grows in quasi-mathematical proportion to the growth of human happiness. Accordingly the audience responds to them rationally. Their calm appearance encourages the spectator to recognise without qualm the symbolic realm of hell, while their morally-oriented statements, including the parallel implied between the fisherman's fate and that of Macbeth, lead the spectator to understand without difficulty the play's moral pattern. Shakespeare's all-embracing conflict between the demonic and the human is confined to one aspect alone, the conflict between virtue and vice. While the major cause of the original Macbeth's downfall is Macbeth himself, in the Weimar adaptation it is caused by the witches. This is apparent from Schiller's rewriting of the Hecate scene, placed as an immediate prologue to Macbeth's visit to the witches. In this, Hecate stirs up antipathy against Macbeth, who now seems almost totally the helpless victim of a fate he has done little to deserve.

> Ich will euch meine Geister senden
> Und solche Truggebilde weben,
> Und täuschende Orakel geben,
> Dass Macbeth, von dem Blendwerk voll,
> Verwirrt und tollkühn werden soll!
> Dem Schicksal soll er trotzen kühn,
> Dem Tode blind entgegen fliehn,
> Nichts fürchten, sinnlos allen wagen,
> Nach seinem eiteln Trugbild jagen.

(I will send you my spirits and weave such phantoms and give deceptive oracles, that Macbeth, full of delusion, will become perplexed and rash! He shall bravely defy fate, fly blindly against death, fearing nothing, senselessly risking everything, hunting his vain phantom.)[34]

The Weimar porter is also a radically different being, serving a purpose diametrically opposed to Shakespeare's. Shakespeare's porter is drunk, speaks in prose and utters remarks bordering on the obscene. The Weimar porter is sober, speaks in verse and does not have a dirty thought in his

---

[33] *Ibid.*, pp. 75–6.   [34] *Ibid.*, p. 130.

mind. Shakespeare's porter, as the guardian of Hell-Gate, is an apt watchman for Macbeth, but the Weimar porter thinks solely of heaven. He enters singing a *Morgenlied*, welcoming the sun as it dispels the gloom of night and evil. He is not entirely humourless – indeed he indulges in authentically Shakespearean word-play when he refers to 'Scotland' as both the country and Duncan – but he is neither coarse nor rudely satirical. Shakespeare's porter is a follower of Macbeth, the Weimar porter of Duncan. His *Morgenlied* revives faith that good will prevail instead of thickening the atmosphere of evil created by the murder.[35] This typifies a fundamental distinction between Shakespeare and Schiller. While Shakespeare's action borders persistently on unmitigated evil and chaos, the Weimar *Macbeth* constantly reassures the audience of what Schiller had earlier called 'a sublime order ... a beneficent will'.[36]

These alterations have fundamental implications for the characterisation of Macbeth. He is no longer a hellhound. Shakespeare's opening description of the battle, important in establishing Macbeth's apocalyptic violence, is muted by Schiller. His Macbeth is a 'heldenmüt'ger Feldherr' ('valorous general'), a good man fighting for his king. The Sergeant's (in the Weimar version, the Captain's) and Ross's speeches do not contain Shakespeare's weighty, savage language, which makes us sense that Macbeth's fury against Duncan's enemies outweighs the cause and anticipates the coming catastrophe. The measured rhythms of Schiller's blank verse are intended not to capture the perilous excitement of the original, but to describe a conventional battle fought by loyal troops, led not by 'Bellona's bridegroom' but by 'Macbeth mit unbezwinglich tapferm Arm' ('Macbeth with invincible, valiant arm').[37] The Weimar Macbeth has neither the size nor the interest of his Shakespearean counterpart. He is a rational man in a rational world. On hearing the witches' prophecy, he speculates calmly on his father's death (which has taken place that very night) and on his chances of succession. His language does not allow us to feel his mental motions. For example, as the idea of Duncan's murder grows on Shakespeare's Macbeth, his words express the furtiveness of his thoughts and communicate his confusion at exactly what it is he wishes to do:

> Stars, hide your fires!
> Let not light see my black and deep desires:
> The eye wink at the hand; yet let that be
> Which the eye fears, when it is done, to see.
>
> (1:4, 50–3)

---

[35] Ian Findlay, 'The Porter's Scene in Schiller's *Macbeth*', *Modern Language Notes*, 88 (1973), 980–7.

[36] Schiller, *Werke*, vol. 20, p. 57. Gundolf argues that Schiller's belief in the existence of a rational order is the most fundamental difference between him and Shakespeare, who saw the world as irrational and chaotic: *Shakespeare und der deutschen Geist*, pp. 288–310.

[37] *Ibid.*, p. 78.

Schiller, by contrast, relates the imagery to the religious symbolism of the play and alters the meaning to clarify it. His non-cryptical language and regular rhythm do nothing to convey Macbeth's confusion and fear.

> Verhüllet, Sterne, euer himmlisch Licht,
> Damit kein Tag in meinen Busen falle, –
> Das Auge selber soll die Hand nicht sehen,
> Damit das Ungeheure kann geschehen!

(Stars, cover your heavenly light, so that no day falls into my bosom. My eye itself should not see my hand, so that the monstrous can happen).[38]

Such generalised language is typical for Macbeth throughout.[39] Consequently, our sense of him as an individual is weakened. He is mainly a pawn in the battle between good and evil. In particular, Schiller carefully avoided any evidence of gross self-interest, cutting such lines as Shakespeare's 'For mine own good all causes shall give way.' The Weimar Macbeth may be wayward, but he is no monster of egoism. To the end he remains a noble, even Olympian sufferer, related to other Weimar tragic heroes in that there is something exemplary in his fate. Unlike Shakespeare's Macbeth, he is not simultaneously terrible and pitiable. Heinrich Vohs, the first Weimar Macbeth, avoided the perplexing ambiguity of such tragedy by playing the final scenes with aloofness, 'with cold disdain for danger', leading one critic to 'admire involuntarily the foundering hero, whose terrible indifference could not even be shaken by the death of his wife'.[40]

If much of the evil is withdrawn from Macbeth, it is transferred to his wife, which places Macbeth and his Lady at melodramatic polarities rather than in uneasy unity. Goethe saw Lady Macbeth as a 'superwitch'[41] who enslaves her husband. Certainly the Weimar Lady Macbeth is even more determined than Shakespeare's. She reproaches her husband for his hesitation more directly and demeaningly and, in an interpolated speech, demonstrates an acute awareness of the political chaos Duncan's murder will cause.[42] Unlike Macbeth, she does not worry in the slightest over causing disastrous civil commotion to achieve her ends. Although the sleepwalking scene is not cut – Schiller puts it into verse and deprives it of its intimacy – it is not prepared for, because the few signs of conscience that

---

[38] *Ibid.*, p. 87.
[39] Paul Steck, in his analysis of the adaptation in *Shakespeare und Schiller*, observes that throughout Shakespeare's language is sensuous, describing the world as felt by individual characters. In contrast, Schiller's is more objective and consciously formed.
[40] From a review by Seckendorf in the journal *Prometheus*, quoted Huesmann, *Shakespeare-Inszenierungen*, p. 126.
[41] 'Shakespeare und keine Ende', *Goethes Werke*, 1st ser., vol. 41, p. 62.
[42] Schiller, *Werke*, vol. 13, p. 94.

W e i m a r,

Sonnabend, den 1. Februar 1812.

Zum Erstenmahle:

Romeo und Julia.

Trauerspiel in fünf Aufzügen,
nach Shackespear und Schlegel,
von Goethe.

Escalus, Prinz von Verona, · · · · · · · · ·	Haide.
Graf Paris, Verwandter des Prinzen, · · · · ·	Dels.
Montague,⎫ Parthey=Häupter, · · · · · · · ·	Frey.
Capulet, ⎭	Malfolmi.
Romeo, Montague's Sohn, · · · · · · · · · ·	Wolff.
Mercutio, Verwandter des Prinzen und Romeo's Freund,	Unzelmann.
Benvolio, Montague's Neffe und Romeo's Freund, ·	Lorzing.
Tybalt, Neffe der Gräfin Capulet, · · · · · · ·	Denn.
Bruder Lorenzo, ein Franziskaner, · · · · · · ·	Graff
Bruder Marcus, von demselben Orden, · · · ·	Durand.
Romeo's Page, · · · · · · · · · · · · · ·	Lorzing.
Ein Apotheker, · · · · · · · · · · · · · ·	Eilenstein.
Gräfin Capulet, · · · · · · · · · · · · ·	Ackermann,
Julia, Capulets Tochter, · · · · · · · · · ·	Wolff.
Juliens Wärterin, · · · · · · · · · · · ·	Engels.
Masken.	
Gefolge.	
Wachen.	

A b o n n e m e n t   s u s p e n d u.

Balkon	,	16 Gr.
Parket	,	12 Gr.
Parterre	;	8 Gr.
Gallerie	;	4 Gr.

Anfang um 6 Uhr.

6 Playbill for first performance of Goethe's *Romeo and Juliet*, Weimar,
1 February 1812

Shakespeare's Lady Macbeth shows have been cut, along with her speech
'Nought's had, all's spent.' She shows no sign of being unable to live with
the consequences of her deeds, a trait that considerably humanises Shake-

speare's Lady. In the Weimar version, she is an unchanging figure of evil. Meanwhile, her husband stands, as monolithically as she does, but for beleaguered nobility.

The most telling omission in the Weimar *Macbeth* is the murder of Lady Macduff and her son. Few scenes demonstrate more effectively Shakespeare's ability to make real to his audience an action that lies beyond their everyday experience. The murder sets Macbeth's cruelty in that much more inhuman a light. But the visceral impact of the scene was beyond the pale of Weimar classicism, while the chatter of the child was probably considered to contrast too strikingly with the high tragedy of the rest of the play. Both the disquiet this scene creates and its stylistic incongruity would have dispelled the calm attention required by Goethe and Schiller of their audiences. Furthermore, it would have cast an unwontedly savage light upon the noble hero. Its omission sums up the criteria by which the play was adapted.

ROMEO AND JULIET

The most radical Weimar rewriting of any Shakespeare play was Goethe's adaptation of *Romeo and Juliet*, first staged on 1 February, 1812 (see plate 6). Goethe had been especially attached to the play since his student days in Leipzig, where he had seen a performance of Weisse's *Romeo und Julie* that deeply disappointed him. He planned to do an adaptation himself, though nothing came of it.[43] Why the play fascinated him then is obvious. With its large cast, violent action and a stylistic range which is broad even for Shakespeare, *Romeo and Juliet* is a prime example of theatre unrestricted by French conventions, 'a beautiful peepshow in which the history of the world flows past our eyes'. But when almost half a century later Goethe came to adapt the play for Weimar, it was these French conventions which he took as his standard. Of all Shakespearean adaptations produced at Weimar, *Romeo and Juliet* was the furthest in form and spirit from the original. While *Macbeth* might still, arguably, be called a translation, *Romeo and Juliet* was unmistakably an adaptation.

Goethe based his adaptation on A. W. Schlegel's verse translation, which is 2,992 lines long. His own text has only 2,033 lines, and of these 488 lines are entirely original. Of the remaining 1,545 lines, 870 are Schlegel's and the remainder are Schlegel retranslated by Goethe. Goethe also rearranged the action so that only twelve scene-changes were necessary in comparison to Shakespeare's twenty-four, while the five-day time-span of the original is reduced to an even more constricted two days.[44] Shakespeare's cast of

---

[43] Georg Heun, *Shakespeares Romeo und Julia in Goethes Bearbeitung* (Berlin, 1965), p. 10.
[44] The figures are taken from Heun, *Shakespeares Romeo und Julia*, pp. 9–10 and 14.

twenty-five characters is cut to seventeen and some of those characters remaining, especially Mercutio and the Nurse, are reduced to shadows of their former selves.

Goethe wished to compress Shakespeare's tragedy, as, like the critics of the later eighteenth century, he considered the street-scenes and the oscillation between lyrical effusion and earthy comedy to be merely attempts to curry the Elizabethan audience's favour. As he wrote a few days before the first performance,

> the principle I followed was to concentrate on [whatever was] interesting and to bring about harmony where Shakespeare, because of his genius, his time and his public, was allowed to assemble many disharmonious trivialities; indeed, he had to, in order to appease the spirit of the theatre that ruled at that time.[45]

In a later letter, he claimed he had made 'a more comprehensible whole' out of the play.[46]

In doing so, he made fundamental alterations. Act I only contains one-tenth of the original; the rest is Goethe. All action up to and including the ball is in two scenes, outside Capulet's house and the ballroom. Shakespeare's action is vastly simplified and develops with absolute clarity. Characters do not wander through Verona with unfettered energy. All that happens is that Romeo and his friends decide to go to the ball so that Romeo may forget Rosalind. Once in the ballroom the plot unfolds swiftly: plans for Juliet's marriage to Paris are made, Tybalt flares up against Romeo, the Prince appears and attempts to bring about concord between the two families by marriage,[47] and Romeo meets Juliet. Only with the balcony-scene, transferred from Shakespeare's Act II to Act I, does the plot begin to move at a more leisurely pace. Goethe also changed the theme of Shakespeare's play. While Shakespeare began with the violence of the feud, Goethe started it with an idyllic song in which Capulet's servants invite the guests to enter the ballroom.

> Zündet die Lampen an,
> Windet auch Kränze dran,
> Heil sei das Haus!
> Feier mit Tanz und Schmaus,
> Capulet der Prächtige
> Richtet sie aus.

(Kindle the lamps, tie garlands to them, hail to the house. Celebrate with dance and banquet. Capulet the magnificent prepares them.)[48]

---

[45] *Goethes Werke*, 4th ser., vol. 22, p. 249.   [46] *Ibid.*, p. 320.
[47] A theme that Goethe then abandons, never to mention again.
[48] *Goethes Werke*, 1st ser., vol. 9, p. 171.

The impression created by this quasi-operatic opening is one of ingratiating harmony rather than of violent discord. It is not deceptive, for the mood is sustained throughout. With the exception of the murder of Mercutio and Tybalt, any representation of the feud is omitted. Characters may talk of it, but it remains in the background, a means of lending pathos to Romeo and Juliet's love and a plot device. Goethe focused exclusively on romantic love, in contrast to Shakespeare who used that love to set in sharper profile the savagery of the Montagues and Capulets. Shakespeare represented Verona in all its immediacy, Goethe held it at a distance. In the Weimar production, this distance was realised physically through a formal staging more associated with opera than with the spoken drama.[49]

After Act I, Goethe followed the original more faithfully, though there are still massive cuts. Almost all action involving the Nurse is excised. The events leading to the deaths of Mercutio and Tybalt are represented completely, though the formal staging of the duel ensured that focus was on the major participants and not on the milieu. Goethe began to depart from the original again at the beginning of Act IV, where, to give Paris more stature, he extended greatly Shakespeare's brief dialogue between him and Juliet. Then he cut all preparations for the marriage, as well as the discovery of Juliet's 'corpse'. The action moves at once from her taking the potion to Mantua, where Romeo is given a long description of her funeral.[50] The final scene is rewritten to centre solely on Paris, Romeo, Juliet and Friar Lawrence, ending with Juliet's death, after which Friar Lawrence delivers a brief homily on the vanity of human striving. Goethe considered Shakespeare's ending weakened the tragic impact of the lovers' deaths, because it was more suitable to comedy and therefore generically impure.

This condensation of Romeo and Juliet brings the action closer to what Schiller had defined as the proper action of tragedy, one that involved 'merely ... single extraordinary moments in the life of man'.[51] The attempt might have been successful, if it were not for the absence of any elements, Shakespearean or Goethean, to give the adaptation life. Whereas the Weimar Macbeth has interest in its embodiment of the idealistic aspirations of Weimar classicism, the changes Goethe made to Romeo and Juliet are not similarly compensating. Ironically, though he concentrated exclusively on romantic love, he failed, where Shakespeare had not, to recapture the experience of that love. Instead he created characters that are unremarkably admirable.

Shakespeare's Romeo is volatile, vulnerable, self-pitying and instantly

---

49 For a detailed description of the staging, see Huesmann, Shakespeare-Inszenierungen, pp. 175–82, and Carlson, Goethe and the Weimar Theatre, pp. 256–7.
50 Goethes Werke, vol. 9, pp. 259–60.   51 Schiller, Werke, vol. 29, p. 265.

responsive to the slightest erotic stimuli. In contrast Goethe's hero is older and more responsible. When he first appears with Benvolio, immediately after the opening song, he is idealistic, contemplative and aware of the world as separate from himself. He asks Benvolio to restrain himself so as to bring peace between the two families, a thought that would never have crossed the mind of Shakespeare's Romeo until the pressure of circumstances had forced it there. Romeo also goes to the ball not to meet Rosalind, but to forget her; indeed, the whole Rosalind affair is presented as past, not living emotion. Later, in the love-scenes, Romeo is self-confident and in control. Goethe represented the male as the dominant partner, where Shakespeare had given the relationship peculiar life by having Juliet take initiatives stronger than Romeo's. In Mantua, he does not instantly determine to die in Juliet's tomb, but only after he has listened to the long account of the funeral. As a result, his decision is a mature one, made by a contemplative mind, not by desolated emotions. The well-measured acting and fine cadences of Pius Alexander Wolff, the first Goethe Romeo, reinforced this image of a stalwart hero who is victim neither of himself nor of society, but is fully in control, taking the wisest course of action. With the exception of the bout of self-pity in Friar Lawrence's cell, Goethe's Romeo is consistent with the ideals of Weimar, but in being so he lacks the vitality of Shakespeare's character.

Juliet is even less interesting, as she is passive and acted upon rather than acting. Not only is she brought to her secret wedding by Romeo, she does not seek out Friar Lawrence to solve the dilemma of her marriage. Instead Goethe, borrowing from Weisse, has him come to see her under the pretext of helping the family mourn for Tybalt. Even though Goethe included in full Juliet's soliloquy before she takes the potion, her positive commitment to the relationship is substantially weakened. Her language is purified of any earthiness and she never refers to her body, the lines

> I'll to my wedding bed
> And death, not Romeo, take my maidenhead

being translated by Goethe as

> Ich will in's Brautgemach
> Nicht Romeo, der Tod, er folgt mir nach.

(I will to my bridal bed. Death, not Romeo, follows me there.)[52]

Most damage is done to the vitality of the play by the positive mutilation of Mercutio and the Nurse, who are, no doubt, prime examples of what Goethe called 'inharmonious trivialities'. As Mercutio appears only spora-

---

[52] *Goethes Werke*, vol. 9, p. 227. Both Heun and James Boyd, in *Goethe's Knowledge of English Literature* (Oxford, 1932), point out that in many cases Goethe changed Schlegel's lines to bring

dically, his death has little impact. He has some Falstaffian humour but none of the original character's wild flights of fancy. The Nurse's coarseness Goethe found utterly inappropriate for tragedy, so the vast majority of her part is cut and she becomes merely a means by which the plot is forwarded.

Even though it was not altogether unsuccessful on stage, Goethe was far from happy with this adaptation. Soon after the first performance he wrote, 'this project was a great lesson for me and I have never looked deeper into Shakespeare's talent. But ... he remains nevertheless unfathomable.'[53] Such was to remain his judgement on Shakespeare for the rest of his life. He continued to see him as a major influence on his imaginative and intellectual development, but he was unable to reconcile the plays with the demands of the practical theatre. This is the main theme of his final major essay on Shakespeare, 'Shakespeare und keine Ende!' ('Shakespeare *ad infinitum!*') (1815), written partially in defence of his *Romeo and Juliet*. Though the essay contains some powerful insights into the difference between Shakespeare and the tragedians of ancient Greece, from the theatrical point of view it is disappointing. Goethe perpetuated the worn idea that as Shakespeare was writing for a primitive theatre, his plays are not suitable for a modern theatre in which representation is realistic. Hence he concluded, even in 1815, that the adaptations of Schröder were more suitable for performance than unaltered versions.

WEIMAR ACTING: PIUS ALEXANDER WOLFF

In fact, Goethe's greatest contribution to the stage history of Shakespeare in Germany may well have been indirect. Throughout his career he was fascinated with *Hamlet*. His Wilhelm Meister grows to manhood partially through his continual imaginative encounters with *Hamlet*. Goethe even had Wilhelm write a perfectly tenable adaptation of the play, which led many to hope that Goethe himself might attempt an adaptation. In fact, Goethe did stage *Hamlet* at Weimar, but never in his own adaptation. In January 1792 he staged the Schröder version, which he revived in 1801 with a tragic ending.

By this time, however, a most significant production had occurred elsewhere. On 15 October 1799, *Hamlet* was given at the Berlin court theatre in the Schlegel translation in as uncut a version as was possible. It was not a great success. Despite strong casting and the care with which

---

them closer to Shakespeare's original meaning. However, Goethe refined the language wherever he felt it would offend the decorum of the stage.

[53] *Ibid.*, 4th ser., vol. 22, p. 270. Note that this letter was written prior to the one cited in note 49.

Iffland, the theatre's director, had prepared for the occasion, the play did not impress the public. A critic complained

> One felt oneself pulled here and there, [one was] slowed down, and had it not been for the funeral procession of Ophelia, the dead march coming at the end of the play, then perhaps the poet would have had to feel the unjust anger of the public.[54]

The heart of the problem was the company's inability to sustain the audience's attention when the form of the play, the 'epic' form as Schiller had called it, did not hold them in the unwavering bonds of suspense.

Goethe produced the Schlegel version at Weimar almost ten years later, in May 1809. Again, this was not a wholly auspicious occasion. Several scenes had been cut, minor changes had been made, and the staging was far from effective. The Hamlet was Pius Alexander Wolff, who, as the leading actor of the Weimar theatre, aroused considerable expectations. In the event, he disappointed too. While his performance contained striking moments, it was felt to lack unity and to be gesturally overladen.[55] This might have been because Wolff, the most complete practitioner of Goethe's restrained and imposing style of tragic acting, did not convey credibly the inner experience of the role. Indeed, the marmorial Weimar style of acting, which was to be widely adopted in the German theatre over the next several decades, was not at all well suited either to the representation of Shakespeare's characters or to the frequently violent action of the plays.[56] Wolff's Hamlet, however, was the exception. His poor appearance in the role at Weimar was in fact only the first of a series of increasingly successful performances that would lead to an interpretation that would dominate German actors' approaches to Hamlet for the rest of the century.[57]

Wolff had his first great success as Hamlet in April 1816, soon after he had left Weimar to become the principal tragedian of the Berlin court theatre. Both in Berlin and on tour in Leipzig and Dresden, he gave an interpretation of Hamlet that accentuated the divisions in the character. In essence, his interpretation was fairly close to Goethe's description in *Wilhelm Meisters Lehrjahre* of Hamlet as a noble young man who is too weak to deal with the corrupt and ruthless world in which he finds himself. This differed considerably from the approach of Schröder, which, despite the extraordinary popularity of the play, was still the dominant model for the German actor. Perhaps the strength of Wolff's performance lay in his combination of nobility with the anger and confusion that had distin-

[54] Quoted in Hans Daffis, *Hamlet auf der deutschen Bühne bis zur Gegenwart* (Berlin, 1912), p. 61.
[55] von Weilen, *Hamlet auf der deutschen Bühne*, p. 108.
[56] Henri Plard, 'Shakespeare mis en scène par Goethe', *Revue d'Histoire du Théâtre*, 16 (1964), 359.
[57] Max Martersteig, *Pius Alexander Wolff* (Leipzig, 1879), p. 57.

guished Schröder's performance. His most exacting but sympathetic critic, Adolf Müllner, identified this precisely.

> The basis [of his interpretation] was unequivocal pain at a crime of which his mother was guilty, and disdainful scorn at the frailty of human morality. On these level foundations, the apparently contradictory elements of the role interweaved and coalesced in the most unaffected manner in the world, and mature connoisseurs ... acknowledged that this Hamlet was as enjoyable as it was new and surprising.[58]

Although this might suggest a naturalistically psychological approach, such as Schröder's, the impact of Wolff's presence was fully dependent on his Weimar training. Critics commented on his impeccable voice production, a fitting quality for a prince – for once the actor who gave advice to the players actually seemed capable of following it[59] – while he maintained consistently the noble posture associated with the Weimar player. But this did not lessen the subtlety of his characterisation. Theodore Rötscher, who would later champion the great realistic actor Karl Seydelmann, commented on the various levels of feeling Wolff was able to realise in the scene with Ophelia,[60] while the writer Holtei found the same scene different each time he saw it,[61] which may well reflect the same multiplicity sensed by Rötscher.

The most distinctive feature of Wolff's performance, however, may well have been his use of the statuesque qualities of the Weimar style in a way that was theatrically arresting and even psychologically authentic. In her *Memoirs*, the actress Karoline Bauer recalls how Wolff registered the pain Hamlet suffers when he hears of his father's death from the Ghost. Against the decorum of the theatre – and very much against the dicta of Goethe's 'Rules for Actors' – Wolff played this scene with his back to the audience as he felt incapable of communicating the pain with his face. Much was therefore left to the audience's imagination. After hearing of the murder, he turned to the audience, his face a mask.

> Youth, life, belief and hope seemed to be extinguished forever from this deathly pale, devastated face. Wan, his lips painfully twisted, he stood there in despair – broken – crushed. His eyes had an expression of nameless sorrow. The words struggled laboriously from his broken heart. The audience was as if enchanted by the inexplicable and barely dared to breathe.[62]

---

58 Quoted Martersteig, *Wolff*, p. 56.
59 *Die Briefwechsel zwischen Goethe und Zelter*, ed. Max Hecker, 4 vols. (Leipzig, 1913), vol. 1, p. 483.
60 Martersteig, *Wolff*, pp. 51–2.   61 *Ibid.*, p. 52.
62 Quoted in Widmann, *Hamlets Bühnenlaufbahn*, p. 197.

Although the classicism that guided Goethe both in his work as a director and adapter and as a trainer of actors may ultimately have contradicted the spirit of Shakespeare, at moments such as this his influence gave to the plays a stature and consequence that had not so far been achieved in Germany.

6

Shakespeare at the Vienna Burgtheater

THE BURGTHEATER AS A NATIONAL THEATRE

Although by the beginning of the nineteenth century Shakespeare's plays were part of the repertoire of the German theatre, their survival was far from assured. This was due chiefly to the persistence well into the century of the eighteenth-century conception of theatre as an institution that guaranteed social cohesion, a conception violated by the unadapted plays of Shakespeare. Over the turn of the century, this incompatibility was most apparent in Goethe's productions at the Weimar court theatre, and because of Goethe's eminence, the ideals of Weimar would continue to have a potent influence over the development of German theatre for several decades. Nevertheless, as the century progressed, the Vienna Burgtheater came to exercise an even greater authority than Weimar did. As the national theatre of the Habsburg territories, the Burgtheater occupied a uniquely prominent position in the social and political life of German-speaking Europe. Hence it became a theatre that was widely admired and imitated.

Perhaps this was because no theatre in German-speaking Europe held so persistently to the principles of its founder, in this case the eighteenth-century emperor, Josef II. A true man of the Enlightenment, Josef had introduced into his territories several far-reaching reforms, designed to transform a society still feudal in structure into a modern state run by an imperial bureaucracy on rational principles. The Burgtheater, constituted as a national theatre in 1776,[1] was a key institution in this reform. Josef was interested in this theatre neither as the provider of entertainment, nor as a means of cultivating the imagination of his citizens. Rather, influenced by the ideas of Josef von Sonnenfels, a Viennese professor whose *Briefe über die*

---

[1] In fact, the Burgtheater had been in existence since 1741, when the Empress Maria Theresa, Josef's mother, ordered the ballroom in the Michaelerplatz to be converted into a theatre. Josef regularised the company's activities. See Franz Hadamowsky, *Die Josefinsche Theaterreform und das Spieljahr 1776/77 des Burgtheaters* (Vienna, 1978).

wienerische Schaubühne (*Letters on the Viennese Stage*) (1768) demonstrated how tenacious the ideas of Gottsched could be, Josef expected the theatre to provide audiences with models upon which they should base their public and private conduct. From the stage they should also feel, aristocrats and commoners alike, the power and beneficence of his rule.[2]

The auditorium of the Burgtheater was not quite as severe or as grandiose a place as its political function might at first suggest. It was not large, so even though classes were separated by the usual division of galleries, any resentment such separation might have engendered was ameliorated in part by the close physical proximity of the lower to the higher classes. All who attended the theatre had the sense of being a personal guest of the Emperor, which grew into the comforting illusion that each audience member was a member of the theatre community. The seemingly classless coterie of the Burgtheater audience could therefore be regarded as a microcosm of the racially pluralistic society which the Habsburg monarchy was attempting to create.

However, Shakespeare, a stylistically pluralistic dramatist if ever there was one, was not welcome in such an environment. For a start, as the Burgtheater was modelled on the Comédie Française, plays seen on its stage were expected to be generically pure and stylistically uniform. As a result, plays from the popular suburban theatres of Vienna were excluded from the Burgtheater repertoire, as they appealed specifically through the sharp juxtaposition of comic and pathetic effects and a spectacle that by its very nature defied the restrictions of the neoclassical unities. Indeed, the exclusiveness of the Burgtheater from the popular tradition was symbolised by Stephanie the Younger's repudiating his popular version of *Macbeth* when he became a member of the ruling board of the theatre soon after it had been constituted as a national theatre.[3] The Viennese popular theatre could, as we have seen, trace its origins back through the *Haupt- und Staatsaktionen* to the English Comedians of the seventeenth century.[4] Though Sonnenfels, the spiritual founder of the Burgtheater, may not have been aware of this historical connection, he certainly recognised affinities between Shakespeare and *Haupt- und Staatsaktionen*[5] and, like Gottsched before him, deplored Shakespeare's tendency to mix high and low and to instil moments of comedy into scenes of great pathos. He complained too about Shakespeare's breach of good taste in making rulers and rabble cohabit on the same stage. His patron Josef II also deplored the unpolished theatre of mixed modes and its capacity to disturb or arouse audiences'

[2] Rudolph Lothar, *Das Wiener Burgtheater* (Vienna: n.d. [1934]), p. 43.
[3] Schumacher, p. 32.
[4] Baesecke, p. 153.
[5] Josef von Sonnenfels, *Briefe über die Wienerische Schaubühne* (rep. Vienna, 1884), p. 220.

emotions unpredictably. To guard against such aberrations on his own stage, in a decree of 1779 he outlined the precise effects that should be aimed at both in the selection and in the representation of plays on the Burgtheater stage. In all things he wished for an ideal balance and moderation.

> Tragedy should be rich in action, exalted in sentiment, without sinking into the terrible or the supernatural; it should arouse pity and fear, but not disgust or horror. The old, good, French poets did not even allow murder to occur in public, even less would they have placed dead bodies [on stage] through the entire act. Such manifestations are revolting. Tragedy speaks in a noble voice, but with no verbiage interwoven with fantasy. The sentimental comedy, whose action stands between the everyday and the unusual, displays special characters, a more probable, more moving action than the tragedy, without sinking into the novelistic; the emotions it arouses should be pleasant without being terrifying. Every character should in the end be instructive, the whole should tend towards the teaching of morals, without becoming tasteless or too wearying. The language should be more elevated than in the comedy but not soar as in tragedy. Comedy involves characters from common life, yet they are not without interest. It includes satire without becoming a lampoon, arouses laughter through wit and nature, not through farce and immodesty. It aims to improve through the represen- tation of its laughable characters. The language is natural, but not taken from the crowd.[6]

Clearly Shakespeare in unedited form was paradigmatic of all the Burg- theater did not stand for. Furthermore, his work was politically suspect. Josef associated him with *Sturm und Drang*, whose 'terrible and nonsensical imitations' of his plays he deplored.[7] In particular, Shakespeare's treatment of the themes of power and authority, his exposé of the fallibility of rulers, was hardly designed to appeal to the authorities of a theatre whose function was to support, not question, the monarchy. During the subsequent reign of Franz I, political freedom was substantially curtailed and the censorship laws of 1797 banned the representation on stage of all material that questioned the legitimacy of royal rule or of the political and social institutions supporting it.[8]

If Shakespeare's plays did not suit the Burgtheater's purpose, they were poor material for the company's distinctive style of acting as well. The picturesque gestures, noble postures and gracious tones associated with French acting were encouraged at the Burgtheater as they accorded well with the image of the actor as a conduit of the Emperor's power. The

---

[6] Quoted Kindermann, *Theatergeschichte Europas*, vol. 5, p. 97.
[7] Stahl, *Shakespeare und das deutsche Theater*, p. 77.
[8] For an account of the laws governing the performance of drama early in the nineteenth century, see Johann Hüttner, 'Theatre Censorship in Metternich's Vienna', *Theatre Quarterly*, 10 (1980), 61–9.

artificiality of such a style had, however, been modified early in the company's history by Friedrich Ludwig Schröder, who, as a leading member of the company between 1780 and 1784, encouraged greater spontaneity and more realistic characterisation. The compromise that evolved was the company's famous, conversational, ensemble style of acting in which each actor behaved self-effacingly on stage, with highly individual or rawly emotional interpretations being discouraged. Owing to the excellent acoustics of the auditorium[9] and the close rapport between actor and audience, speech and gesture on stage could be effectively elegant and subdued. In tragedy, actors would not attempt to represent the superhuman dimensions of suffering, as these would be too enlarged and strident. Instead, they would project an image of gracious and ingratiating nobility. As a result, in the early years of the nineteenth century, the most favoured plays were the sentimental pieces of Iffland and the melodramas of Kotzebue. Later in the century, the French salon play was to feature most prominently in the repertoire.

But, despite these barriers, Shakespeare was not entirely absent from the Burgtheater stage. Heufeld's *Hamlet* had received its first performance here, before the theatre had been elevated to 'national' status, and in the following decade, during his brief stay with the company, Schröder had introduced his versions of *King Lear* and *Henry IV*. Some adaptations from Shakespearean originals were also performed. But, by the turn of the century, these had gone. All plays attributable to Shakespeare had been dropped and only Schiller's *Macbeth* found its way to the stage in 1808.[10]

Given these circumstances, it is most surprising that the Burgtheater was to play a crucial part in the assimilation of some relatively complete versions of Shakespeare's major plays into the German theatre. These versions and their staging were the responsibility of a man who initially might have seemed unlikely to take on the task, the liberal writer and journalist Josef Schreyvogel.

JOSEF SCHREYVOGEL

In 1814, Schreyvogel was appointed general secretary and dramaturg to the Burgtheater, a fitting choice because as a young man he had spent some time in Weimar, where he had come under the influence of Goethe.[11] His

---

[9] See Herta Singer, 'Die Akustik des alten Burgtheaters', *Maske und Kothurn*, 4 (1958), 220–9.

[10] Between 1776 and 1800, fifty-five performances of Schröder's *Hamlet* were given (104 from 1776 to 1820), twenty-two of Schröder's *King Lear*, eighteen of *Imogen* (a version of *Cymbeline*), and two of *Coriolanus*. There were no new productions of Shakespeare between 1789 and 1808, when Schiller's *Macbeth* was staged. The next new production was to be Schreyvogel's *Romeo and Juliet* in 1816.

[11] See Rudolf Payer von Thurn, 'Joseph Schreyvogels Beziehungen zu Goethe', *Jahrbuch der Grillparzer Gesellschaft*, 10 (1900), 96–128.

Weimar experience was reflected in his consistent and generally successful endeavours at building an ensemble of exemplary actors, who formed the basis for the succession of great acting companies that were to compose the Burgtheater for the rest of the century.

Like Goethe, Schreyvogel was fascinated by Shakespeare. To judge from his diaries, he began reading him seriously just before his appointment to the Burgtheater. But from the very start, he did not see Shakespeare as the wild genius that had appealed to *Sturm und Drang*. Neither did he consider the plays to arouse unruly passions in the reader or spectator, as his eighteenth-century forebears had. Instead, he considered that 'his works display and at the same time awake in the spectator a certain peace and deliberation of reason over the emotions and, like all entirely true pictures of nature, even have an open interest in reason'.[12] In Schreyvogel's reading at least, Shakespeare seemed rather to accord with than fly in the face of the Burgtheater's stated purposes.

In fact for his time Schreyvogel's reading seems rather forced, but the reasoning behind it might be gathered from his choice for the first of Shakespeare's plays that he would introduce to the Burgtheater stage, Goethe's adaptation of *Romeo and Juliet*. His enthusiasm for this version of the play did not, however, last for long. Soon after he had started work on the script in February 1816, Schreyvogel determined that Goethe had ruined Acts IV and V,[13] so he set out to rework them and found himself going back to Schlegel's original translations. This convinced him – and Schreyvogel was possibly the first to posit the idea – that there did not necessarily have to be that great a difference between the reading and performance versions of a play. He then returned to Goethe's Act I and revised it totally, once again depending far more than Goethe had done on Schlegel's translation. Although there is evidence to suggest that the version of *Romeo and Juliet* performed at the Burgtheater on 20 December 1816 was possibly closer to Goethe's adaptation than the edition of Schreyvogel's text published in 1841,[14] the latter eventually came to be performed in the Burgtheater and was, with the exception of the 1799 *Hamlet* in Berlin, probably the closest to a complete Shakespeare text that had been done on the German stage until that time.

In fact, to make the play acceptable to the imperial censors, the Burgtheater administration and public taste, Schreyvogel still had to make significant cuts and alterations. In particular he had to satisfy the singular prudery of the censors. This is most apparent in his treatment of the Nurse

[12] *Josef Schreyvogels Tagebücher: 1810–1823*, ed. Karl Glossy, 2 vols. (Berlin, 1903), vol. 1, p. 62.
[13] *Ibid.*, vol. 2, p. 161.
[14] See Eugen Kilian, 'Schreyvogels Shakespeare-Bearbeitungen: 3. *Romeo und Julia*', *Shakespeare-Jahrbuch*, 41 (1905), 151–2.

Romeo.

7 Costume for Romeo in Schreyvogel's *Romeo and Juliet* (first
performed at the Vienna Burgtheater, 20 December 1816)

and Mercutio, who are even shadowier versions of figures already severely reduced by Goethe. Not the slightest double-entendre or risqué expression was allowed to escape from the lips of the actors. Accordingly any references to physical love, particularly when uttered by Juliet, were cut. Furthermore, given the strong ties between the Habsburg monarchy and the Catholic church, the integrity of religious institutions and the beneficence of divine providence could never be questioned. As a result, Lawrence is no longer a Friar, a member of a recognised religious order, but a hermit. In his opening speech (Shakespeare, II:3, 1–30), all references to poisonous plants are cut, as they would be unseemly in the mouth of a religious man, however minor his status, while later in the play Juliet cannot utter her suspicion that Lawrence wants her dead to escape from the consequences of the marriage (IV:3, 24–9). Also, she cannot say that she will have faith in heaven only if Romeo is there (III:5, 205–8). Small as these cuts might seem, often amounting to no more than a phrase or two, they have a curiously levelling effect, depriving Shakespeare's characters of much of their defiant vitality and emotional individuality.

Of course, such excisions cannot be attributed solely to the pressure of censorship. In some regards, Schreyvogel was still guided by principles of adaptation that had been common since the eighteenth century, or even earlier, especially those that guaranteed a fast-moving action. Hence, he often cut passages of verse in which characters elaborate on their thoughts and feelings, while any lines which essentially repeat what has been said before are always omitted. This means that throughout the play sharp personality traits are blunted. Capulet is not like Shakespeare's original character, a contradictory blend of generosity, vindictiveness, cruelty and doting love. To develop such a character holds up the action, so his cruel physical threats are considerably cut and modified and his ravings over Juliet's 'corpse' have gone, probably because they invited too confused a response from the audience and went against the general habit of showing fathers to be kindly old men.

The character who suffers most is Romeo. Although Schreyvogel restored much of Shakespeare's Act 1, even including some references to Rosalind, she is not a major presence in Romeo's love life. Instead, as in Goethe's version, the early Romeo is quite an uncomplicated young man, less volatile than Shakespeare's character. The long dialogues of word-play between him and his companions in which this volatility is notably apparent are cut. As a result, the role has no emotional lability and the range of Romeo's growth in the course of the play is distinctly diminished. Schreyvogel followed Goethe in having Romeo take the initiative in the matter of the marriage, so that Shakespeare's unorthodox treatment of the active woman and the passive man is reversed to accord with contemporary ideas about the relationship between the sexes.

Despite the cuts, Schreyvogel's *Romeo and Juliet* was a considerable achievement. By starting the play with the street fight between the Montagues and Capulets, he restored the focus of the play lost by Goethe. Certainly Schreyvogel had not escaped totally from Goethe's un-Shakespearean dramaturgy – his Act I is still greatly simplified and the final scene in the crypt is shortened so that the audience has no time to contemplate the action before the curtain descends – but by including more of the original episodes than Goethe did and by staging the play's bellicose conflicts, Schreyvogel realised for the first time Shakespeare's original theme.

Exactly how successful the production was is difficult to judge. Schreyvogel admitted that the first-night reception was lukewarm, mainly because the Viennese taste for a happy ending was thwarted. Also, he felt the physical demands of the play militated against conditions of performance. The frequent scene-changes unsettled the audience, while a large number of the subsidiary roles were poorly acted.[15] The latter point is pertinent, as Schreyvogel had still not formed a large and thoroughly integral ensemble. Only when that was achieved would the whole of a Shakespeare play have a chance to work effectively on stage. As it was, *Romeo and Juliet* attracted a few full houses but was taken off a little less than a month after its first performance and was not seen again until 1820.

Schreyvogel was not disheartened by the comparative failure of his first excursion into Shakespeare. Over the years, until his notorious dismissal from the company in 1832 – for personal differences with the administration – he staged other important Shakespearean works. These included a revival of Schiller's *Macbeth* in 1821, *King Lear* in 1822, *Othello* in 1823, *Hamlet* in 1825, *The Merchant of Venice* in 1827, and *All's Well That Ends Well* and *Henry IV Parts 1 and 2* in 1828. *The Merchant of Venice*, unlike all other contemporary adaptations, maintained the original order of the scenes so as to emphasise the thematic interdependency of Venice and Belmont,[16] but the grandest achievement, possibly of Schreyvogel's whole tenure at the Burgtheater, was his production of *King Lear*, first seen on 28 March 1822.

This was not the first time *King Lear* had been given at the Burgtheater. Schröder had played it back in the early 1780s in a performance legendary for the power of his anger and the moving reunion with Cordelia. Schröder's adaptation had shown remarkable durability since then. It was still in regular use throughout Germany in the 1820s and on a notable occasion in April 1816 had been used by the now ageing Josef Lange – the

---

[15] Schreyvogel, *Tagebücher*, vol. 2, p. 225.
[16] Something not even the Meininger managed. See chapter 8.

Heufeld Hamlet of 1773 – for a performance at the Theater an der Wien, with the first scene restored. When, therefore, Schreyvogel came to revive the play at the Burgtheater, he had the performance tradition of a fairly full text to draw upon. Unlike his British contemporaries Edmund Kean and Macready, he did not have to compete against a popular sentimentalisation of the play such as Nahum Tate's *History of King Lear*.

Perhaps this performance tradition is one of the reasons why a play which otherwise might seem to fly so completely in the face of Burgtheater tradition was allowed on the stage. Certainly the strength of Schreyvogel's adaptation, based on the verse translation of Johann Voss (Schlegel had not translated the play),[17] is the unusual completeness of the text. His *Romeo and Juliet* is only two-thirds of the length of Shakespeare's play, but his *King Lear* is just a few hundred lines shy of the original.[18] Naturally the hand of the censor can be detected, notably where graphic sexual statements are suppressed and in those passages where it is clear that the relationship between Edmund and Goneril and Regan is more than sentimental. But the most notorious change, insisted on by the censor and validated by public taste, was the so-called 'Viennese ending'. The deaths of Lear and Cordelia were regarded as both unnecessary and indecorous; hence they must live. Schreyvogel did not, like Nahum Tate, prepare for this happy catastrophe long before it occurs; rather he followed Shakespeare through to Lear's final line – 'Look there, look there!' – only to have Cordelia revive and the curtain descend on the rapturous reunion of father and daughter.

What is most remarkable about Schreyvogel's adaptation is that it flies in the face of Sonnenfels's old condemnation of Shakespeare. Schreyvogel retained the vast majority of the Fool's lines and even adapted his jokes to the understanding of a contemporary Viennese audience. He also kept Edgar as Poor Tom, who has a distinctly unnerving effect that would have earned the thorough disapproval of the now long-dead Josef II. The double plot, which violates unity of action, was also kept intact, and even though Schreyvogel followed Schröder by having the blinding of Gloucester take place off-stage, on the whole he sustained admirably the Shakespearean tension between catastrophic tragedy and grotesque parody.

If the very presence of *King Lear* on the Burgtheater stage was exceptional, even more remarkable was the success of the performance with its audience; it was greeted, as Schreyvogel observed, with 'thunderous applause'.[19] Whether this was in acknowledgement of the completeness

---

[17] In fact, *King Lear* only appeared in the Schlegel/Tieck edition of Shakespeare in 1833, in a translation by Wolf von Baudissin.

[18] While Shakespeare's *King Lear* is approximately 3,300 lines long, Schreyvogel's *König Lear* (Vienna, 1841) is approximately 2,800 lines, an unusually full length for an adaptation in the early nineteenth century.

[19] Schreyvogel, *Tagebücher*, vol. 2, p. 337.

8 Heinrich Anschütz as Lear

of the text is doubtful. Rather, it was caused primarily by the performance of Heinrich Anschütz in the central role, an interpretation that would enrapture audiences for decades (see plate 8). Anschütz's interpretation was so complete and striking that it alone recommended the play and may well have hidden features that audiences might otherwise have found objectionable.

Few performances in the nineteenth-century German theatre were so widely written about as Anschütz's Lear. Indeed, until his death in 1865, it was paradigmatic of all that Burgtheater acting stood for. Lear, in Schröder's version, had long been a celebrated role for the German actor. Schröder had been terrifying in his immense rage, while Iffland, the most celebrated technical actor of his generation, used the role to depict the pathos of old age.[20] The great Romantic actor, Ludwig Devrient, had represented with disturbing accuracy the destruction of Lear's sanity.[21] Anschütz's Lear was different.

Despite his apparent objection to the 'Viennese ending',[22] his reading of the role may well have grown from it. After Lear and Cordelia are reunited, Albany offers Lear his kingdom back again, but the old man responds by pointing to Cordelia's breast and ends the play with this speech.

> Nein, nein! Hier ist mein Platz. – Regiere Du,
> Albanien! Du bist der Krone werth.
> Mich lässt in diesen Kindesarmen ruh'n.
> Bis mich die Götter auf in ihre nehmen.
>
> (No, no! Here is my place. – You reign/Albany! You deserve the
>   crown/Leave me here to rest in this child's arms,/Till the gods
>   take me up into theirs.)[23]

Ludwig Speidel, an important Viennese drama critic, writing of Anschütz from memory, recalls that the centre of his performance was 'the child in the old man, the helpless child',[24] and that while other aspects of his performance were unusually striking, such as the eruption of anger at Cordelia's refusal to flatter him and the descent into madness, the helplessness of the King remained the dominant theme of the performance, which was brought most fully to the fore when Lear and Cordelia were reunited. The novel atmosphere which this dimension gave the role was identified by the essayist Gustav Kühne as being particularly Viennese. The

---

[20] Heinrich von Collin, extracted in Jacobs, *Schauspielkunst*, pp. 319–20.
[21] Karl Costenoble, *Aus dem Burgtheater*, 2 vols. (Vienna, 1889), vol. 2, p. 334.
[22] Heinrich Anschütz, *Erinnerungen aus dessen Leben und Wirken* (Leipzig, n.d. [1900]), p. 199.
[23] Schreyvogel, *Lear*, p. 139.   [24] Ludwig Speidel, *Schauspieler* (Berlin, 1911), p. 87.

Viennese, Kühne claimed, wish only to be moved by their tragedy, not frightened, hence this 'incomparably beautiful . . . weeping Lear'[25] was least effective when he was angry, most moving as he slipped from madness into the relief of second childhood.

But not all critics saw the same qualities in Anschütz's performance. Ludwig Tieck, for example, found that he represented splendidly the 'egoism, heroic anger and weakness of the king',[26] which is reminiscent of the harsher style of Schröder, but even he found the awakening to Cordelia indescribably beautiful, as if this were the moment the whole part was tending towards. Perhaps the most celebrated discussion of all came not from a critic but from the novelist Adalbert Stifter. In his major novel, *Der Nachsommer* (*Indian Summer*), Stifter's hero Heinrich visits the Burgtheater to see Anschütz, whose performance as Lear was considered to be 'at the highest level that a man in this branch of art could achieve'. It was quite possibly the greatest performance 'in the German language on any German stage'.[27] Stifter does not give a detailed account of how Anschütz played the role, but the impression it made upon the hero was unforgettable. At the end, Heinrich, like the rest of the audience, was totally absorbed, painfully moved to tears by Lear's predicament. Pity, not fear, was the essence of Anschütz's interpretation.

The success of Schreyvogel's *King Lear* was due mainly, it can be plausibly argued, to the poetic world of decline so attractively conjured up by Anschütz. It invited the audience to feel powerful empathy with Lear's predicament and gave the illusion of being a universal condition. Equally importantly, never once were the audience unnerved by his madness, as those who saw the haunting performances of Ludwig Devrient had been.[28] Anschütz remained faithful to the Burgtheater ethos in that he reassured rather than disturbed. Under the cover of that reassurance, Schreyvogel managed to stage an unusually complete version of *King Lear*, without its potentially unpalatable ambivalence ever becoming apparent. There is, of course, no way of knowing how conscious he was of this deception, but no doubt Anschütz as Lear realised perfectly Schreyvogel's own view of Shakespeare as a writer who aroused 'a certain peace and deliberation of reason over the emotions'. Despite the fullness of Schreyvogel's Shakespearean texts, in some important respects he acceded to those principles of the Burgtheater that Shakespeare's plays seemed to challenge.

[25] Gustav Kühne, *Portraits und Silhouetten*, 2 vols. (Hannover, 1843), vol. 2, p. 305.
[26] Ludwig Tieck, *Kritische Schriften*, 4 vols. (Leipzig, 1848), vol. 4, p. 34.
[27] Adalbert Stifter, *Der Nachsommer*, (n.p. n.d. [1956]), p. 192.
[28] Georg Altman, *Ludwig Devrient* (Berlin, 1926), p. 147.

HEINRICH LAUBE

The years following Schreyvogel's dismissal were relatively un-distinguished and it was not until 1850, with the appointment of the Saxon playwright and essayist Heinrich Laube as director, that the theatre was again to become prominent in the German-speaking world. Laube was not specially enthusiastic about Shakespeare. He had made his name in association with the *Junges Deutschland* group of writers, whose cynical, realistic outlook on the world was a reaction to the excesses of Romanticism. This led them to suspect the unquestioning worship of Shakespeare associated with the Romantics.[29] When he was a critic in Leipzig, Laube, not unlike generations of critics and audiences before him, showed himself intolerant to all aspects of the plays that did not directly further the dramatic action. In *A Midsummer Night's Dream*, for example, he found the main action to be lacking in interest, the low comedy completely inappropriate, the last act unnecessary and the language entirely unsuited to be spoken on stage.[30] Once he was appointed director of the Burgtheater, his attitude changed somewhat as Shakespeare formed part of his larger plans. His most pressing ambition, beyond the development of an integral acting ensemble, was to foster a repertoire that would incorporate all major works of the various phases and national schools of the modern theatre that 'are well-formed and do not contradict our customs'.[31] Shakespeare had, therefore, to occupy a prominent though not necessarily pre-eminent position in Laube's repertoire.

Although Laube sometimes discomfited the Burgtheater administration by insisting on staging Shakespeare, his tastes in drama were on the whole in accord with the theatre's traditions. Among contemporary genres, he most favoured the French well-made play for its rigorous structure; among German-language plays he enthusiastically sanctioned conversation-pieces set in the salons of Vienna, which allowed his actors to display their graceful deportment. Shakespeare's irregular works were not to his taste. Indeed, Laube shared the objection, first voiced by Gottsched over a hundred years earlier, to the way in which Shakespeare mixed high and low elements,[32] while his unshakable belief in the efficacy of the structure

---

[29] This did not imply a rejection of Shakespeare himself. See for example the writings of Heinrich Heine, a leading essayist of the period, who reacted primarily against the idealism of the Romantics. Much of his writing on Shakespeare recalled the work of *Sturm und Drang*. See Wolfgang Stellmacher (ed.), *Auseinandersetzung mit Shakespeare: Texte zur deutschen Shakespeare-Aufnahme, 1790–1830* (Berlin, 1985), pp. 31–6.

[30] Heinrich Laube, 'Ein *Sommernachtstraum* in Leipzig', *Theaterkritiken und dramaturgische Aufsätze*, ed. Alexander von Weilen, 2 vols. (Berlin, 1906), vol. 1, pp. 41–52.

[31] Heinrich Laube, *Das Burgtheater*, in *Schriften über das Theater*, ed. Eva Stahl-Wisten (Berlin, 1955), p. 177.

[32] *Ibid.*, p. 252.

of the well-made play led him to pour scorn on such seemingly formless works as the history cycles, which he considered entirely unperformable:

> The action does not progress rapidly and within distinct limits. Much happens, but the event stands in the foreground; what remains hidden is the action, the actual dramatic source of the event, the actual power of the drama, the personal development of human beings through logical action. We are therefore uncertain about to whom we should direct our interest, and in plays we must be interested in people; we scatter our sympathy among parties, in individual scenes – we have no impression of a coherent action.[33]

But despite these objections, there were pressing reasons why Laube wished to stage Shakespeare. Like his predecessors, he valued the plays' wealth of characterisation. Shakespeare's figures, he felt, were grounded in a realistic perception of life that complemented the particular ambience of the mid-nineteenth century, an age Laube recognised as being marked by an unprecedented growth of trade and industry.[34] Also, like Goethe before him, Laube sensed a magnitude in Shakespeare's works that transcended sheer utility, 'a philosophy of life', he wrote, 'which allows itself to be bound by no dogma and presents us with revelations that are deeply compatible to us'.[35] This alone compelled Shakespeare's inclusion in any repertoire that was to reflect the whole range of Western drama.

Although Laube could not work independently of the censor, he benefited from the greater liberalism of outlook that accompanies improvements in economic conditions and that in Vienna was also partially a consequence of the civil disturbances of 1848. As a result, he could introduce a wider selection of plays than Schreyvogel had been able to, some of which had distinctly republican, one might even argue anti-monarchical, implications.[36] For example, one of Laube's first major productions after taking over the directorship was *Julius Caesar* (1850). Two years later, he introduced *Richard III*, while his last Shakespearean production was *Richard II* (1863), possibly the play most critical of royalty. Even though he did not drop old favourites such as *Hamlet*, *Lear* and *Romeo and Juliet*, Laube was more interested in plays with public themes, which centred around issues of state, in contrast to the plays favoured by earlier

---

[33] *Ibid.*, p. 397.

[34] Frederick Abeles, 'Shakespeare-Aufführungen am Burgtheater unter Laube' (unpublished dissertation, University of Vienna, 1935), p. 13.

[35] Laube, *Burgtheater*, p. 267.

[36] The Shakespeare plays produced during Laube's directorship were *Julius Caesar* (1850), *Henry IV*, *Hamlet*, *King Lear*, *Coriolanus*, *The Merchant of Venice*, *The Comedy of Errors* (all 1851), *Richard III*, *Much Ado About Nothing* (1852), *Twelfth Night*, *Cymbeline* (1853), *Antony and Cleopatra*, *A Midsummer Night's Dream* (1854), *Othello* (1855), *Macbeth* (1856), *The Winter's Tale* (1862), and *Richard II* (1863). Productions of *The Taming of the Shrew* and *Romeo and Juliet*, first staged by earlier managements, were also revived.

generations, who had preferred sentimental family pieces and tragedies of fate in which characters are subject to supernatural forces they can do nothing to withstand.[37]

Although Laube's energetic and pragmatic theatre direction and his attachment to the dramaturgy of the well-made play made him very much a man of his time, in actuality these attributes had a conservative influence on the adaptation and performance of Shakespeare. Laube in fact reversed the trend towards unadapted texts that had been initiated by Schreyvogel. He was not as radical an adapter as some of his eighteenth-century predecessors had been, but he did more to make the texts conform to Burgtheater taste than Schreyvogel had done. He simplified them, often cutting soliloquies and reforming them as dialogue. Ideas and motives were clarified and made less ambiguous and scenes were often reshaped to bring the most important issues more into the foreground and to give them climaxes that would hold the attention of audiences accustomed to a drama of suspense. As far as possible he did not alter the pattern of Shakespeare's action. Taking advantage of the comparatively liberal climate in which he worked, he restored the death of Lear – though Cordelia still remained alive. He made few alterations to those plays that accorded fairly closely to his own dramaturgical principles, so, with the exception of some rather drastic editing of the battle in Act v, his *Julius Caesar* is very close to Shakespeare's original. This is not, however, the case with *The Merchant of Venice*. Ignoring the advances made by Schreyvogel, Laube returned to the older custom, established by Schröder, of grouping all the Belmont scenes together, hence obscuring the thematic unity of the play.[38] *Antony and Cleopatra* with its thirty-eight scenes and forty characters was drastically reduced to twelve scenes and twenty-three characters, while the problematic *Cymbeline*, retitled *Imogena*, had to be virtually rewritten so that it could be adapted to the proscenium stage and the exigencies of the well-made play.

In keeping with the Burgtheater's tradition of mildness on stage, Laube reduced much of the violence of Shakespeare's action. He also pared down the language, reducing long and complex sentences to more manageable proportions as he considered the Schlegel/Tieck translation to be virtually unspeakable.[39] Laube, who has been recognised as an early director of the realist school,[40] also had an intense suspicion of poetry on stage. Accordingly he expected his actors to tone down their voices in lyrical passages and instructed them to transfer the conversational technique they had

---

[37] Abeles, 'Shakespeare-Aufführungen', p. 4.

[38] Alexander von Weilen, 'Laube und Shakespeare', *Shakespeare-Jahrbuch*, 43 (1907), 112.

[39] Laube, 'Briefe über das deutsche Theater', *Schriften über Theater*, pp. 62–3.

[40] Marvin Carlson, 'Montigny, Laube, Robertson: The Early Realists', *Educational Theatre Journal*, 24 (1972), 227–36.

mastered in contemporary drama to the speaking of Shakespearean verse. Of course, this meant that the verse itself had to be severely pruned. To take one example, in Laube's adaptation of *Antony and Cleopatra*, Enobarbus's lavish description of Cleopatra in her barge is cut down to the minimum required to convey the information necessary, no attempt being made to conjure up the exotic sexual allure cast by the queen. Shakespeare wrote

> she did lie
> In her pavilion, – cloth-of-gold of tissue, –
> O'er picturing that Venus where we see
> The fancy out-work nature; on each side her
> Stood pretty dimpled boys, like smiling Cupids,
> With divers-colour'd fans, whose wind did seem
> To glow the delicate cheeks which they did cool,
> And what they undid did.
>
> (II:2, 198–205)

This Laube rendered less colourfully as

> In goldgewirkten Zelte lag sie da
> Wie Venus selbst; an beiden Seiten Knaben,
> Schön, wie Cupido, die mit bunten Fächern
> Balsamisch fächelten, nicht Kühlung, nein,
> Entzündung.
>
> (There she lay in a tent woven with gold, like Venus herself; on both sides boys, beautiful like Cupid, with coloured fans made balmy winds, not cooling but inflaming.)[41]

While the exclusion of Shakespeare's complex images in this passage was no doubt due partly to the prudery of the Burgtheater on sexual matters, it also demonstrates that Laube, like Schröder seventy years before him, had an ineradicable suspicion of any passage that strongly draws the audience's attention away from the flow of the action.

As director of the Burgtheater, Laube's greatest achievement was the formation of an acting company of possibly even a higher quality than Schreyvogel's. Even the smallest roles came to be performed with expertise and integrity, which, given the size of Shakespeare's casts and the importance of incidental figures in his plays, was an important condition for the successful production of his plays. However, the particular quality he expected from his actors was not altogether suited to the representation of Shakespeare's characters. Laube remained true to the founding ideals of the Burgtheater in that he valued his actors not so much for their ability to

---

[41] Quoted Georg Altmann, *Heinrich Laubes Prinzip der Theaterleitung* (Dortmund, 1908), p. 71.

portray unusual and striking individuals as for their capacity to serve as models for a cultivated and highly sophisticated urban culture. Indeed, the status of the actor as substitute aristocrat reached its zenith during his direction, while the quality of the ensemble had never been higher.[42] Laube was not, therefore, interested in actors whose métier was the representation of psychic forces that were irrational, even destructive. His theatre should reassure its audiences, not sow doubts in their midst. Laube reiterated Josef II's validation of the theatre as an agency of social cohesion, not as an institution designed to question or undermine the social fabric. He therefore encouraged his actors, in addition to mastering the physical and vocal language of high society, to act with a simplicity that disregarded division, that projected an image of 'simple truth'[43] and, in the name of social harmony, engaged the audience's closest sympathy for the actors and the characters they portrayed.

That such a genteel and pleasing style is not entirely suited to the performance of Shakespeare was apparent from the career of Adolf von Sonnenthal, who for over fifty years, from 1856 to 1909, was doyen of the company and widely regarded as the most complete embodiment of Laube's philosophy of theatre. His principles of professional collegiality and of simplicity, truth and integrity in acting were identical to the principles Laube tried to instil in the company. It is, therefore, significant that in a career that was longer than that of almost any other German actor, few of Sonnenthal's most celebrated roles were from Shakespeare. He was most successful when portraying amiable characters who radiated warmth and benign humour. In fact he claimed he could never play a part which went against his personality, nor one that was not a shining example of moral worth.[44] Those qualities which make a dramatic character exciting were therefore of little importance to him, which is probably why one of his most perceptive critics, Helene Richter, claimed that 'his road to Shakespeare was long and tiresome'.[45]

In fact, even though he did not achieve great distinction in them, Sonnenthal attempted almost all the major roles in those plays of Shakespeare that were staged during his career. Richter felt that only two of them, his Henry IV and Lear, were successful. His unceasing concern to represent warmth and goodness meant that he could not come to terms with problematical figures such as Hamlet or Macbeth, who are torn by contradictions and whose very being is to realise and resolve or founder within those contradictions. However much nobility and goodness Shakespeare's tragic heroes have, they also possess daemonic aspects of character

[42] Lothar, *Burgtheater*, pp. 175–6.   [43] Laube, *Burgtheater*, p. 292.
[44] Jakob Minor, *Aus dem alten und neuen Burgtheater* (Zurich, 1920), p. 62.
[45] Helene Richter, *Schauspieler-Charakteristiken* (Leipzig, 1914), p. 39.

SONNENTHAL

„als König Lear".

9 Adolf von Sonnenthal as Lear

which counteract and often devastate that nobility, only to have it reveal itself in its true strength as the play comes to an end. It was this complex way in which nobility manifested itself that Sonnenthal failed to understand. He succeeded only when the role required the simple unfolding of a consistently noble character.

Essentially his Lear was a refinement of Anschütz's. From the very beginning he was a figure of pathos, a hero who had reached senility. Throughout the scenes where Goneril and Regan isolate him, he responded to them with attitudes of weakness, confusion and servility. Even his curse on Goneril ended not on a climax of rage, but in an outburst of tears. The following scenes with Regan were equally tearful, once again calling solely on the audience's pity. The storm-scene was strangely soft. Sonnenthal's Lear did not hold conversation with the elements; there was hardly a scrap of defiance in him and, when madness finally descended on him, it did so as if it were a blessing.[46] This Lear did not reach the limits of human tolerance; instead he quieted down and madness served as a salve for the injuries the unjustly persecuted old man had suffered. The reconciliation with Cordelia, marked by extended pathos-laden pauses, and the final scenes were played as if Lear had reached a stage of sublimity in which the cares of the world could no longer touch him. Later in Sonnenthal's career, the death of Cordelia was allowed on stage. When she died, it seemed merely a natural step towards their final reunification. As Richter pointed out, one could never imagine that this gentle Lear had struck Cordelia's hangman dead.[47] Violence, anger and defiance were all absent from Sonnenthal's interpretation.

In later years, the genial world of the Burgtheater was to be challenged, by actors such as Friedrich Mitterwurzer and Josef Kainz, who stressed division in their characters, and by directors such as Franz Dingelstedt, who shifted attention away from the ensemble towards physical production. Nevertheless, however limited Schreyvogel's and Laube's endeavours may have appeared to later generations, by remoulding Shakespeare in a way that was compatible with the ethos of the court and national theatre, they did much to establish his plays on the stages of German-speaking Europe.

[46] Ferdinand Gregori, 'Adolf von Sonnenthal: König Lear', *Shakespeare-Jahrbuch* 40 (1904), 87.
[47] Richter, *Schauspieler-Charakteristiken*, p. 45.

7

Shakespeare and the German actor

Shakespeare's plays were beginning to appear on the stages of Germany just as the country's first great actor, Konrad Ekhof, was ending his career. Ekhof was noted both for his grave stage presence and for the quiet, moving realism of his acting. As this came to be imitated by other actors, it led the German stage away from the rhetorical excesses of a style of acting developed from the French theatre, that had been widely practised in Germany through to the middle decades of the eighteenth century.[1] Given the nature of his contribution to the development of acting, Ekhof might have been expected to welcome the advent of Shakespeare's comparatively realistic plays, but he did no such thing. Rather, as he explained in a letter to his pupil August Iffland, he feared them, as he felt they 'will utterly spoil our actors. Each one who speaks the splendidly powerful language has nothing else to do except to say it. The rapture that Shakespeare excites makes everything easy for the actor.'[2] Clearly for Ekhof, Shakespeare's greatness as a writer threatened the independence of the actor's imagination and therefore the potential vitality of theatrical performance. Nevertheless, the importance of the part Shakespeare was to play in the history of German acting is perhaps reflected in the fact that, despite his antipathy, the last role Ekhof played before his death in 1779 was the Ghost in *Hamlet*.

In some ways, the realism of Friedrich Ludwig Schröder's acting represented a progression on Ekhof's innovations, though Schröder did not display the gentlemanly restraint that had marked the work of the older actor; instead he gave harsher representations of character that often incorporated unpalatable traits of personality. Because of this, he was far more enthusiastic than Ekhof had been about the potential which Shake-

---

[1] For an account of this style of acting, the so-called 'Leipzig school', see Simon Williams, *German Actors of the Eighteenth and Nineteenth Centuries: Idealism, Romanticism and Realism* (Westport, Conn., 1985), pp. 6–10.
[2] Quoted in Eduard Devrient, *Geschichte der deutschen Schauspielkunst*, ed. Rolf Kabel and Christoph Trilse, 2 vols. (reprinted Munich, 1967), vol. 2, p. 410.

speare's plays offered the fledgling art of German acting. They were certainly a prime basis for his own work. 'The son of nature, Shakespeare', he is reported to have said, 'makes everything so easy and so satisfying for me.' This is because, despite the reduction of his own adaptations of the plays, Schröder found poetic style and character to be at one in Shakespeare. In other playwrights, he claimed, 'I must fight and exert myself to harmonise several very admirable and poetically brilliant passages with nature . . . soften them so that they do not contradict the characters.' But in Shakespeare Schröder found a unity between character and language. The plays also allowed him to mature as an actor. He did not, probably with justice, see himself as a virtuoso artist, concerned mainly with displaying technique. He did not, in his own words, wish 'to shine and to be conspicuous, but to fill out and to be. I wish to give to each role whatever belongs to it, nothing more and nothing less. In this way each must be what no other can be.'[3] Shakespeare was, therefore, the ideal playwright for him, and, in concert with the theoreticians of his day, he considered Shakespeare's prime contribution to the theatre to be the creation of powerful, unique individuals. His roles were a gift to the actor, not a threat to his stature as an artist.

When seen in the context of the repertoire of the German theatre of the late eighteenth and early nineteenth centuries, Schröder's appreciation of Shakespeare is understandable. The court and national theatres, which were the backbone of the system, did not specialise in 'high' drama to the exclusion of the 'popular', as did, for instance, the exemplary Comédie Française in Paris. Opera and lighter musical plays, usually performed by the same actors that appeared in the spoken drama, took up a considerable portion of the repertoire, as did the effective melodramas of Kotzebue and sentimental pieces of Iffland. Although these were important in building a native, popular German repertoire, the range of human emotions encompassed in the plays' characters was so limited and conventional that few, if any, calls were made on the actor's imagination or skills. In fact, actors rarely had the opportunity to appear in plays that allowed them to develop characterisations in depth. As Ludwig Tieck, an inveterate campaigner against whatever was stultifying in theatre, put it,

> These representations, vulgarly snatched from life, have the disadvantage of making the art of acting almost superfluous, and accustom the spectator to understand only the natural, the insignificant, without any connection with art, and to accept clumsy imitation as being true and pure.[4]

---

[3] Meyer, *Schröder*, vol. 1, p. 338.   [4] Tieck, *Kritische Schriften*, vol. 3, pp. xi–xii.

The same could as justly have been said about the plays of Raupach and the several adaptations of Scribe that dominated the German repertoire in the middle years of the nineteenth century.

From the late eighteenth century on, a 'classical' German repertoire, centred around the plays of Goethe and Schiller, was also being established in the theatres. But in performing these works, actors almost universally adopted the formal posture and elevated diction of Weimar classicism, which enabled them to project ideal images of mankind. Schiller's dramas, for example, challenged the actor to give a theatrically credible presence to characters whose dramatic function was more symbolic than psychological. The style of acting his plays required was inappropriate when it came to the representation of Shakespeare's characters in which the psychological was regarded as being the prime consideration. Shakespeare could be more appropriately acted by followers of the realistic Hamburg school, which had had its genesis in the career of Schröder. For most of the nineteenth century, however, the Hamburg school was far less widely followed than the Weimar school.

As we have seen, there were several reasons why Shakespeare was not especially prominent in the repertoire of the early nineteenth century. His plays could not be easily adapted to the generally integrative function of the contemporary theatre. They also challenged severely the physical limitations of the illusionistic stage. But in addition to this, the favour given to the Weimar style of acting in tragedy and the public's taste for the so-called 'trivial' drama of Kotzebue, Iffland and their successors were active obstacles in the way of frequent performances of the plays. The meteoric rise of *Hamlet* in the late 1770s was the exception, not the rule. One or two other plays that offered arresting central roles, such as *King Lear* and *The Merchant of Venice*, were seen with some frequency in various theatres in different parts of the country, but they were far from being among the plays most frequently performed. A good example of how Shakespeare fared in the repertoire of the late eighteenth and nineteenth centuries is offered by the theatre at Mannheim. This was an important institution, as in 1779 it had become the first purely German theatre to be constituted as a court and national theatre after the model of the Burgtheater. It has also been considered one of the key institutions in the introduction of Shakespeare into Germany,[5] for it was here that *Julius Caesar* received its first performance in German and several other of the plays were given sound and conscientious production under the aegis of the theatre's great intendant Heribert von Dalberg and the young August Iffland. But analysis of the repertoire indicates that Shakespeare was not to

---

[5] Stahl, *Shakespeare und das deutsche Theater*, pp. 137–77.

be seen that often in Mannheim. As we have seen, between 1779 and 1839, seven of his plays in versions bearing a relatively close similarity to the original were given a total of fifty-eight performances, making for an average of almost exactly one performance a year. Of these fifty-eight performances, twenty-seven, or a little under half, were of the Schröder adaptation of *Hamlet*. *King Lear* and *Julius Caesar* found some popularity, but the rarely-seen *Timon of Athens* was given only twice and *Coriolanus* once.[6] The fifty years between 1839 and 1859 were distinctly better for Shakespeare, but even then only 384 performances of thirty plays were given, which makes for an average of a little under eight performances per year. Admittedly, among the classic German playwrights, only Schiller fared better than Shakespeare. Between 1779 and 1839, twelve of his plays were given 276 performances for an average of somewhat less than five performances a year, and between 1839 and 1889, sixteen of his plays were given 402 performances for an average of eight a year. The fact is that for over a hundred years, the *Trivialdramatik* of the day prevailed. In terms of sheer number of performances, Iffland and Kotzebue and their successors dominated the spoken drama. Moreover, no single dramatic author even approached in popularity the operas of Mozart.[7]

But there is one notable way in which Shakespeare's plays do stand out statistically from the *Trivialdramatik* in the hundred years covered by these statistics. No single play by a popular playwright of the time received a significantly larger number of performances than did a major play by Shakespeare. The repertory of the popular drama changed as popular taste changed, but Shakespeare survived and eventually predominated. The reason for this lay substantially in the capacity of his plays to withstand changes in taste, or, more accurately perhaps, in their ability to appeal to contemporary taste at each phase of its development. Certainly the depth and richness of Shakespeare's characters invested the plays with a dimension lacking in almost all other drama seen on German stages. Although the foremost purpose of the popular drama was to entertain, from the

---

[6] All figures are taken from Walter, *Archiv und Bibliothek des Grossh. Hof- und Nationaltheaters in Mannheim*, vol. 2. A precise tabulation of the repertoire is provided only for 1779 to 1803, which indicates that *Hamlet* (twenty-seven performances), *King Lear* (eleven performances) and *Julius Caesar* (ten performances) were the most popular Shakespearean plays early in the theatre's history. The other plays given over these years, not including complete rewritings, were *The Merchant of Venice* (four performances), *Macbeth* (three performances), *Timon of Athens* (two performances) and *Coriolanus* (one performance).

[7] In Mannheim as elsewhere in Germany, Mozart's operas were by far the most frequently performed of all theatre works. The play most often given between 1779 and 1889 was in fact Rautenstrauch's comedy *Jurist und Bauer* (*Judge and Peasant*), which was given seventy-two times. Mozart's *Die Zauberflöte* was given 115 times, *Don Giovanni* 100, and *Die Entführung aus dem Serail* eighty-nine. The most popular Shakespeare play was *Hamlet* in Schröder's version, which was last given during the 1830s. It was given a total of forty-six performances (Walter, *Archiv*, pp. 256–7).

mid-eighteenth century on it had a moralistic bias, generally encouraging the audience to cultivate the conventional virtues and loyalties to family, social custom and country. German classical drama had loftier considerations, but it too was ambitious to improve its audiences, primarily by cultivating their taste and expanding the range of their minds according to the principles enshrined in Weimar classicism. Shakespeare's dramas, with their focus on the inner, often turbulent life of the character, seemed to have no such objective.

The difference between Shakespeare and German drama had important ramifications for the actor, as his plays challenged the generally-held idea of the actor as moral preceptor or social model for the audience. Instead they encouraged him or her to explore character free of any moralistic bias that might otherwise stand in the way of an unalloyed representation of character. Furthermore, they undermined a major institutional restraint of the German theatre. Until well into the nineteenth century, both actors' careers and the nature of stage performances were stringently limited by the *Fach*, or typecasting, system, by which actors limited themselves to playing only certain character-types and playwrights wrote to accommodate solely those types. Shakespeare's characters could not easily fit into the *Fach* system and so they challenged that system's validity. They also provided the ambitious actor, prepared to escape its confines, with the opportunity to develop his or her acting powers independently. Hence, through Shakespeare the actor could appear as an interpretative artist, as had already been evident in the difference between Schröder's and Brockmann's Hamlets in the late eighteenth century. The *Trivialdramatik* provided no such opportunity. Furthermore, in order to give Shakespeare's roles their fullest stature, the actor had to combine the prevailing and seemingly contradictory schools of German acting. While he or she had to practise the psychological realism of the Hamburg school, at the same time Shakespeare's roles have a symbolic status which is often as manifest as Schiller's; this is felt especially through the poetry. In the context of the time, this symbolic dimension could most appropriately be realised through the Weimar style. For this reason, Eduard Devrient, the major historian of German acting, considered Shakespeare to be at the basis of all that was most productive in the evolution of the art.

> In Shakespeare the full, pure truth of human nature ... was perfected. Here it was, with all the diversity of life, with all the tiny details of intimate nature, but the grandeur of conception, carved throughout with a wholeness, so that the performer had to grow with his role.[8]

---

[8] Eduard Devrient, *Geschichte*, vol. 1, p. 467.

By amplifying the art of the actor, by extending and making more apparent the skills required in a successful performance, Shakespeare's plays allowed the German actor to mature. They also helped the acting profession gain respect in the public's eyes at a time when it was struggling for social recognition. So, while Kotzebue's celebrated melodrama *Menschenhass und Reue* (*Misanthropy and Repentance*) received far more performances than *King Lear* did over the turn of the eighteenth into the nineteenth century, in the long run *Lear* would prove to be the more important and enduring play.

Of course, the full impact of Shakespeare could only be felt when more complete versions of his plays were staged than those almost universally used in the early nineteenth century. Only then could the full potential of the roles, their complex and contradictory aspects of personality and the use of poetry as a delineator of character, become apparent to the actor. As the century progressed, more complete versions of the plays came to be given. Consequently, actors and audiences became increasingly familiar with the wealth of Shakespeare's characterisation, though this was not a process that had been completed even by the start of the twentieth century.

SHYLOCK

This growth in German actors' and audiences' awareness of the complexity of a Shakespearean role can be exemplified in the history of the interpretation of Shylock. From its first performance at Hamburg in November 1777, *The Merchant of Venice* proved to be one of the most resilient of Shakespeare's plays on the German stage. In two ways, this was peculiar. First, because the taste for French dramaturgy prevailed until well into the nineteenth century, German audiences were predisposed towards generic purity in the drama they saw. *The Merchant of Venice* did not cater to this preference, for it is difficult to disguise the fact that it is a comedy with a distinctly tragic sub-plot in the figure of Shylock. In actuality, it was treated more as a tragedy than a comedy, first by purging the grosser comic elements, the Gobbos, then by the most drastic and usually unsatisfactory editing of Act v. But the very presence of Shylock provided the second objection to the play. The eighteenth-century audience's desire to see represented on stage environments and experiences close to their own survived more than just vestigially until well into the nineteenth century. The role of Shylock flies in the face of that partiality. After all, it demonstrates Shakespeare's capacity to make his audience aware of the limitations of their own world and perceptions. Shylock is a notable example of the Shakespearean character who neither conforms to nor confirms the moral outlook of the audience. Instead he disturbs their judgement, first by making them sympathetic towards a figure – the vindictive businessman and miser – who was normally represented unsympathetically on the stage, secondly by subverting racial prejudices, fairly widely held if not overtly advocated.[9] The dramatic context of Shylock encourages audiences to question the very process by which those prejudices are arrived at. Notwithstanding the hostility that might have been aroused by the play, it grew in popularity, no doubt in considerable part because of the confusing attraction offered by the role of Shylock. It allowed the actor to test his power over the audience by inviting them to identify with an alien belief and a racial difference that had historically aroused the fear, at times the open hostility, of the majority of German society. Furthermore, it allowed the audience to extend their understanding to a generic figure who was normally despised and rarely represented with much sympathy.

The first notable Shylock in Germany was Schröder himself. As Schröder reduced Shakespeare's final act to nothing more than a few lines after the trial scene, in which disguises are explained and loose ends tied up,[10] Shylock's downfall became the central as well as the final experience of the play. Far less was written of Schröder's Shylock than of his Hamlet. What little there is suggests that he used the role in an attempt to extend the audience's understanding of a world that was alien to them. A historian of the Hamburg theatre referred to his performance as 'a splendid imitation of Jewish customs and demeanour',[11] while his major biographer compared him to Macklin,[12] no doubt because Schröder managed to represent Shylock's malignity while drawing the audience's sympathy towards him. The sympathy they felt might have grown the more they recognised the necessity of that malignity.

That Shylock can be interpreted in a way that in later years might have been described as anti-semitic is apparent from the interpretation given by August Iffland. In addition to being one of the most widely performed playwrights of his time, Iffland was the most celebrated actor in Germany after Schröder's retirement in 1799. After several years at Mannheim, he was appointed director of the Berlin court theatre, a post he kept until his death in 1815. As an actor, he was noted for his highly polished technique that allowed him to represent vividly the slightest nuances and minutiae of his characters' physical behaviour. He was concerned also to find a personal, moral identity in the roles he played. The actor, he considered,

[9] This covert anti-semitism is one of the themes in Alfred D. Low, *Jews in the Eyes of the Germans* (Philadelphia, 1979).
[10] The scene is quoted complete in Adolf Hauffen, 'Schröders Bearbeitung des *Kaufmann von Venedigs*', *Vierteljahrschrift für Litteraturgeschichte*, 5 (1892), 94–5.
[11] Johann Friedrich Schütze, *Hamburgische Theatergeschichte* (Hamburg, 1794), p. 461.
[12] Meyer, vol. 1, p. 297.

10 August Iffland as Shylock

must be noble so that he can inspire the audience to be noble too. 'It is not possible to represent nobility', he wrote, 'without having noble feelings oneself.'[13] In order to exercise this influence effectively, the actor must win the total trust and confidence of his audience. To do this, in his acting, as in his playwriting, Iffland avoided representing extremes of experience. Instead, he portrayed and thereby dignified the average.

Not surprisingly, Shakespeare did not feature that prominently in Iffland's repertoire. When he did appear in his plays, it was usually in subsidiary roles, as in the first production of Schlegel's *Hamlet* in Berlin in 1799, when he played Polonius. Shylock was one of his few major Shakespearean roles,[14] and it is distinguished from almost all other interpretations of the part as the one audiences found 'entirely agreeable and pleasant'.[15] Iffland was not prepared to risk alienating his audiences' sympathies, so he played the Jew as he appeared through the eyes of prejudice. His costume made the character somewhat ridiculous, dressed as he was in a blue coat with fur trimming, a caftan and red stockings (see plate 10). His performance was an aggregation of small mannerisms, commonly accepted as typical of the Jews. He pattered across the stage with mincing footsteps, he walked in circles when worried, he crumpled his cap in distress during the trial scene. The main through-line of his performance was the character's greed, a trait that audiences associated with his race. Accordingly, in the scene with Tubal, where Shylock's greed and vindictiveness is most apparent, he struck his critics as being entirely Jewish.[16] Iffland gave no stature to Shylock. In his interpretation, the character remained what it can be in a performance of the unadapted text, a subsidiary figure, a dispensable menace, a nuisance rather than a threat. This was apparent particularly in his choice of a knife with which to carve Antonio's flesh. Normally this was a large, forbidding instrument, but Iffland used a small penknife that could hardly be seen from the auditorium. When he collapsed at the end of the trial, he struck a contemporary as being little more than 'a laughable scarecrow'.[17]

However limited Iffland's range and depth as an actor, as director of the Berlin court theatre he was capable of recognising the quality of work very different from his own. He rather uneasily associated for a few years with the celebrated intuitive actor Ferdinand Fleck, but some years after Fleck's death, he was responsible for bringing to Berlin the greatest of all Romantic actors, Ludwig Devrient. Ludwig Tieck had sensed in Ferdi-

13 Wilhelm Koffka, *Iffland und Dalberg* (Leipzig, 1865), p. 461.
14 Lear was another, which he played as a pathetic old man.
15 Hans de Leeuwe, 'Shakespeares Shylock: europäische Darsteller einer berühmten Rolle', *Kleine Schriften der Gesellschaft für Theatergeschichte*, 23 (1969), 9.
16 Johann Gustav Büsching, extracted in Jacobs, *Schauspielkunst*, pp. 346–7.
17 August Haake, *Theater-Memoiren* (Mainz, 1866), p. 171.

11 Ludwig Devrient as Shylock, with Lebrun as Graziano

nand Fleck a touch of unearthliness, a pathos that seemed specially suited to realise the full stature of Shakespeare's roles.[18] Certainly, on days when he was inspired, Fleck was capable of projecting the illusion of a complete and complex character by arousing his audiences to sense unfamiliar powers in the character, which he never fully expressed so his audience never fully understood them. Fleck was also able to introduce a touch of humour into even the most tragic of Shakespeare's heroes; both his Macbeth and Lear were remarkable for this. This ambivalence, to which audiences were generally unaccustomed, was ideal for a role like Shylock. In it, Fleck used such contrasts that different people saw totally different things. Initially, his Shylock was an aristocratic figure, distinguished by his

---

[18] Tieck, quoted by Devrient, *Geschichte*, p. 525.

distance from and superiority to the Christians. But in the scene with Tubal, he gave way to his lust for revenge with a passion that seemed distinctly vulgar. To Ludwig Tieck, who was most sensitively attuned to Fleck's acting, his Shylock was the soul of greed and envy, but he ended the play 'terrible and ghostlike, but never common, always noble'.[19]

If there was something vague, almost mystical, in critical assessments of Fleck's acting, audiences and critics could speak far more precisely about the appeal of Romantic acting after they had seen Ludwig Devrient. Devrient's Shakespearean repertoire was remarkably small,[20] but the sheer compass of his acting opened up a realm of mental and emotional experience that was 'Shakespearean' in its scope. In essence, Devrient concentrated more completely than actors before him on the unconscious motivation of tragic characters. He represented them as being under the control of powerful forces they could do little to withstand, which often led to their destruction. While occasionally his characters struck audiences as being haunted by supernatural forces, more frequently they recognised such forces as having their genesis within the character. Hence it was easier to understand and more viscerally feel them than the irrational forces that drove Fleck's characters. More than either Schröder or Fleck, Devrient, by making this normally hidden realm of experience the foremost stratum of the role, was able to disturb and confuse the sympathies of his audiences.

Devrient was not the most vigorous of actors, due no doubt to his chronic alcoholism, which started to drain his energies severely soon after he arrived in Berlin from Breslau, where he had first performed most of his major roles. It may, however, have made the realms of unconscious experience more accessible to him than to other, more sober actors. His Shylock was, anyway, a quiet figure, a 'bowed man, weakened by age, at the end of a life of servitude'.[21] Nevertheless, as the rich clothes he wore demonstrated, he was wealthy. His life had been spent building up resentment against the hated Christians; in fact, this hatred was the dominant concern of his life, making his demand for Antonio's flesh an act of desperate rebellion, a necessary consummation, yet a triumphant culmination of years of bitterness, suffering and martyrdom.[22] Devrient accentuated rather than hid racial differences, playing Shylock either with a distinctly dark skin[23] or speaking in a recognisably Jewish accent, dressed as a Venetian Jew (see plate 11),[24] or as a Polish or Hungarian Jew.[25] But he

[19] Tieck, extracted in Jacobs, *Schauspielkunst*, p. 344.
[20] The only Shakespearean roles he played were Lear, Shylock, Hubert (*King John*), Parolles, Falstaff (*Henry IV*), and, towards the end of his career when he was dying, Richard III.
[21] Altman, *Devrient*, p. 215.
[22] Ludwig Rellstab, *Gesammelte Schriften*, 9 vols. (Leipzig, 1860), vol. 9, pp. 335–6.
[23] *Ibid.*, p. 335.   [24] *Die Briefwechsel zwischen Goethe und Zelter*, pp. 426–7.
[25] Haake, *Theater-Memoiren*, p. 170.

always took care that the character's nobility – a quality which audiences constantly associated with European culture – was persistently to the fore. Consequently he so carried the audiences' sympathies with the character that at the end they were unable to determine precisely how they should feel towards him.[26] Not surprisingly, given both the contrasts in the role and the focus on the unconscious, hidden experience of Shylock, where the roots of his obsessive hatred lay, audiences and critics were split in their reaction to what they saw. For some, Devrient was typical of all Jews, a symbolic figure of suffering;[27] his revenge was the revenge of his race, which made entirely plausible his refusal to accept money in place of the pound of flesh. Even more significantly, the power of Shylock's need made his demand seem essentially right.[28] Others, however, depending perhaps upon when they saw the performance – Devrient's drinking made him not the most reliable or consistent of performers – found the end of the role not to be logically the conclusion of the beginning.[29] But almost all spectators felt the defeat of Devrient's Shylock as a shattering experience. He gave an appalling cry as he realised that he had been outwitted and defeated by the Christians, and, by his broken gait as he left the stage, it was clear he was going to his death. Perhaps no German actor so completely embodied the tragic dimensions of the role.

Within approximately fifteen years, the Berlin theatre-goer would have seen three different Shylocks, one of which, Iffland's, contrasted sharply with the other two, Fleck's and Devrient's. In accounting for that contrast, the theatre-goer might have recognised one of the key contributions made by Shakespeare to the development of German acting, that is that his roles were so constructed as to withstand definitive interpretation. If the late 1770s introduced Germany to the interpretative potential of a character as limited as Hamlet in Schröder's adaptation, as Shakespeare's plays came to be performed more widely and in fuller texts, the public became increasingly aware that the actor's art consisted, among other things, in a series of choices. Such choices and the unity that could be created from them gave the actor an enhanced status in the theatre as a creative artist.

No actor more clearly demonstrated the expanded potential for interpretation than Karl Seydelmann, a celebrated virtuoso of the post-Romantic generation. Seydelmann, more than any of his predecessors, was known as a soloist, who developed interpretations in isolation, rather than as a member of a company. Ludwig Devrient had toured, almost to the end of his life in 1832, but Seydelmann, whose career reached its apogee in the

---

[26] *Ibid.*, p. 171.
[27] August Klingemann, *Kunst und Natur*, 3 vols. (Brunswick, 1828), vol. 3, p. 350.
[28] Rellstab, *Gesammelte Schriften*, p. 336.
[29] Eduard Gans, extracted in Jacobs, *Schauspielkunst*, pp. 355–6.

late 1830s, was able to take more advantage of improved communications and a burgeoning network of theatres to become the first of a steadily increasing number of touring virtuosi. As this number grew, Shakespeare's plays came more to the fore because of the opportunities they provided for the actor to demonstrate his powers of characterisation. As a concomitant to this, the variety of interpretation his roles offered became even more apparent than in the earlier decades of the nineteenth century.

In several ways, Seydelmann's acting was a reaction to Ludwig Devrient's. While Devrient heightened the unconscious motivation of the character, Seydelmann avoided such dangerous territory, ensuring that each character he represented had clear motives, comprehensible both to the character and to the audience. Furthermore, while Devrient struck all who saw him as an intuitive actor, everything Seydelmann did was obviously planned to the last detail. He ensured that each of his roles had hard, distinct outlines, which the audience could grasp without difficulty and accept or reject at will. Seydelmann therefore aroused clearly articulated and strikingly divided critical responses. The division was intensified by his difficult personality. For Seydelmann life was a constant battle. He idealised hard work and spoke out uncompromisingly against the pervading mediocrity of the theatre and the overall slackness of the profession. He also suffered from chronic ill health, which led to his early death at the age of fifty in 1843. His struggles had made him many enemies. Eduard Devrient, a noted actor and director as well as a theatre historian, abominated the man, finding everything he did morally suspect, while Heinrich Laube idealised him as a clear-eyed realist after the excesses of Romanticism. Hence, while Devrient castigated him as an exhibitionist, who acted purely for theatrical effect, one who was typical of all that was worst and most excessive in modern acting,[30] Laube lauded the 'simplicity, clarity and beauty' of his performances.[31]

Seydelmann recorded some of his most frequently performed roles in his prompt-books, which provide an unusually complete insight into his interpretation for this comparatively early phase of the modern theatre. Shylock is among the roles he set down, inserting personal comments and stage-directions for his interpretation in the dialogue.[32] It is clear from his comments that Seydelmann was primarily concerned with the growth of Shylock's anger and the birth of his revenge from it. His Shylock grew on

---

[30] Eduard Devrient, *Aus seinen Tagebüchern*, ed. Rolf Kabel, 2 vols. (Weimar, 1964), vol. 1, p. 85. It should, in fairness, be noted that Devrient had an acute sense of the historic importance of Seydelmann, since he devoted more pages to him than to almost any other single actor in his *Geschichte der deutschen Schauspielkunst*.

[31] Laube, quoted in S. Troizkij, *Karl Seydelmann: Die Anfänge der realistischen Schauspielkunst* (Berlin, 1949), p. 98.

[32] Karl Seydelmann, *Aus seinen Rollenheften und Briefen* (Berlin, 1955), pp. 40–59.

12 Karl Seydelmann as Shylock

stage, his development occurring in terms of present action, not in the past as Ludwig Devrient's had seemed to have done. In the opening scene, Seydelmann's Shylock was mild, a pragmatic businessman who came surprisingly close to being friends with Antonio. Only when the pound of flesh was mentioned did Seydelmann allow a slight tone of malice to creep into Shylock's voice. His anger grew as he became increasingly aware of his difference from the Christians, to explode into wildness as he heard of Jessica's betrayal. This led to the climax, which was not the trial, but the speech 'Hath a Jew eyes?' This so logically came at the apex of Shylock's suffering that it must virtually have compelled the audience's sympathy. Not surprisingly, there are mixed reports on the performance. Eduard Devrient felt he exaggerated and overloaded the role with inconsequential details; in the trial he felt he wantonly distorted the character and therefore the balance of the play.[33] Others did not see the humane figure Seydelmann described in his prompt-book; instead they felt he emphasised too strongly the greed and commonness of the character.[34] But Theodor Rötscher, Seydelmann's major biographer, considered his Shylock to be a powerful symbol of an undertrodden race.[35] Most remarkably, in direct contrast to the fatalism of Ludwig Devrient's ending and in some ways reflective of a growing pragmatism in society at large, Rötscher did not feel that Seydelmann's Shylock was defeated at the end. He left the stage unbowed, ready to fight again.

The most celebrated of the virtuosi of the middle decades of the nineteenth century was the first Jewish actor to play Shylock in the German theatre, the Polish-born Bohumil Dawison, whose career flourished during the 1850s and 1860s. Energy rather than harmony was the hallmark of Dawison's acting. Like the earlier English Romantic actor Edmund Kean, Dawison employed sharp, seemingly sensational contrasts, often changing from liveliness to indifference, from lassitude to wildness, not always with the logic for such changes being apparent.[36] He also rejected the rhetorical pathos of the Weimar style and rarely tried to ask for the audience's sympathy for the characters he played. In expressing passion he was 'sharp and cutting'[37] rather than soft and ingratiating. Not surprisingly he did not last long at the Burgtheater, where his rough acting and tendency towards solo virtuosity aroused the ire of Heinrich Laube.[38] But one of the leading critics of the time, the Berliner Karl Frenzel, considered that Dawison's angularity made him the ideal player of Shakespeare though it entirely unsuited him to act the calmer, idealised

---

[33] Devrient, *Geschichte*, vol. 2, p. 329.   [34] Kühne, *Portraits*, vol. 2, p. 333.
[35] Heinrich Theodor Rötscher, *Seydelmanns Leben und Wirken* (Berlin, 1845), p. 206.
[36] Devrient, *Geschichte*, vol. 2, p. 305.
[37] Bürde, quoted by Peter Kollek, *Bohumil Dawison* (Kastellaun, 1978), p. 154.
[38] Laube, *Das Burgtheater*, pp. 233–5.

13 Bohumil Dawison as Shylock

figures of German classical drama.[39] Dawison filled his roles with colour and went for the individuality of the part rather than for an aesthetic purity of line and nobility of form. He was especially good at providing credible motivation for difficult characters, such as, for example, Leontes, a figure who until then had been considered almost incomprehensible.

Although Dawison was acting at a time when more complete versions of Shakespeare were gradually appearing on the German stage, he insisted that when he played Shylock, Act v must be cut, so that his downfall was the final impression left with the audience. His early interpretations of the role were apparently too detailed and he failed to grasp a consistent through-line, but by the time he had reached maturity in the mid-1850s, he seems to have mastered it. He was noted for adopting what was recognised as a distinctly Jewish accent, though not the quaking voice of anti-semitic caricature, but one that was 'full-toned and powerfully demanding'.[40] Frenzel was convinced by it, finding his Shylock to be a good, proud man, driven by a sense of his own right. No doubt Dawison felt the racial prerogatives of the part more personally than his predecessors, but by the end he had transcended those considerations to make a statement that went far beyond the particular experience of the Jews. He became, Frenzel wrote, 'a hero of hatred, a martyr to the absolute, to noble custom and the gruesomely wounded right of beautiful humanity'.[41]

Dawison gave what was possibly the most idealised of all nineteenth-century Shylocks. In the final decades of the century, when the first stirrings of modern anti-semitism were being felt in the German-speaking world, less sympathetic representations of the role began to appear on the stage. Perhaps the most notable Shylock in this period was Friedrich Mitterwurzer. Mitterwurzer, himself no anti-semite, was, unusually for the theatre, a deeply religious man who often agonised over the seeming irreconcilability of his vocation and his beliefs. Archaic as this struggle might have seemed in the latter half of the nineteenth century, it provided him with a fruitful basis for his representation of the dilemmas of modern man as dramatised in the works of Ibsen and other contemporary playwrights. According to Laube, he could only act 'fissured' characters,[42] a judgement made more exact by the critic Julius Bab, who saw in Mitterwurzer's acting the struggle of modern man split between the reality of his physical, biological being and his longing for the immaterial.[43] Mitterwurzer frequently fastened on pathological elements in the characters he played, in direct antithesis to the Weimar style, which still had a tenacious hold on German acting, or to the elegant realism of the

---

[39] Karl Frenzel, *Berliner Dramaturgie*, 2 vols. (Erfurt, n.d.), vol. 2, p. 271.
[40] Kollek, *Bohumil Dawison*, p. 176.
[41] Frenzel, extracted in Jacobs, *Schauspielkunst*, p. 361.
[42] Quoted in Minor, *Aus dem alten und neuen Burgtheater*, p. 165.
[43] Julius Bab, *Kränze der Mimen* (Emsdetten, 1954), p. 267.

14 Friedrich Mitterwurzer as Shylock

Burgtheater, where he was contracted on three different occasions but never easily settled into the company.

Mitterwurzer's primary historical importance is as one of the first great German actors of Ibsen, but he also invigorated the classical repertoire by treating the major roles in a way to which his audiences were entirely unaccustomed,[44] as if they were exercises in pathological psychology. His Macbeth, for instance, did not prepare for battle with the exalted resignation of a Weimar hero, but was quite clearly drunk, as if to hide from himself his imminent nervous collapse.[45] Such unidealistic acting meant that for the majority of his career Mitterwurzer had to fight for recognition. Only in the 1890s, when naturalism was beginning to prevail in the contemporary repertoire, did he achieve widespread recognition and acclaim.

Shakespeare, of course, provided him with a mine of roles, and, in his several years of restless touring, he acted most of the major parts. Shylock was among the most celebrated. Mitterwurzer wrote on the part in a little-known essay entitled 'Style', in which he rejects the well-rounded, 'polite' acting of the court theatres. Instead, he argues for an acting that is 'sharp and angular', that reflects the sharpness and angularity of life outside the theatre.[46] The actor playing Shylock, he claimed, should therefore represent the reality of the Jewish situation and the utter malice that the conditions he has lived under have created in him. He will take any opportunity to revenge himself on Antonio in the cause of his suffering race. On appearing at the trial, he should be dressed in his most splendid robes, ready to commit murder in defiance of the whole Signoria. The only thing that holds him back is his greed for Antonio's money, which is as great as his hatred.

In performance, Mitterwurzer seems to have captured some aspects of his theoretical discussion of the role (see plate 14). His desire to revenge himself on the Christians was so great that, unlike earlier actors, he made no attempt to hide it and so may have lost some credibility.[47] But what was most remarkable about his performance was the mixture of burlesque with passages of powerfully naturalistic acting. He attempted no great tragic moments, but oscillated between styles of acting that must have had a most disconcerting effect on audiences who prized stylistic unity above all in their actors. So Mitterwurzer began Shylock with a 'terrible, inextinguishable anger'[48] which became so immense that he showed the character as terrified of himself. For example, when he was cursing Jessica, in wishing her dead he actually summoned up her corpse in his imagination and his fury was suddenly checked by his fear at the sight. This principle of contradiction informed the complete

---

[44] Max Burckhard, *Anton Friedrich Mitterwurzer* (Vienna, 1906), p. 103.
[45] Maximilian Hardén, *Köpfe*, 9th edn (Berlin, 1910), p. 373.
[46] Friedrich Mitterwurzer, 'Styl', *Vor den Kulissen*, ed. Josef Lewinsky (Berlin, 1881), vol. I, p. 186.
[47] Eugen Guglia, *Friedrich Mitterwurzer* (Vienna, 1896), pp. 70–1.
[48] Richard Fellner, extracted in Jacobs, *Schauspielkunst*, p. 364.

role, for while he was in himself a figure of fury, to the Christians he was an object of ridicule, a 'Jewish Hanswurst', an insignificant creature whose downfall was entirely to be desired. Mitterwurzer challenged the idealism of the generation prior to his own by reaching back to the interpretations of the early nineteenth century. He revived the impressively morose and turbulently angry Shylock, but set him in a context that is distinctly reminiscent of the interpretation given the role by Iffland. In this clear disjunction, by which a deeply pathetic, even tragic experience is seen in a framework that ultimately devalues it, Mitterwurzer was no longer looking back to the past, but looking forward to the stylistic incongruity of the twentieth-century theatre.

8

Romantic legacy: Shakespeare and spectacle

For both institutional and technical reasons, German theatres at the end of the eighteenth century could not realise on stage the vision of Shakespeare that had been offered by *Sturm und Drang*. However, the Romantic critics who began writing some twenty years later, August Wilhelm Schlegel and Ludwig Tieck, had a more direct influence than *Sturm und Drang* critics upon how the plays were staged. Indeed, in Schlegel's and Tieck's different understandings of Shakespeare we can identify the origins of the two major traditions of Shakespearean production that were to provide an alternative to the eighteenth-century legacy, which, in the influence of Weimar and the work of the Burgtheater, extended well into the nineteenth century.

A. W. Schlegel's contribution to the cause of Shakespeare was invaluable as, through both his essays and his translations, he guaranteed a permanent home for the plays in the German theatre and greatly increased people's understanding of them. His *Vorlesungen über dramatische Kunst und Literatur* (*Lectures on Dramatic Art and Literature*) included the first comprehensive survey of Shakespeare's work to be written in German, while his translations provided Germany with versions of the plays that in their vitality and variety were a fitting complement to the English originals and, despite the doubts of people such as Heinrich Laube,[1] were generally proved to be stageworthy.

Schlegel's strength as a critic can be gauged from his essay on *Romeo and Juliet*, published in 1797 in Schiller's periodical *Die Horen*.[2] It demonstrates his sound practical criticism, as he methodically covers different aspects of the play, always keeping in view their relationship to the whole. This, combined with his acute sense of the psychological accuracy of Shakespeare's characterisation, made the essay a major contribution to the critical discussion that had continued unabated since *Sturm und Drang*. Schlegel was

---

[1] See chapter 6, p. 122.
[2] Published in English in 1820 in the obscure *Olliers Literary Miscellany*, 1 (1820).

a terse and economical writer, who used images as direct as the play-wright's. 'Romeo's youth', he wrote, 'is like a thundery day in spring, where sultry odours enwrap the most beautiful, luxuriant blooms.'[3] But the most remarkable aspect of his essay was his further exploration of an idea that had already been introduced by Gerstenberg, that Shakespeare's plays resemble pictures, in contrast to the neoclassical perception of drama as an enclosed, sculptural form. With greater comprehension than Gersten-berg, Schlegel demonstrated how this is so. For example, while most critics and practitioners had problems with *Romeo and Juliet*'s wealth of char-acters, Schlegel did not. Mercutio was usually regarded as an incidental character at best, but Schlegel saw him as crucial to the spirit of the whole, as he embodies the extremes that fuel the play: 'love and hate, [that which is] sweetest and most bitter, joyful rejoicing and dark foreboding, caressing embraces and the sepulchre, blossoming youth and self-annihilation'.[4] Through him the play's theme is extended to include more than the lovers' experiences. As in a crowded picture, a bystander, though not closely involved in the action, can be used to condition and deepen our under-standing of it. The Nurse, Schlegel pointed out, serves a similar function.

Schlegel also understood how themes are realised by visual represen-tation. He argued that the conflict between the families impresses the audience because it is represented in a fight that engages everyone from the servants to the highest ranks. His appreciation of Shakespeare's language was unique to his time as well. Word-play had offended even Shakespeare's most ardent advocates, and in tragedy especially it was considered childish. Schlegel points out that Romeo and Juliet's word-play is actually highly suitable, as love frequently brings out childishness in lovers.

This critique of *Romeo and Juliet* is based on a reading that is accurate, imaginative and willing to take Shakespeare's plays as they are.[5] In miniature it anticipates the vast scope of Schlegel's major critical achieve-ment, the *Vorlesungen*, delivered in Vienna in 1808 and published between 1809 and 1811. So coherent and persuasive was Schlegel's grasp of the development of Western drama and of Shakespeare's place in it that his criticism had a major impact upon English Romantic critics and gave Germany the reputation of being a country where Shakespeare was taken as seriously as he was in England.[6] Throughout the lectures, Shakespeare is Schlegel's measure of dramatic excellence. The sections specifically on him include first a survey of the whole canon, then critical comments on all the

[3] August Wilhelm Schlegel, 'Über Shakespeares *Romeo und Julia*', *Kritische Schriften und Briefe*, 7 vols. (Stuttgart, 1962), vol. 1, p. 126.
[4] Schlegel, *Kritische Schriften*, vol. 1, p. 133.
[5] Schlegel takes David Garrick severely to task for his alterations to *Romeo and Juliet*.
[6] See Thomas G. Sauer, *A. W. Schlegel's Literary Criticism in England, 1811–1846* (Bonn, 1981) for a detailed account of Schlegel's influence on the English Romantics.

plays and several of the apocryphal works as well, a critical undertaking until then unparalleled in German scholarship.

Schlegel's understanding of the artistic process was similar to Herder's in that he regarded form as an organic, not a mechanical, phenomenon. He saw strong parallels between the mental gestations of the artist and biological growth. Artistic forms therefore vary according to 'the direction taken by the poetic sense'.[7] This led Schlegel to make a clear distinction between classical and Romantic drama. Following Herder, he regarded the unities of the classical drama as indigenous to certain times and places. 'Romantic' drama also grew from specific social conditions. Among such 'Romantics' Schlegel includes Shakespeare and the dramatists of the Spanish Golden Age, all of whom displayed a delight in mixtures and fascination with 'a chaos, which is always experiencing new and wonderful births, hidden in the ordered universe, even in its very bosom'. Ancient tragedy has the limited dimensions of sculpture, but Romantic drama is a large picture where, in addition to the main characters, 'all that surrounds the figures must also be portrayed'.[8] Nothing can be omitted.

As in the *Romeo and Juliet* essay, the distinction of Schlegel's criticism was his analysis of the 'picture' created by every one of Shakespeare's plays. He demonstrated how the pictures are composed and the special effects achieved by the juxtaposition of different elements. He acknowledged that they are the product of an age no more barbarous than his own and was energised rather than appalled at its idiosyncrasies, such as its delight in anachronism, a sign, he claimed, not of weakness but of the age's confidence in itself.[9] Schlegel thought concretely and saw Shakespeare as a concrete thinker too, aware of the structure of each play, placing each scene where it can achieve its maximum impact upon the audience. He also continued the eighteenth-century enquiry into Shakespeare as a master of characterisation, praising his ability to enter into all characters so that they behave according to their own inner laws. They seem impelled by a 'self-existent energy', which allows the audience to see to the innermost centre of their minds.[10] While not all of this is original, Schlegel's observation that these recesses are revealed through characters' relationships and conflicts within those relationships is. Furthermore, Schlegel was the first to recognise Shakespeare as a master of irony through skilful juxtaposition of the play's elements. This led him to understand as none had before the importance of comic characters and sub-plots.

[7] A. W. Schlegel, *Vorlesungen über dramatische Kunst und Literatur, Kritische Schriften und Briefe*, vol. 6, p. 110.

[8] *Ibid.*, p. 112.   [9] *Ibid.*, pp. 123–4.   [10] *Ibid.*, pp. 129–30.

In Shakespeare's dramas the comic scenes are the antechambers of the poetry, where the servants dwell; these prosaic attendants should not speak so loudly as to drown the conversation in the great hall; nevertheless, in those intervals when the ideal society has withdrawn, they deserve to be listened to; their daring mockery, their presumptious imitations, can provide much information about the circumstances of their masters.[11]

Schlegel's detailed knowledge of Shakespeare was due in part to his experience as a translator. While the *Vorlesungen* established him as an international scholar, the translations had already made him a national figure. Until the 1790s, the only version of Shakespeare widely available was the prose translation of Wieland, augmented by Eschenburg. No comprehensive attempt had been made to translate the complete canon so as to recapture accurately the energy of the verse and observe the difference between verse and prose. Schlegel wrote of the need for such a translation in an essay he published on the appearance of *Wilhelm Meisters Lehrjahre*. In it, he argued that 'plasticity is the most distinguished excellence of our language'[12] and as such it is ideal for recapturing the essence of Shakespeare's verse. He demonstrated a strong grasp of the technical aspects of dialogue, pointing out that because the dramatic form is so compressed, stage language performs more functions than normal speech does in real life. As verse is more concentrated in meaning than prose, it is a natural stage language. It is not unnecessary, not 'decoration and oratory', but the means whereby whatever is truly poetic, 'the most evident depiction of mental images, the most inward expression of feelings', is realised.[13] The alternation between verse and prose Schlegel recognised as indicating primarily differences between certain characters or between moods in the same character – Prince Hal, for example, speaks in verse and prose – and secondarily differences in rank. All this, plus the wealth of Shakespeare's imagery, Schlegel was to attempt to create in German.

The translation was an unusually extended project. Schlegel himself translated sixteen of the plays, published between 1791 and 1801, followed by one more in 1810.[14] He gave up as his interests changed; when urged to resume the project, he said he had lost the knack of translation. Eventually his publishers gave Ludwig Tieck the responsibility for completing it, apparently with Schlegel's approval, but Tieck lacked the stamina to take

[11] *Ibid.*, p. 138.
[12] A. W. Schlegel, 'Etwas über William Shakespeare bei Gelegenheit *Wilhelm Meisters*', *Kritische Schriften und Briefe*, vol. 1, p. 101.
[13] A. W. Schlegel, *Kritische Schriften und Briefe*, vol. 1, p. 110.
[14] *Romeo and Juliet, A Midsummer Night's Dream, Julius Caesar, As You Like It* (all published 1797), *The Tempest, Hamlet* (published 1798), *The Merchant of Venice, Twelfth Night, King John, Richard II* (published 1799), *Henry IV Parts 1 and 2* (published 1800), *Henry V, Henry VI Parts 1, 2 and 3* (published 1801), and *Richard III* (published 1810).

on the undertaking single-handedly and eventually the translations were completed under his supervision by his daughter Dorothea and Wolf von Baudissin.[15]

Despite the several hands that completed the Schlegel/Tieck translation, it is remarkably uniform in style, sticking faithfully to Schlegel's original intention,

> to reproduce [the text] faithfully and at the same time poetically, following step by step the literal meaning and yet catching at least a part of the innumerable, indescribable beauties which do not lie in the letters but hang about it like a ghostly bloom.[16]

The translations are faithful to the original without being prosaic, demonstrating a resourcefulness and imagination that often finds close German equivalents to Shakespeare's English. The alternation of verse and prose was scrupulously observed and the only changes allowed were either the excision or alteration of obscure references and obscenities. The German verse was flexible, pleasant to hear and rhythmically light, which made it ideal for the stage, while Shakespeare's ambiguous and multiple meanings were surprisingly well sustained in the German.[17] But the reason why this translation is historically pre-eminent is that it appeared at a time when German literature was at a crucial stage in its development. By the start of the nineteenth century, it was no longer purely of local and national interest. The works of Goethe, Schiller and the Romantics had expanded the scope and flexibility of German as a literary medium. The Schlegel/Tieck translations, by demonstrating that German could achieve a range and expressiveness equal to Shakespeare's English, validated the advancement of German literature to European status. So, while several other complete translations of Shakespeare have since appeared, the Schlegel/Tieck version has always commanded a remarkable loyalty.[18]

---

[15] Baudissin translated *All's Well That Ends Well*, *Antony and Cleopatra*, *The Comedy of Errors*, *Henry VIII*, *King Lear*, *Measure for Measure*, *The Merry Wives of Windsor*, *Much Ado About Nothing*, *Othello*, *The Taming of the Shrew*, *Titus Andronicus*, and *Troilus and Cressida*. Dorothea Tieck translated *Coriolanus*, *Cymbeline*, *Timon of Athens*, *The Two Gentlemen of Verona*, and *The Winter's Tale*. Tieck collaborated on two translations, on *Love's Labour's Lost* with Baudissin and on *Macbeth* with Dorothea Tieck. *Pericles* was not translated.

[16] Schlegel, *Kritische Schriften und Briefe*, vol. 1, p. 101.

[17] See Peter Gebhardt, *A. W. Schlegels Shakespeare-Übersetzung* (Göttingen, 1970) for a detailed analysis of the translations, with specific emphasis on *Hamlet*.

[18] See K. G. Kagler, 'Weshalb immer noch die Shakespeare-Übertragungen der Romantiker vorzuziehen sind', *Shakespeare-Jahrbuch*, 92 (1956), 90–5 for some thoughts by a theatre director as to why the Schlegel/Tieck version is still to be preferred. In the 1984–5 season, of the sixty-three new productions of Shakespeare in West German, Austrian and German Swiss theatres, twenty-three used or were based on the Schlegel/Tieck translation. See Ingeborg Boltz and Christian Jauslin, 'Verzeichnis der Shakespeare-Inszenierungen und Bibliographie der Kritiken. Spielzeit 1984–85', *Shakespeare-Jahrbuch* (Heidelberg, 1986), 177–97. In 1985, in the German Democratic Republic, five of the fifteen new productions of Shakespeare were

Nevertheless it is not perfect. In his concern to prove Shakespeare's consummate artistry, Schlegel had failed to translate one crucial aspect of the plays that had been central to Herder's appreciation of them, that is their roughness. Shakespeare wrote for a popular theatre, and while Schlegel understood this critically, his translations frequently seem directed towards creating the image of Shakespeare as a harmonious writer whose language is designed never to offend the sensibilities of his audience. The major drawbacks of the translation, which date it and ensure that it is not definitive, were best summarised by the mid-nineteenth century writer Gustav Freytag. Schlegel and Baudissin, he wrote,

> together created a dramatic style for Shakespeare which ever strives at moments of great emotion to preserve coherence with a measured language. In order to achieve a greater unity of tone, in words, images and idioms, they carefully evaporate and moderate whatever strikes our feeling as common, raw and awkward, even though it was probably not understood as such in Shakespeare's day.[19]

As a later critic saw it, the ruggedness of Shakespeare's language had been subjected to 'a general process of smoothing, tidying and levelling of the versification'.[20]

This judgement of the translation may well account for its popularity. It identifies one regard in which Schlegel perpetuated rather than inhibited the eighteenth-century desire for congruity and harmony in theatre. Practitioners quickly accepted the Schlegel/Tieck translation as the verse was pleasingly sonorous and, despite Laube's objections and the practice of others who would simplify the language still further, was relatively easy to speak. The provision of a practical alternative to the eighteenth-century prose versions was partly the cause of an increase in the number of productions of Shakespeare in the course of the nineteenth century. As a reading text it went through innumerable editions and raised Shakespeare to a level of literary prestige possibly greater in Germany than in England. This may well have been because, as the translators' syntax was modern and archaic vocabulary was avoided, German readers found the plays easier to read than their English counterparts did.

based on Schlegel/Tieck. See Armin-Gerd Kuckhoff, 'Shakespeare auf den Bühnen der DDR im Jahre 1985', *Shakespeare-Jahrbuch*, 123 (Weimar, 1987), 153–64.

[19] Quoted in Alois Brandl, 'Ludwig Fulda, Paul Heyse, und Adolf Wilbrandt über die Schlegel–Tiecksche Shakespeare-Übersetzung', *Shakespeare-Jahrbuch*, 37 (1901), xxxix.

[20] Margaret E. Atkinson, *August Wilhelm Schlegel as a Translator of Shakespeare* (Oxford, 1952), p. 33.

FRANZ DINGELSTEDT

New concerns regarding the performance of Shakespeare grew from Schlegel's criticism and translations. First, as the plays were conceived to be structured as pictures and as visual effects came to be understood as integral to their impact, the pictorial aspects of performance started to attract increasing attention. Secondly, as characters were revealed through relationships rather than in isolation, the concept of an ensemble approach to the production of Shakespeare gradually gained ground, even though the virtuoso soloist remained a powerful counterforce until the end of the century. Finally, as harmony was the essence of the Schlegel/Tieck translations, the productions based upon them often strove to achieve a complementary visual harmony.

The first attempt to produce Shakespeare as a grand stage spectacle took place in the opening decades of the century at the Berlin court theatre in productions supervised by Iffland.[21] Goethe had also attempted a notably spectacular production of *Julius Caesar* at Weimar in 1803.[22] But it was not until the middle of the century, with the installation of versatile gas-lighting and scenic systems in the theatre and the growing demand of audiences for spectacle, that the full visual potential of Shakespeare's plays came to be explored.

A key figure in this development was Franz Dingelstedt, who did much to popularise Shakespeare's work by exploring the variety of his plays, applying the practice of ensemble performance to them and utilising lights and scenery to create an attractive atmosphere for the dramatic action. From the moment he took over direction of the Munich court theatre in 1851, it was clear Dingelstedt favoured the classics. Before him, the classics had been done on an average sixteen times a season, but for the six years of his intendancy they were given on average forty times a season, with Shakespeare prominent among them.[23] Dingelstedt's finest achievements in Munich were probably his adaptations of *Macbeth* and *The Tempest*, the latter of which was the play's professional première in Germany.[24] After Munich, Dingelstedt took over the Weimar court theatre, where he stayed until 1867. The Weimar years were even more notable for his work on Shakespeare. Here he was responsible for 105 performances of twenty-four

---

[21] Schlegel's versions of *Hamlet*, *Julius Caesar* and *The Merchant of Venice* were staged at the Berlin court theatre during Iffland's intendancy, as were Schiller's *Macbeth* and Goethe's *Romeo and Juliet*. Kindermann, *Theatergeschichte Europas*, vol. 5, pp. 217–36.

[22] See Huesmann, *Shakespeare-Inszenierungen*, pp. 139–48.

[23] See Otto Liebscher, *Franz Dingelstedt: Seine dramaturgische Entwicklung und Tätigkeit bis 1857* (Halle, 1909), p. 94.

[24] Stahl, *Shakespeare und das deutsche Theater*, p. 382.

of the plays,[25] including *The Winter's Tale*, never seen in Germany before, and the two history cycles, performed together over an eight-day period. This is generally regarded as the crowning achievement of Dingelstedt's career and as one of the most important events of the nineteenth-century German theatre, comparable in stature to Wagner's *Ring* cycle.[26] Dingelstedt finished his career as director of both the Vienna court opera and the Burgtheater. In fact, Dingelstedt rather than Schreyvogel or Laube has been credited with finally establishing Shakespeare as a 'dominating presence' at the Burgtheater,[27] even though his work here was mainly a refinement of his Weimar productions. He revived the history cycles with a better cast than in Weimar and staged *Antony and Cleopatra* in a not especially successful production. In summary, while Dingelstedt's repertoire as a stage director was comprehensive, ranging from Greek tragedy through to modern drama, Shakespeare always remained 'the great love and the great occurrence of [his] life and creative career'.[28]

In the mid-nineteenth century, the most consistently popular theatrical genre was grand opera, and the prime significance of Dingelstedt's work was the staging of Shakespeare's plays to appeal to the tastes of that operatic public. As a young man he would not have believed this possible. He wrote in 1843,

> Dress a Shakespearean drama in all the arts and accomplishments of the modern theatre and they will paralyse each other. There are certain things between heaven and earth, which, if they are to be brought into the realm of the senses, must be made to appear not completely tricked out, but in classic nudity and in their most primitive, most childlike simplicity.[29]

But when he came to stage Shakespeare, 'primitive . . . childlike simplicity' was the last thing on Dingelstedt's mind. The principles he used for adapting the plays were set out in his introduction to his versions of *Macbeth* and *The Tempest*,[30] and in an afterword to his adaptation of the history cycles.[31] In some ways they were not very different from the principles of his eighteenth-century predecessors, and they often ignored the advances achieved by Schlegel.

---

[25] Rudolf Roennecke, *Franz Dingelstedts Wirksamkeit am Weimarer Hoftheater* (Greifswald, 1912), pp. 135–6.

[26] Ludwig Eckardt, 'Shakespeares englische Historien auf der Weimarer Bühne', *Shakespeare-Jahrbuch*, 1 (1865), 391.

[27] Lothar, *Burgtheater*, p. 240.

[28] Friedrich Rosenthal, *Unsterblichkeit des Theaters* (Munich, 1924), p. 177.

[29] Quoted in Karl Glossy, *Aus der Briefmappe eines Burgtheaterdirektors* (Vienna, 1925), p. 110. Glossy's 175-page introduction to this collection of letters is the most complete biography of Dingelstedt available.

[30] Franz Dingelstedt, *Studien und Copien nach Shakespeare* (Budapest, Vienna and Leipzig, 1858), pp. 1–28.

[31] Franz Dingelstedt, *Theater*, 4 vols. (Berlin, 1877), vol. 4, pp. 459–95.

When faced with the practicalities of production, Dingelstedt, like most theatre people of his own and previous generations, had no difficulty in thinking of the stage version as something different from the printed version. On stage, he argued, Shakespeare's text must be 'mundgerecht' and 'bühnengerecht'. By 'mundgerecht' – 'easy to speak' – he meant that all obscurities should be clarified and the language made easy for the actor to deliver and equally easy for the audience to understand. Contorted expressions should be made intelligible and metrical irregularities smoothed out. By 'bühnengerecht' – 'fit for the stage' – he meant that the action should be so simplified that the audience is never uncertain about what is happening, while characters' motives should be made explicit and characterisation less complex. Explanations should be added wherever there are puzzling jumps in the action and the rhythm of the play should be regularised.[32]

In his discussion of staging, Dingelstedt was no more original. He believed firmly in the basic premise of the illusionistic theatre, that the audience's attention should be enchained by as unbroken a span of action as possible.[33] As the means of changing scenery was still fairly cumbersome, Shakespeare's frequent scene-changes should be reduced, with several scenes taking place in the same location, and the play edited to ensure that this is possible. But here also was the novel core of Dingelstedt's attraction to Shakespeare. He was drawn to him primarily by the opportunities the plays offered for spectacle and he would allow the demands of spectacle to determine the structure of the action, in contrast to earlier adapters who in part reduced the plays to the reduced capacity of the theatre to create spectacle. But for Dingelstedt, Shakespeare was important first and foremost as the creator of singular and exciting environments.

It is a cliché of nineteenth-century theatre history that Dingelstedt and Laube, the 'Dioscuri' of their time, represented irreconcilable opposites. Laube, denying all spectacle, placed sole emphasis on the word, while Dingelstedt accentuated physical appearances: 'in place of the dullness and insufficiency of the prevailing decor he sought to create a brilliant decorative milieu'.[34] But theoretically he was aware of the dangers of spectacle. When he visited the Parisian theatre as a young man, he had been unimpressed by the prodigious spectacle of the boulevard theatres,[35] and even though he appreciated some of Charles Kean's productions, he deplored the English theatre, 'which wishes', he wrote, 'to enter into competition with the Crystal Palace and place the scene-painter, the machinist, the costume designer and the properties manager over the

[32] Dingelstedt, *Theater*, vol. 4, p. 494.   [33] Glossy, *Briefmappe*, p. 111.
[34] Eugen Kilian, *Aus der Praxis der modernen Dramaturgie* (Munich, 1914), p. 259.
[35] Glossy, *Briefmappe*, pp. 110–11.

playwright and actor'.[36] Instead he felt the director should seek an 'equipoise between poetry and scenery',[37] each reinforcing the impact of the other. Physical production, he claimed, should not swamp the play but nourish it, penetrating 'the poetic intention, bringing hidden beauties to light, concealing obvious faults'.[38] The director should encourage the actors to work in harmonious ensemble and 'arrange the crowds to be lively and yet discrete and assemble scenery and costumes with good taste'. In Dingelstedt's productions acting, poetry and spectacle should work as one.

Whether they did or not is questionable, as Dingelstedt's visual sensibility prevailed over the aural and mimetic. His career began just as gas-lighting was being installed in German theatres, and he used this new technology to create marvellous atmospheric effects, 'softening contours and toning down the colours in a Corot-like vagueness'.[39] Also he created the illusion of historical accuracy, several of his productions being done in collaboration with leading historicist painters, Kaulbach and Piloty in Munich and Makart in Vienna. His stagings, therefore, had an alluring look that satisfied both the audiences' senses and their growing appetite for the apparent resurrection of the past in all its details. Despite his reservations about the English theatre's fascination with production, Dingelstedt utilised the vast personnel of the modern theatre – actors, dancers, designers, musicians, technicians – and its increasingly sophisticated machinery to give Shakespeare grand operatic treatment. In Munich he was also known for initiating spectacular productions of Wagner, and indeed his practice has been seen as an actualisation of Wagner's theory of the total work of art.[40]

The quality of his productions can be recaptured through the published adaptations, which include detailed stage directions. But while the history cycles occupy pride of place in his work, the essence of Dingelstedt's staging can perhaps be more efficiently comprehended through two adaptations that were even more widely performed than the histories, Macbeth and The Winter's Tale.[41]

Although Dingelstedt deplored the habit of piecing stage versions together from different translations, he was quite capable of doing it himself. Macbeth was compiled from three available translations – Schiller,

[36] Dingelstedt, Theater, vol. 4, p. 475.   [37] Dingelstedt, Studien, p. 25.
[38] Franz Dingelstedt, Literarisches Bilderbuch (Berlin, 1878), p. 221.
[39] Paul Lindau, Nur Erinnerungen, 2 vols. (Stuttgart and Berlin, 1919), vol. 2, p. 254.
[40] Kindermann, Theatergeschichte Europas, vol. 7, p. 170.
[41] Dingelstedt's adaptation of the histories has been the subject of much critical discussion. Perhaps the most extensive is the one to be found in Roennecke's book. A good account of the adaptation and of the Weimar performances can be found in Robert K. Sarlos, 'Dingelstedt's Celebration of the Tercentenary: Shakespeare's Histories as a Cycle', Theatre Survey, 5, 2 (1964), 117–31.

Kaufmann and Schlegel/Tieck – with 'the pathos [borrowed] from Schiller, the characterisation from the other two, to make from all these a fourth, occasionally original version'.[42] In fact, there are not as many original passages in *Macbeth* as in other of Dingelstedt's adaptations. Although he reduces Shakespeare's twenty-eight scenes to twelve, he only materially cuts Shakespeare's expository scenes, between Ross, Macduff and the Old Man (II:4) and Lennox and the Lord (III:6). He included the murder of Lady Macduff and Macduff's agony at hearing of it, which gives Act V a renewed impetus. The main rearrangement of Shakespeare's action is in this act, which is divided into three scenes, scene 1 covering the assembly of the English and Scottish troops, scene 2 all the events in Macbeth's castle, and scene 3 the final battle. This makes the action easier to follow than in Shakespeare, but it is less moving. For example, the sleepwalking scene follows the first army scene, which makes it of interest only as an incident in the decline of the Macbeths, not as an insight into the psychology of guilt. The Witches are restored to their original form, as is the porter, though nineteenth-century distaste for the public discussion of physical functions means that his scene is radically cut. To make up for this, he appears throughout the play as an ubiquitous messenger, which detracts even further from the disturbing eruption of drunken commentary in Shakespeare.

   Dingelstedt's characterisation is unremarkable. While he claims he took it from Kaufmann and Schlegel/Tieck, he follows Schiller's lead in making Macbeth an errant, noble soul and his wife an irredeemable villainess. The 'mundgerecht' language deprives them of dramatic life, imagery is simplified, passages of tortured meaning are cut or paraphrased, and retarding passages exploring character alone disappear. Rich lines such as Macbeth's

> If th'assassination
> Could trammel up the consequence, and catch,
> With his surcease, success
>
> (I:7, 2–4)

are rendered prosaically as

> Wenn der Meuchelmord
> Auch aller Folgen uns entledigte

(If the assassination also exempted us from all consequences)

while 'Screw your courage to the sticking place' becomes, inaccurately, 'Halte nur Stand' ('Stick to your position') and 'men-children' become 'Söhne' ('sons'). While Schiller's alterations incorporated a reinterpre-

---

[42] Dingelstedt, *Studien*, p. 148.

tation, Dingelstedt's are designed not to strain the imagination of a possibly inattentive audience.

Whether this *Macbeth* achieved 'equipoise of poetry and scenery' is doubtful, for the weak poetry was balanced by striking visualisation. To twentieth-century eyes, Dingelstedt's direction would seem to have been over-emphatic, but for an age that had a strong appetite for visual stimulus, it brought the play to life. Notable was the way in which characters' states of mind and the atmosphere of the action itself were actualised in the scenery, not the poetry. For example, Macbeth's demand that the stars hide their fires was accompanied by a sudden withdrawal of the back of Duncan's tent to reveal a panorama of the stars. The events leading up to the murder were staged atmospherically, as the lighting declined gradually from the brightness of the banquet, seen through doors at the back of the stage, to total darkness. While the realism by which this was achieved, by having servants extinguish lights, has been dismissed as 'pedantic hair-splitting',[43] the optical effect complemented the darkening mood well and the final onset of darkness, caused by the extinguishing of light in Duncan's room when he was murdered, must have been distinctly chilling. The appearance of Banquo's Ghost was also exciting, as Dingelstedt staged it so that the audience could see how confused the court was at Macbeth's behaviour,[44] an example of attention to the overall context of the action.

If Dingelstedt's production was historic for his use of scenery and staging to animate the drama, he ensured its popularity by relying on operatic conventions. This was most apparent in the formal processions, which occurred whenever Duncan entered and when Macbeth came on for the banquet. Hecate was also operatic. While the Witches have a primitive energy, Hecate, who appears where she does in Schiller's version, arrives 'solemnly and slowly', dressed in a 'black dress with a long train', veiled, wearing 'a silver diadem, to which is attached a new moon'.[45] Perhaps Dingelstedt was alluding to Mozart's Queen of the Night. Romantic Italian opera may also have influenced his historically inaccurate decision to designate the architecture of Macbeth's castle as Norman–Gothic, a canny choice as such an atmosphere would strike audiences familiar with the operas of, for example, Donizetti, as particularly apposite for the play.

Dingelstedt's *Macbeth* was instantly successful and soon performed throughout Germany. His adaptation of *The Winter's Tale*, first produced at Weimar in 1859, was even more important as this was the first time the play had been seen in Germany. It was a difficult play for audiences to accept, as they still prized unity of tone in the drama and this the play

[43] Schumacher, *Macbeth auf der deutschen Bühne*, p. 193.
[44] Liebscher, *Dingelstedt*, pp. 118–19.
[45] Dingelstedt, *Studien*, p. 100.

distinctly does not have. A contemporary critic found this a major problem. *The Winter's Tale*, he claimed, involves 'the most surprising fluctuations between the deepest seriousness and most bitter pain', an unpleasant oscillation which the adapter must modify by 'abbreviating, recasting, eliminating and moderating' moments, even whole scenes.[46] Dingelstedt did this thoroughly. He so simplified the notoriously complicated language of the first three acts that the characters no longer seem to struggle with words to express the tortuous quality of their feelings. This transfers the conflict to a more reassuring plane, for it now occurs solely on the surface of consciousness and between characters, rather than both between them and between the character and his or her painfully confusing experience of the irrational. In particular, Leontes does not express his jealousy as brutally as in Shakespeare, while Polyxenes is more temperate when he discovers Florizel and Perdita in love. Meanwhile the demonic Autolycus is reduced to a jolly fellow who sings conventional *Wanderlieder*. In Shakespeare, the violent irrationality of character is complemented by a natural world that is unaccountably harsh, especially in the central transitional scenes, where Antigonus abandons Perdita and is killed by the bear. In Dingelstedt, these scenes are cut and the necessary information communicated through calm expository speeches.

More attention is paid to pathos of situation than to pathological psychology. This meant that Dingelstedt could not use scenery as resourcefully as he had done in *Macbeth*. Instead, he had recourse to music. The success of the production may have been due as much to Friedrich von Flotow's celebrated score as to the adaptation. Dramatic moments were reinforced with music in the manner of melodrama and opera. Music gave an idyllic cast to the scene between Hermione and Mamilius before Leontes's jealousy tears them apart, while at the trial it was used unashamedly to muster audience sympathy for the beleaguered Hermione. Music also accompanied Hermione's coming to life at the end of the play. Formal features of the musical theatre, such as elaborate processions at the trial and extended dances during a banquet that opens the play and the sheep-shearing also helped make Dingelstedt's *Winter's Tale* popular.

The trial-scene demonstrated Dingelstedt's skill as a director of large crowds. He was probably most in his element when directing massed groups of actors to create a highly-charged atmosphere or to highlight dramatic climaxes.[47] His battles were especially celebrated. In *The Winter's Tale* there is, of course, no battle, but the trial-scene offered a spectacle as exciting (see plate 15). Dingelstedt juxtaposed three different moods, represented by three groups: the ceremonial grandeur of the judges, the

---

[46] Quoted in Roennecke, *Franz Dingelstedts Wirksamkeit*, pp. 58–9.
[47] Lindau, *Nur Erinnerungen*, pp. 253–4.

15 Trial-scene from Dingelstedt's *The Winter's Tale*, Berlin National
Theatre

surly Leontes with his soldiers and an excitable crowd, which constantly threatened to break down the barriers that surrounded the trial-space. As the trial proceeded, tension developed between the two latter groups, when the crowd reacted angrily to Leontes and cheered Hermione. As a result, the centre of attention was withdrawn from her to the crowd's discontent with Leontes's rule, giving the scene a political cast. The climax was reached when a deafening clap of thunder followed Leontes's denial of the oracle and the crowd fled in terror. The conflict was expressed not within or even between characters, but by a larger impersonal entity that magnified and simplified the divisions within the action of the play.

Dingelstedt has not been the most sympathetically treated of nineteenth-century directors. Despite the care with which he put together productions, he acquired the reputation of being a dilettante, playing with appearances and not penetrating to the heart of a play. In contrast to the dour Laube, a none-too-friendly professional rival, Dingelstedt seemed a 'cool and slippery' diplomat, concerned as much with his own social eminence as with artistic integrity, or an entrepreneur turning out entertainment for a society oppressed by its own luxury, one that valued only masks and appearances and lush art.[48] There may have been some

[48] Rosenthal, *Unsterblichkeit*, pp. 151–80.

truth in this. Dingelstedt's success, especially in Vienna, has been attributed to the *arriviste* audiences that filled the Burgtheater auditorium in the early 1870s.[49] He certainly was far from realising Shakespeare in the form envisaged by August Schlegel, but his productions mark the first attempt to use the totality of the theatre in realising Shakespeare on stage. As such his work was preparatory for the most celebrated German company of the last decades of the nineteenth century, the Meiningen court theatre.

THE MEININGER

Dingelstedt understood the similarity between his work and that of the Meininger. 'Look at that,' he said sadly when the company first visited Vienna, 'that's how it is. That is what *I* did. Perhaps I did too much. And now they call it the Meininger.'[50] Probably this is true. Before taking over the government of his duchy and its court theatre, Georg of Saxe-Meiningen had travelled widely, and he apparently knew Dingelstedt's work well by 1857.[51] Given Georg's parallel interest in contemporary historicist painting, it is therefore likely that he would be influenced by him. However, the particular rigour with which Duke Georg applied his principles led to the Meininger having a far greater influence on the development of German and European theatre.

Initially there seems to have been little difference between Dingelstedt's work and the famous Meininger production of *Julius Caesar*, so rapturously received when it was first performed at the Friedrich Wilhelmstädtisches Theater in Berlin in May 1874. Its success was due to three factors, all of which might be considered attributes of Dingelstedt's work as well: the crowd scenes, the energy of the ensemble and the fidelity of the design to the historical period, down to the smallest details of costumes and personal props.[52] Like Dingelstedt, the company had rescued a play that was in danger of becoming a lifeless classic, by giving it new immediacy. In particular, the great scenes in the Forum were remarkable for 'mood and passion everywhere, realistic truth and expression proper to the situation'.[53] Although there were some dissenting voices, the general opinion

---

[49] See Fritz Fuhrich, 'Burgtheater und Öffentlichkeit von Laube bis Dingelstedt', in *Das Burgtheater und sein Publikum*, ed. Margret Dietrich (Vienna, 1976), pp. 335–67, for an analysis of the audience of the time.

[50] Lothar, *Burgtheater*, p. 242.

[51] Anne Marie Koller, *The Theater Duke: Georg II of Saxe-Meiningen and the German Stage* (Stanford, 1984), p. 18.

[52] Stahl, *Shakespeare und das deutsche Theater*, p. 446.

[53] B.S., 'Das deutsche Theater und die "Meininger"', in *Die Meininger: Texte zur Rezeption*, ed. John Osborne (Tübingen, 1980), p. 117.

was that the Meininger used the stage as a 'living and lively' picture,[54] in which the various skills of the actor and elements of physical production were used to give as complete a realisation of Shakespeare's play as possible. How then did their work differ from Dingelstedt's?

As one reads contemporary accounts of the Meininger tours, the difference becomes clear. First, all critics agreed that the presence of the production in itself was of paramount importance; often they felt it to be overwhelming. No one could ignore the roaring mobs in *Julius Caesar* or the feverishly active street-scenes in *The Merchant of Venice*. Likewise, everybody commented on the authenticity with which periods of history were seemingly recreated. Above all, critics were impressed by the thoroughness of research, the deliberation of effect and determination not to neglect the most insignificant passage in the action or portion of the stage picture. Even if the company offered little that was new, it combined all theatrical elements into a unique totality. All this was the result of several years of preparation in the obscurity of Meiningen. While Dingelstedt had to work under the pressure of a constantly changing repertoire,[55] the Duke of Saxe-Meiningen could painstakingly prepare his major productions. The repertoire in Meiningen was not so demanding and his personnel, devoted solely to the production of spoken drama, was much larger. As the Meininger productions were constantly repeated on the company's tours between 1874 and 1890 – *Julius Caesar* was given 330 times, *The Winter's Tale* 233 and *Twelfth Night* 132[56] – it was not surprising that the technical standard of production was more efficient than that of a company with a regularly changing repertoire. A further novelty that played up the quality of production was the constant focus on ensemble in which no individual stuck out, in which actors acted 'passively' – i.e. in reaction to others on stage – as well as 'actively',[57] and in which there was no casting by the *Fach* system, which the Duke refused to tolerate. If this theatre had a virtuoso, it was the director alone.

But while the Duke has earned a reputation as the first stage director in the modern theatre,[58] he would not have admitted to it if, by director, one meant an independent artist creating from his own imagination and not the playwright's. In fact the Duke and several of his contemporaries considered his most significant achievement to be the restoration to the German

---

[54] Hans Herrig, *Die Meininger: ihre Gastspiele und deren Bedeutung für das deutsche Theater* (Dresden, 1879), p. 25.

[55] For example, in 1864, the year he staged the history cycles, Dingelstedt was responsible for producing thirty-seven plays and eleven operas. Roennecke, *Franz Dingelstedts Wirksamkeit*, pp. 224, 227 and 230–1.

[56] Koller, *The Theater Duke*, p. 195.

[57] Max Martersteig, *Das deutsche Theater im 19. Jahrhundert*, 2nd edn (Leipzig, 1924), p. 643.

[58] John Osborne, *The Meiningen Court Theatre, 1866–1890* (Cambridge, 1988), p. 171.

theatre of the original texts of classic playwrights, with only the minimum adaptation for contemporary theatrical conditions. The whole apparatus of the theatre was being used solely for this purpose. So the Duke's declared intention of representing the play alone and the critical reaction that concentrated primarily on physical production are highly contradictory. Nowhere is this more apparent than in the Meininger productions of Shakespeare.

In his old age, the Duke claimed that the main reason for sending his court theatre on tour was to provide a model for Shakespearean production. 'I was annoyed that Shakespeare was so badly played in Germany', he told his associate Max Grube,[59] and he intended to remedy this. He did so by appealing, like Dingelstedt, to contemporary tastes for a pictorial art, realistic to the tiniest detail and historicist in subject matter. His visual senses, as Wolfgang Iser has pointed out,[60] took priority over his aural, so he favoured pictorial images above the verbal. With plays like Shakespeare's, that were written for a theatre in which the potential for spectacle was limited, that presents a problem. As Iser explains, in *The Merchant of Venice* language fulfils the function that scenery served in the later illusionistic theatre. For example, the minor characters Solanio and Salerio consistently evoke Venice as a city of restless activity, devoted to the hazardous pursuit of trade. Through them character and environment are felt as one, through their language environment becomes an expression of character. This develops in two directions. On the one hand, the recurrent discussion of shipping and trade leads the audience's imagination away from Venice towards a wider realm of enterprise, the imagery of the language pointing towards the horizon the city itself aspires to. On the other hand, the imagery of trade enters into the private realms of the play so that the whole Belmont plot, while it retains the aura of a fairy-world, is actually conceived in terms of the 'real', Venetian world of trade. The similarity of the two worlds gives the play unity. Furthermore, as relationships are often described in terms of commerce, the external environment becomes an image for emotional change within the characters.

The main limitation of the Meininger undertaking was its failure to capture this characteristic dynamic of Shakespearean drama. Iser explores these limitations in their production of *The Merchant of Venice*. The production opened with 'the bustle of a market and a ballet, with the Doge

---

[59] Max Grube, *The Story of the Meininger*, trans. Anne Marie Koller (Coral Gables, Florida, 1965), p. 21. It should, however, be noted that a few pages later Grube, without any awareness of contradiction, points out that according to the Duke's stage director Chronegk the tours were necessary in order to finance the lavish productions.

[60] Wolfgang Iser, '*Der Kaufmann von Venedig* auf der Illusionsbühne der Meininger', *Shakespeare-Jahrbuch*, 99 (1963), 72–94.

carried over the stage in a sedan chair, roared at, cheered by a multitudinous throng of a hundred extras',[61] while later scenes included carnivals, atmospheric effects with gondola lights, genre studies of Venetian life and, during the trial, a large crowd in a gallery responding with lively interest to the reversals that occur in the course of the trial. This heavy emphasis on the visual was complemented by several cuts, such as, for example, Salerio's speech on the dangers of trade (I:1, 22–40) and Bassanio's meditation on the caskets (III:2, 54–101), in which the imagery clearly refers both to Bassanio's state of mind and to the outer environment of trade and barter. In the Meininger production, Iser argues, word and picture did not support each other as ideally they should have done; rather they competed for the audience's attention as neither was relevant to the other. The elaborate production grounded the action in a literal environment that drew attention to itself rather than completing in physical terms the poetic range suggested by the language. Production lay beyond, not in, the language.[62]

While contemporary nineteenth-century criticism was not as methodical as Iser's, several writers found the effect of the Meininger productions to be most disjunctive. The hostile, conservative Viennese critic Ludwig Speidel, a partisan of Dingelstedt's, did not like his expectations of the play to be confounded by a production that overwhelmed him:

> I wish to enjoy a poem and they come at me with rich clothing materials and bedaubed canvas; I want to delight in the warm breath of an artist and they fling whole hordes of gesticulating, buzzing and shrieking extras at me; I wish to be moved, edified, impressed, and instead they make me into a blinded, confused and confounded gaper.[63]

Hans Hopfen, a discriminating critic, who also found the Meininger productions difficult to accept, objected to scenery taking precedence over the actor, arguing that this priority was like that of

> a painter who wishes to paint the furthest subjects in the background of his painting with greater accuracy and truth to nature than what he has brought into the foreground, who, as it were, wishes to stand the perspective relation on its head.[64]

Those who agreed with Hopfen's idea of reversed perspective also felt, not surprisingly, indifferent to the characters and therefore to the progress of the dramatic action. After all, as eighteenth-century critics of Shakespeare had realised, an audience can be held only when invited to participate imaginatively in the lives of the characters. With the primary focus on the

---

[61] Adolf Winds, *Geschichte der Regie* (Berlin and Leipzig, 1925), p. 93. Quoted Iser, 'Der Kaufmann von Venedig', p. 76.

[62] *Ibid.*, p. 78.   [63] Ludwig Speidel, 'Die Meininger in Wien', in Osborne, *Rezeption*, p. 90.

[64] Hans Hopfen, 'Die Meininger in Berlin', in Osborne, *Rezeption*, pp. 69–70.

physical setting, this was not possible.[65] The total realism of the production and the self-contained completeness of the Meininger play-world could isolate audience members too, because, however exciting this world appeared to be within itself, its very insistence on its completeness meant it lay outside the boundaries of the audience's immediate experience and therefore did not excite them. This sense of isolation was best articulated by the English critic William Archer, who reviewed the Meininger *Julius Caesar* when the company played at Drury Lane in 1881. Archer considered Ludwig Barnay an excellent Antony, who delivered his address 'with absolute mastery', but the excitement he could have created was undermined by the production's insistence that he pay attention solely to the crowd on stage and not to the audience. Consequently, the impact of his speech was felt through the crowd's reactions and not directly. For Archer, Barnay would have been more effective had he also appealed to the imagination of the audience, so that they could feel the effect of 'his strokes of invective and pathos in [their] own imagination' and not 'by inference'.[66]

The Meininger concern with total illusion also affected the structures of the plays they performed, which undercut their claim to be staging the 'original' text. Again Iser, quoting Granville-Barker, observes how in *The Merchant of Venice* the Venetian and Belmont lines of action intertwine, underscoring the interdependence of the two worlds, also established in the language. To execute each of the frequent changes of scene that Shakespeare requires to create a visceral stage-impression of this intertwining posed a formidable problem to the nineteenth-century stage, where scene changes were cumbersome, in contrast to the momentary changes accomplished on Shakespeare's stage. Hence the Meininger had to minimise scene-changes that broke the illusion and destroyed the rhythm. In *The Merchant of Venice* this meant that short scenes in which the action moved from one locale to another, such as the crucial arrest of Antonio in Venice (III:3), were cut while the three scenes of the wooing of Portia by Morocco and Arragon (II:1; II:7; II:9) were made into one, a grouping that had first been effected by Schröder in Hamburg, one hundred years before, and repeated by Laube at the Burgtheater. As a result, Venice and Belmont still appeared to be two very different worlds, confronting each other rather than interdependent. However, in the Meininger production, as Act v was fully restored, the fairy-tale values of Belmont rather than the perilous world of Venetian enterprise ended as the dominant presence.

Such changes altered the balance and meaning of the play and changed its

---

[65] Iser, '*Der Kaufmann von Venedig*', p. 88.
[66] William Archer, 'The German Plays. *Julius Caesar* and *Twelfth Night*', in Osborne, *Rezeption*, p. 127.

16 Set for Meininger *Julius Caesar*, Act v

atmosphere. A similar effect could be observed in other productions. For example, to avoid scene changes, the whole of Act v of *Julius Caesar* was played on a single set representing a gorge by Philippi (see plate 16), while the company's ill-starred production of *Macbeth* was set almost entirely within a single castle. Such consolidation of scenes, which often won applause for ingenuity, undoubtedly helped build tension and kept the audience within the grip of the illusion. Nevertheless, the sense of enclosure they created militated against Shakespeare's intention to create the sense of a broader, even limitless world in which great historical changes occur, one often open to the most unpredictable and catastrophic forces of change. The circumscribed limits of the Meininger stage expressed a more rational world where such forces stay under control

Whatever the shortcomings of the Meininger, however, not even their most bitter opponents could deny that, like no company before them, they increased the popularity both of Shakespeare and of other classic dramatists. On the most rudimentary level, they achieved this by applying to the classics production techniques usually seen in popular musical theatres such as the Victoriatheater in Berlin.[67] But some of the changes they effected were more fundamental than a simple appeal to popular taste and they arose, paradoxically, from the very tendency that Iser finds obstructed a successful production of Shakespeare's text. Robert Prölss, a Dresden critic, one of the Meininger's most enthusiastic apologists, in his analysis of the company's work[68] took as his theme the Duke's love of painting. He argued that the Meininger productions were 'mahlerisch' – 'pictorial' or 'like pictures' – thereby implying a contrast to the 'Plastik' – 'sculpture' – of the neoclassical tradition of Goethe and the Burgtheater directors. 'Mahlerisch' suggests attention to environment as distinct from sole focus on the subject as in 'Plastik'. It also implies a production style particularly suited to Shakespeare's plays, which, as we have seen, had for over a century been described by critics as pictures.

One of the best examples of Shakespeare as a 'mahlerisch' playwright is the murder of Cinna the poet by the mob in *Julius Caesar*. This scene had first been restored to the play by Laube at the Burgtheater, but it was the Meininger who revealed its effectiveness. As this role, like most minor roles, was cast with a strong actor,[69] it had a particularly powerful effect on the audience; in it, the true danger of mob violence becomes clear and the heady turbulence of the Forum scenes is set in an ironic light. Another prime example is the murder of Lady Macduff and her son. The few critics who saw the Meininger production of *Macbeth* commented specially on this scene, as the unsettling contrast between the mother's lighthearted banter and the approaching murderers encapsulated the evil of Macbeth more effectively than a hundred storming extras.[70] Both moments characterise an important aspect of Shakespeare's 'pictorial' dramaturgy, until this time largely ignored in the German theatre. Such dramaturgy comprises the use of scenes not inextricably part of the action to make a most forceful comment on the action that might not effectively be made in a continuous plot. The very separateness of the scene directs the

---

[67] Herrig, *Die Meininger*, p. 22.
[68] Robert Prölss, *Das herzoglich Meiningen'sche Hoftheater* (Leipzig, 1887).
[69] Karl Frenzel, 'Zwei Shakespeare-Vorstellungen in Meininger', in Osborne, *Rezeption*, p. 54.
[70] Schumacher, *Macbeth auf der deutschen Bühne*, p. 200.

audience's attention to the issues it is addressing. From it the audience achieves a more comprehensive view of the action. Gerstenberg and August Schlegel had drawn attention to this pictorial quality in Shakespeare's action. Schiller, with the same technique in mind, described it as 'epic'. Some decades after the Meininger had stopped touring, Bertolt Brecht would use the same term to describe a similar phenomenon. The theatre that used such means asked for a more active and imaginative response from the audience than the neoclassical adaptations of Shakespeare had required.

The indeterminate nature of the Meininger's work is indicated by the absence of any experiments in non-illusionistic theatre that such scenes readily invite. But they led the company to focus with special intensity on how any dramatic moment could be given interest in and for itself rather than as part of a larger structure in which the scene contributes towards the building of suspense. Through their productions, Shakespeare's plays were treated not as headlong, suspense-filled actions, but as panoramas of life. Despite the formal similarities between the Meininger *Merchant of Venice* and Schröder's, their productions were a far cry from the tight eighteenth-century adaptations, which dealt with the lives of only a limited number of people. As a critic commented when seeing a production of *Cymbeline* at Meiningen before the tours began, their productions were not for audiences who wished their plays to proceed with haste towards a resolution, but for ones who relished scenes that retarded the action and embellished it.[71] To hold their audiences' attention, the Meininger had to present such scenes in an original way.

Naturally, they were equally careful in their representation of scenes essential to the action, which accounts for the vivid impression so many people had of their productions, despite complaints by some of not being involved in the characters. For example, in *Julius Caesar*, the conspirators spoke in whispers, ostensibly because they did not wish to be heard from neighbouring gardens, but in reality because this held the attention of the audience and gave a visceral impression of conspiracy. Striking visual details abounded, such as the appearance of Caesar's ghost to Brutus before Philippi, achieved by a single electric spotlight played on the actor's head, which seemed disembodied as the actor was wearing a red toga against the similar red of the tent walls. One of the Meininger's most successful productions was *Twelfth Night*. Performed on a fixed setting, with two smaller settings rolled on when necessary, the production was noted for the quality of ensemble and for the actors' ability to enliven the action with original comic moments, the most unusual being a positive wave of laughter that overcame Sir Toby and company as Maria first told them of Malvolio's change of clothes.

The attention to detail that highlighted individual scenes complemented the

[71] W. Rossman, 'Ueber die Shakespeare-Aufführungen in Meiningen', in Osborne, *Rezeption*, p. 34.

17 Forum-scene, Meininger *Julius Caesar*

historicist gravitation of the productions. But even though some felt their historicism went too far, giving their work 'a doctrinaire flavour',[72] the company could demonstrate a sensitivity to the potential of the scenic environment as metaphorical expression which belies those who accused them of unalloyed historicism. Not all their productions involved a disjunction between word and pictorial effect. For example, the Meininger were praised for their authentic re-creation of ancient Rome in *Julius Caesar*, with scenery based on the sketches of the curator of the Vatican collection. But it has since been convincingly demonstrated that the Duke knowingly employed anachronism by including in his stage-forum buildings, especially the temple on the backdrop, that were not put up until several decades after Caesar's death (see plate 17). Also he rearranged the known proportions of the Forum to achieve heightened dramatic effect.[73] Fidelity to history may only have been used to persuade the audience to accept the production, not as an end in itself. *The Merchant of Venice* failed when first produced in 1874 in the 'historically faithful' setting of Venice in the Middle Ages, but it succeeded when revived in 1886 in a Renaissance environment that, despite Iser's reservations, had some

[72] Speidel, 'Die Meininger in Wien', in Osborne, *Rezeption*, p. 83.
[73] See Inge Krengel-Strudthoff, 'Das antike Rom auf der Bühne und der Übergang vom gemalten zum plastischen Bühnenbild', in *Bühnenformen – Bühnenräume – Bühnendekorationen*, ed. Rolf Badenhausen and Harald Zielske (Berlin, 1974), pp. 160–76. An admirably detailed account of this important production can be found in Osborne, *The Meiningen Court Theatre: 1866–1890*, pp. 88–110.

relation to the play's theme. In particular, the setting in the Jewish ghetto 'with its dilapidated houses, its ragged washing hanging from lines stretched over the streets'[74] might effectively have suggested the economic realities by which Shylock had been conditioned. The Meininger production that was second only in popularity to *Julius Caesar*, *The Winter's Tale*, given in the original and not in Dingelstedt's adaptation, was not at all historicist. While Dingelstedt had set his production in ancient Greece, the Meininger were more imaginative, conjuring up a fairy-tale world by idyllic backdrops of Sicilian land- and seascapes and costumes from sources as diverse as the paintings of Botticelli and the national dress of Bohemia.[75] Leontes's anger in the first part of the play was imaginatively reflected in the dark figures of gods painted on the walls,[76] possibly suggesting that his jealousy is as unaccountable as divine wrath.

Perhaps the greatest of the Meininger achievements would have been their *Macbeth*, had the production not been crippled by weak performances in the central roles. In fact it was seen only ten times, in Berlin and Breslau. Stahl calls it 'one of the densest productions atmospherically of the great Meininger classic repertoire, which would have caught correctly the sinister and gruesome mood of the work in an exceptional way'.[77] Here the Duke's historical knowledge served him well, for instead of setting the play in Dingelstedt's Norman–Gothic environment, he went back to tenth-century, tribal Scotland. The heavy rock cliff of the opening scenes was converted into the walls of the castle so there was a symbolic affinity between Macbeth and the natural or supernatural forces that impel him. The production abounded in details. The Witches, dressed in the same colour and material as their surroundings, were truly 'bubbles' of the earth, the murderers of Banquo spoke to Macbeth from a trapdoor, appearing to be half below the ground as if part of the underworld, while the murder of Lady Macduff, as already mentioned, was peculiarly effective. Furthermore, while the Meininger confined most of the action to one castle and so limited one's sense of the historical range of the action, they still used the limitation for a strongly symbolic conclusion, as Macbeth was slain by Macduff on the very steps which earlier he had ascended to murder Duncan. The revenge of divine right was graphically realised.

It is difficult to place the Duke of Saxe-Meiningen and his company in the history of stage direction. The company was not, as has often been pointed out, innovative; what they did was to combine the resources of the theatre that were available to them at that time.[78] But this very combination drew attention to the fact of production as something separate from the text and

[74] Grube, *The Story of the Meininger*, p. 102.   [75] *Ibid.*, p. 89.
[76] Prölss, *Das herzoglich Meiningen'sche Hoftheater*, p. 55.
[77] Stahl, *Shakespeare und das deutsche Theater*, p. 454.
[78] Thomas Wiecke, 'Meiningen und die Meininger: Acht Thesen', *Theater der Zeit*, 29, 6 (1974), 11. Osborne, in *The Meiningen Court Theatre*, painstakingly establishes the company in the cultural and theatrical context of its time.

therefore as capable of interpreting that text to an audience. Shakespeare, it would seem, both suffered and benefited from this. He suffered because even though the texts were supposedly given in their original form, the striking physical environment could divert attention from the action. But he benefited from the company's skill at filling out the action with the finest details and using these to create an atmosphere that often engrossed audiences and opened up a more complete play than they had until this time experienced.

What is undeniable in the Meininger achievement is the effect they had on the placement of Shakespeare in the German repertoire. While it is not strictly accurate to claim that Shakespeare was an 'unpopular' dramatist in Germany before the Meininger,[79] after their tours audiences had a more complete idea of the range, size and nature of his drama. The company also stimulated more performances of the classics. Karl Grube, an early historian of the company, has estimated that three times the number of performances of Shakespeare, Schiller, Goethe and Kleist were given in the German theatre between 1880 and 1900 than between 1860 and 1880, an increase he attributes solely to the Meininger.[80] As Ludwig Barnay, one of the few great actors who worked with the Meininger in his years of maturity, observed in his *Memoirs*, the Meininger elevated the classics to a position of eminence in the German theatre so that they were no longer 'Cinderella' to the 'proud, richly-dressed sisters . . . opera . . . [and] operetta'.[81] While this change did not always meet with the approval of contemporary critics and while they depended on production techniques that soon dated, the Meininger managed to bring Shakespeare to unprecedentedly large audiences and stage him in a manner they found attractive and which complemented the idea of the plays as a picture of life. As Karl Frenzel observed, with the Meininger 'performances were no longer an Eleusinian mystery that only the initiated could understand'.[82] They were accessible to all who wished to attend.

With the Meininger Shakespeare achieved the popularity that critics a hundred years before had first claimed for him.

[79] Lawrence F. McNamee, 'The Meininger Players and Shakespeare', *Drama Survey*, 3, 2 (1964), 264.
[80] Karl Grube, *Die Meininger* (Berlin and Leipzig, 1904), p. 40.
[81] Ludwig Barnay, *Erinnerungen*, 2 vols., 2nd edn (Berlin, 1903), vol. 1, p. 247.
[82] Frenzel, 'Zwei Shakespeare-Vorstellungen', in Osborne, *Rezeption*, p. 63.

9

Romantic legacy: the 'Shakespeare-stage'

THE REACTION AGAINST SPECTACLE

Through the Meininger, Shakespeare's plays achieved a popularity that had so far been unequalled in the German theatre, but not all critics or scholars unquestioningly agreed that they were doing the cause of Shakespeare a service. Some felt his plays to be radically distorted by the Meininger's attention to production values and by the company's concern that all performances should be as visually attractive and as historically 'accurate' as possible. Even though their scenic stage appeared to complement the fullness of Shakespeare's text, critics were concerned that it was directly antithetical to the stage for which Shakespeare actually wrote. The plays, their argument went, were seriously misrepresented when visual spectacle appeared to be the prime consideration. The most vociferous of all such critics was Rudolf Genée, a historian well acquainted with theatrical conditions of the past, who had published in 1870 the first major book-length study of the history of Shakespeare in the German theatre.[1]

In 1887, Genée published an essay, 'Die Natürlichkeit und die historische Treue in den theatralischen Vorstellungen' ('Naturalness and Historical Accuracy in Theatrical Performances'), that was to have some influence on future production. The essay was read in 1889 by the intendant of the Munich court theatre, Karl von Perfall, who then commissioned one of his directors, Jocza Savits, and his resident designer, Kurt Lautenschläger, to construct a stage that would allow for an alternative approach to Shakespearean production than that practised by the Meininger. In his essay, Genée had discussed at length the relationship between stage design and the inner action of the play, positing the equation that standards of acting fall in direct relationship to the emphasis placed on spectacle. Using an argument that echoed certain of Goethe's and Schiller's precepts on the drama, Genée

---

[1] Rudolf Genée, *Geschichte der Shakespeare'schen Dramen in Deutschland* (Leipzig, 1870).

claimed that spectacle violates the very essence of dramatic art, for drama is dependent wholly upon 'symbolic' action, which can only be understood when the stage suggests reality rather than manifests it. He wrote

> The dramatist has done enough when he awakens in us the impression of inner truth, when he knows how to express the inner being by the symbolism of appearance, so that we survey the whole by means of concentrated images, from whose accumulated lines the picture is assembled.[2]

Genée went on to call for a theatre in which artistic effects were achieved solely through the words of the poet and the performance of the actor. The spoken word, he argued, was the single most important element in performance. Gesture and movement should only be permitted when they give external form to the 'inner truth' of the word. In the severely restricted theatre envisioned by Genée, scenery had one function only: to support the actor. It was therefore most successful when the audience was least aware of it. If it were reduced to the necessary minimum, Genée considered Shakespeare's plays could be played in a manner that would allow the symbolic nature of the action to unfold and appeal in full to the imagination of the audience.

In the context of late nineteenth-century theatre, when the Meininger seemed to stand as a culmination for all that was progressive, Genée's writings sound puritanically radical. His ideas, however, were not entirely original, something he acknowledged himself through his constant citation of the writings and practice of two earlier writers, both of whom had advocated and experimented with the idea of playing Shakespeare on a stage that either approximated to the one for which he wrote or was designed on principles similar to those of the Elizabethan stage. These writers were the Romantic poet, novelist and critic Ludwig Tieck and the late Romantic dramatist and novelist Karl Immermann. Neither had been exclusively a theatre person, but their enthusiasm for the imaginative world they had discovered in their reading of Shakespeare led them to attempt to find an effective way to realise it on stage.

LUDWIG TIECK'S WRITINGS ON SHAKESPEARE

Few German writers have been so devoted to Shakespeare as Tieck.

> The centre of my love and knowledge is Shakespeare's spirit [he wrote], to which, involuntarily and often without knowing it, I refer everything. Everything, whatever I experience and learn, is related to him, my ideas as

---

[2] Genée, 'Die Natürlichkeit und die historische Treue in den theatralischen Vorstellungen', *Die Entwicklung des szenischen Theaters und die Bühnenreform in Deutschland* (Stuttgart, 1889), p. 67.

well as nature. Everything explains him and he explains the other beings and so I study him incessantly.[3]

Throughout his long writing career, which lasted from the earliest phase of Romanticism through to the middle of the nineteenth century, Tieck was constantly involved with Shakespeare's work, alluding to him literally hundreds of times in his notes, essays, novellas, literary and theatrical histories and critical works. He supervised the continuation of the Schlegel translation,[4] and though his skill as a translator was limited, the conclusion of the project did not betray the high standards with which it had been initiated. He was also one of the first Germans to show an active interest in theatre history, particularly of the Elizabethan age, and while his understanding of this was far from complete, it was fruitful in that it furthered German awareness of the physical conditions that helped create Shakespeare's plays. But Tieck's crowning Shakespearean achievement, a book that would survey his whole work, was never written. He constantly claimed to be on the verge of completing it, but never did. It remained a series of notes, articles and reviews, to be published as such only in his extreme old age and not under his editorship.[5] Apart from reviews of individual plays and performances that appeared throughout much of his lifetime, Tieck's most sustained judgement on Shakespeare is contained in two early essays, 'Shakespeares Behandlung des Wunderbaren' ('Shakespeare's Treatment of the Marvellous'), written when he was a student in Göttingen and published as an introduction to his translation of *The Tempest* in 1793, and 'Briefe über Shakespeare' ('Letters on Shakespeare'), published in his *Poetic Journal* in 1800.[6]

From these two essays, it is clear that Tieck's ideas were strikingly different from those of the *Sturm und Drang* critics. *Sturm und Drang* had prized Shakespeare as a genius who intuited the universal and natural order, but for Tieck he was most important as an artist who carefully crafted his material. Tieck regarded the plays not as simply the spontaneous outpourings of a creative mind, but as deliberate strategies aimed at engaging completely the attention of their audience. In fact his interest in Shakespeare as a dramatic strategist, in how he arranged the play to achieve its effect upon the audience,[7] was to deepen considerably German understanding of his dramaturgy. Furthermore, as he was interested more in the

[3] Ludwig Tieck, 'Briefe über Shakespeare', *Kritische Schriften*, (Leipzig, 1848; reprinted Berlin and New York, 1974), vol. 1, p. 141.
[4] See Henry Lüdecke, 'Zur Tieck'schen Shakespeare-Übersetzung', *Shakespeare-Jahrbuch*, 55 (1919), 1–6.
[5] Nikolaus Delius, *Die Tieck'sche Shakespearekritik* (Bonn, 1846).
[6] Ludwig Tieck, 'Shakespeares Behandlung des Wunderbaren' and 'Briefe über Shakespeare', *Kritische Schriften*, vol. 1, pp. 35–74 and 135–84.
[7] Henry Lüdecke, *Ludwig Tieck und das alte englische Theater*, (Frankfurt, 1922), p. 63.

comedies than the tragedies, Tieck helped expand awareness of the range of the Shakespearean canon.

Herder, it will be recalled, had compared Shakespeare's plays to dreams. In his essay on the 'Marvellous', Tieck specified this general observation by demonstrating how Shakespeare used the stage to create in the audience a condition akin to sleep. This he did by maintaining their pleasure in the stage illusion so constantly that they are never allowed the freedom to transfer their thoughts to the real world. When seeing *The Tempest*, for example, Tieck argued that the spectators become so absorbed in the action that 'in unceasing perplexity [they] lose the yardstick with which [they] are accustomed to measure the truth'.[8] Shakespeare disorients them not by engaging their interests in certain characters, but by the arrangement of scenes, which move like a journey from the opening storm into the heart of the dream-world of the island. The illusion is also sustained by the careful balance of characters. Tieck argued that if the action were to involve mainly magic figures such as Ariel and Caliban, the audience would soon lose interest and escape from the dream, so Miranda and Ferdinand were introduced as a counterweight to sustain it. Shakespeare was equally careful to ensure that the lovers do not attract too much attention, because if they do the magic world of the island will strike the audience as intrusive or even uninteresting, so in this way too the illusion of dreaming will be lost. He maintained balance also by avoiding situations in which characters display extreme passions because these would call for a correspondingly strong emotional response from the audience that would disrupt the dream. The complexity of a character, Tieck pointed out, is determined solely by its function in the action. So in *The Tempest* comic characters are simple, uncomplicated figures, which is all they need to be, since if a character as complex as Falstaff were suddenly to appear, the balance of the play would be seriously disrupted.

Tieck's critique of Shakespeare was not limited to the comedies. His early comments on *Romeo and Juliet* foreshadowed Schlegel's famous critique of the play,[9] while in both early and late essays on *Hamlet* he wrote of Claudius as a powerful monarch and Polonius as an effective statesman, so emphasising the wholeness of Shakespeare's play-world and not the figure of Hamlet alone.[10] In direct contrast to much eighteenth-century criticism of Shakespeare, he demonstrated how character is subordinate to the overall design of the play, how it functions within a larger framework and is not the ultimate objective. He considered Shakespeare's plays as aesthetic wholes, not as fragments of world history or as expositions of

---

[8] Tieck, *Kritische Schriften*, vol. 1, p. 44.   [9] Lüdecke, *Tieck*, p. 77.
[10] Ludwig Tieck, 'Bemerkungen über einige Charaktere im *Hamlet*, und über die Art, wie diese auf der Bühne dargestellt werden könnten', *Kritische Schriften*, vol. 3, pp. 248–9.

mighty personalities. Also, while Tieck was far from subscribing to a neoclassical viewpoint, his understanding of Shakespeare resolved the dilemma that had been raised in Goethe's and Schiller's discussion of the nature of drama. Schiller had faulted Shakespearean structure as it did not, like drama of a neoclassical mould, hold the audience in its grip. This he could only see as being achieved through observation of the unities and the construction of an action that maintained dramatic momentum.[11] Tieck, however, found a series of more variable dynamics by which the audience could be drawn without resistance into the action.

Not all of Tieck's fragmentary writings on Shakespeare were confined to structural analysis. As the centre of his criticism was the impact of the action on the audience, he grew deeply interested in the conditions under which the plays were first produced and, accordingly, became the first German scholar to conduct detailed research into the Elizabethan theatre. His interest was not, however, solely antiquarian, for in two ways he hoped it would lead to a revival or re-energising of contemporary theatre. First, he prized Shakespeare and other contemporary dramatists because they were writing at a time of artistic and social vigour very different from the one in which he lived, which he considered to be suffering from 'a lameness in all limbs', crippled by the 'melancholy memory of a heroic age that has flown'.[12] But in Shakespeare's plays the energy and form of popular theatre is used to express the imaginative freedom of an active society escaping from the bonds of feudalism and becoming a self-sufficient Protestant state. Tieck hoped the boundless energy of the plays could stimulate his own age and encourage the writing of the highest poetic drama that is 'enchained by no moral anxiety, no prudery'.[13] Shakespeare is a Hercules who might purge the age of its weakness. If this sounds like Romantic disenchantment and nostalgia, the other reason for Tieck's interest in the Elizabethan theatre was more practical. In the 'Briefe über Shakespeare', he described a visit to a popular theatre in which there is no representational scenery. The setting is left up to the audience's imagination, and it engages their attention far more effectively than would sophisticated modern scenery with its 'great probability and accuracy in design'.[14] On a stage such as this, Tieck claimed, Shakespeare's imaginative world could most effectively be conjured up, whereas stages equipped for elaborate spectacle, which by the early nineteenth century were becoming increasingly common in the larger German cities, could only be a barrier to the free reign of the imagination. Moreover, without the interposition of scenery, the audi-

---

[11] See chapter 5.   [12] Tieck, *Kritische Schriften*, vol. 1, p. 153.
[13] Lüdecke, *Tieck*, p. 104.
[14] Tieck, *Kritische Schriften*, vol. 1, p. 166.

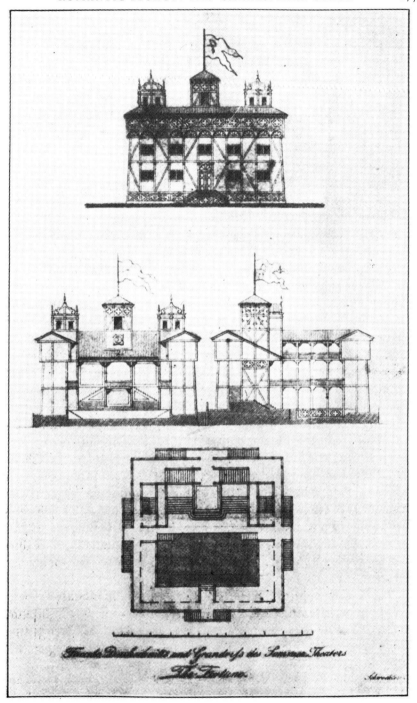

18 Tieck's reconstruction of the Fortune Theatre, 1836

ence would have easier access to the heart of the play and the imaginative world of the playwright.

> The idea of the unity and organisation of a work of art cannot grow with time, but must originally lie in the soul of the artist, or he is no artist. This completion is his soul, everything else is only husk and clothing.[15]

So that Shakespeare's stage-world could easily take hold of the mind and imagination of the audience, Tieck argued for a stage closer to the audience than was possible in the early nineteenth-century theatre with its broad orchestra pit. He was already aware of what critics of the Meininger would complain about later in the century, that heavy, realistic scenery not only hindered the imagination of the audience, but, by preventing swift transitions from one scene to another, destroyed the rhythm of the play as well.[16] Naturally the Elizabethan theatre was the prime model for that stage. In addition to publishing some scholarly works on the Elizabethan theatre,[17] in 1836 Tieck completed, with the help of the architect Gottfried Semper, a reconstruction of the Fortune Theatre.[18] It was not entirely accurate, primarily because Tieck worked from the questionable assumption that all stages evolved from one original form and that the Elizabethan theatre must therefore share features with the stages of ancient Greece.[19] As a result, he represented the Fortune as having a broad, shallow relief stage rather than one that thrust into the audience. From this stage two conspicuous flights of stairs led to a substantial upper stage (see plate 18). There is little hard evidence for any of this, but despite the inaccuracies, this reconstruction provided one of the first potentially viable alternatives to the ubiquitous scenic stage of the nineteenth century.

Despite his deep interest in Shakespeare's plays as theatre pieces rather than as literary works, Tieck was not particularly successful in the practical sphere. As dramaturg to the Dresden court theatre between 1825 and 1842, he managed to advance the cause of Shakespeare by having the plays performed in versions more complete than the late eighteenth-century adaptations, which, despite the availability of the Schlegel translations, were still in use.[20] He was, for example, responsible for the first performance of *Romeo and Juliet* that almost entirely restored Shakespeare's original

---

[15] *Ibid.*, p. 150.   [16] *Ibid.*, vol. 3, p. 173.

[17] In addition to his writing on Shakespeare, Tieck's most considerable contribution to scholarship on the Elizabethan theatre is his introductory essay to a volume of Elizabethan plays, 'Das altenglische Theater' (1811, 1823, 1828), in *Kritische Schriften*, vol. 1, pp. 215–322.

[18] See Gertrud Hille, *Die Tieck-Semper'sche Rekonstruktion des Fortunatheaters: Ein Beitrag zur Geschichte der Bühnenreform des 19. Jahrhunderts* (Berlin, 1929).

[19] Karl Immermann, *Werke*, ed. Benno von Wiese, 5 vols. (Frankfurt, 1971–3), vol. 4, p. 135.

[20] The Shakespeare plays produced at Dresden while Tieck was dramaturg there were *The Merchant of Venice, Hamlet, Romeo and Juliet, King Lear, Julius Caesar, Othello, Henry IV Parts 1 and 2, Much Ado About Nothing* and *Macbeth*. See Robert Prölss, 'Shakespeare-Aufführungen in Dresden vom 20. Oct. 1816 bis Ende 1860', *Shakespeare-Jahrbuch*, 15 (1880), 173–210.

text.[21] Sometimes he influenced effectively the way in which the plays were staged. In an 1836 production of *Macbeth*, a specially constructed upper stage provided an effective playing area for the Witches and for scenes on the battlements,[22] though there was a fair amount of irrelevant spectacle, including a full-scale ballet for the Witches during Act IV.[23] In fact, a reconstruction of the Fortune Theatre stage, or anything even remotely approaching it, remained purely within Tieck's imagination. He could only bring it to life in his writing. In his novella, *Der junge Tischlermeister* (*The Young Master Carpenter*) (1828), he described an imaginary production of *Twelfth Night*, staged by amateurs in the hall of a large mansion on a stage that ran the length of the hall. In the centre of this long, narrow ramp stood

> the upper balcony or gallery . . . supported by free-standing pillars, the ionic capitals of which were elegantly gilded. Below was the smaller, inner stage, hidden by curtains of red silk. The steps [to the inner stage] were also designed with colourful coverings, so that the stage could be itself, whatever one wanted.[24]

The key appeal of this fictional stage was its lack of definite locale. Its sparseness and the absence of representational scenery did not 'contradict the poet's work', but gave the spectator the right to imagine whatever space the playwright wished to be represented in it. Crucially, the all-encompassing illusion that Tieck wanted the stage to create was enhanced rather than destroyed by the non-realistic presentation, while the uninterrupted performance, as described by Tieck, maintained the rhythms of the play undisturbed. As a result, the audience had freer access to Shakespeare's imaginative world than they would have had with a conventional scenic stage.

FIRST SHAKESPEARE-STAGES

Tieck's researches into the Elizabethan theatre bore most immediate practical fruit in the work of Karl Immermann, who, as intendant of the Düsseldorf Theatre between 1834 and 1837, is possibly best known for training a company of actors whose standards of ensemble playing were to become a yardstick for the German theatre in the middle years of the century.[25] Immermann was a disciplined man who favoured economy in

---

[21] Since, for reasons best known to the censor, Juliet was not allowed to be seen going to confession, Tieck was obliged to follow Goethe's version of Act IV.

[22] Stahl, *Shakespeare und das deutsche Theater*, p. 283.

[23] Schumacher, *Macbeth auf der deutschen Bühne*, pp. 166–7.

[24] Tieck, 'Der junge Tischlermeister', in *Romane* (Munich, n.d.), p. 418.

[25] Richard Fellner, *Geschichte einer deutschen Musterbühne* (Stuttgart, 1888), pp. 199–206.

the theatre for artistic as well as financial reasons, and for him, as for the later Genée, the essence of theatre was the spoken word rather than spectacle:

> Like all poetry, dramatic poetry should attempt to attain its effect by *audible* signs. The visual, the mimetic must come to the fore, but only as a supplementary means. The pure basis of performing art remains speech; beautiful recitation is primary and most important.[26]

This led Immermann to adopt simple settings that provided no distraction from the poetry and to cultivate ensemble as a deliberate antidote to the prevailing virtuosity among actors. He had hoped such a company would allow him to develop a repertoire centred around the classics,[27] but he was prevented from doing this by the taste of the local audience, who preferred comedy and contemporary dramas of family life. In fact during the three years of his intendancy, only fifteen performances of eight of Shakespeare's plays were given, but these did include a *Romeo and Juliet* even more complete than Tieck's had been in Dresden.[28] As Immermann's devotion to Shakespeare was greater than that of most of his contemporaries in the German theatre, such figures might be taken as a reliable indication of how rarely the plays were given in Germany during the first half of the nineteenth century.[29]

As a general concern, Immermann was acutely aware of the need both to create a close rapport between actors and audience and to arrange the physical production of a play so as to display the major features of its action clearly. To find ways to bring the actors closer to the audience, Immermann both visited and corresponded with Tieck, who discussed with him his ideas of the generic form that gave rise to the Greek and Elizabethan theatres. This led Immermann to speculate on the possibility of an open stage without scenery. Even before taking on the intendancy at Düsseldorf, he had sketched out a basic plan for such a theatre, which, though not identical with Tieck's reconstruction of the Fortune, clearly showed his influence as he set the stage in relief to the audience.[30] In such a theatre, Immermann realised, 'human action remains the main point of the drama',

---

[26] Karl Immermann, 'Über das Theater zu Düsseldorf im Winter 1832–1833', *Werke*, vol. 1, p. 679.

[27] Benno von Wiese, *Karl Immermann* (Bad Homburg, 1969), p. 157.

[28] Immermann's version was almost complete, though for some unknown reason he cut the Apothecary-scene and the brief Act v scene 2 in Friar Lawrence's cell. See Eugen Kilian, 'Schreyvogels Shakespeare-Bearbeitungen', *Shakespeare-Jahrbuch*, 39 (1903), 118.

[29] The plays performed were *Hamlet, Macbeth, King John, King Lear, The Merchant of Venice, Romeo and Juliet, Othello* and *Julius Caesar*. See Richard Fellner, 'Karl Immermann als Dramaturg', Karl Immermann, eine Gedächtnisschrift zum 100. Geburtstage des Dichters (Hamburg and Leipzig, 1896), p. 179.

[30] Immermann, *Zwischen Poesie und Wirklichkeit: Tagebücher 1831–1840*, ed. Peter Hasubeck (Munich, 1984), p. 75.

and any scenic decoration, which he describes as a 'lifeless' element, fulfils a purely supportive function.[31] In the Düsseldorf theatre, he was unable to attempt even the most approximate reconstruction of the Elizabethan stage, constrained as he was by the permanence of the proscenium arch. Nevertheless, the groundplans for his staging of *Hamlet* show a sensitivity, unusual for his time, to the potential contribution that can be made by the arrangement of actors on stage to the audience's understanding of the action. For example, he blocked the play-scene, which he considered the crisis of the play, so that the audience could see the reactions of the various characters to the play in full face rather than in profile, an arrangement that required considerable ingenuity.[32] In his production of *Macbeth*, he made sure that the reactions of the minor, but nevertheless important, characters of Malcolm and Donalbain to the murder of Duncan were fully apparent.[33] In his use of space to define the relationship of characters and to make clear their motives, Immermann introduced a welcome clarity to the production of Shakespeare.

Some years after he had stood down from the intendancy, Immermann had a unique opportunity to combine an intimate actor–audience relationship with an open stage modelled on the Elizabethan theatre. He was commissioned to produce *Twelfth Night* with amateur actors for the Fasching celebrations of 1840, not in a regular theatre but in a large hall. Here, with the help of a Professor Wiedmann, he constructed a stage which, while not an exact replica of the Elizabethan, by combining Elizabethan and Renaissance elements provided an effective and flexible setting for the play. The fore-stage, which was broad, shallow and in relief to the audience, was backed by four entrances and a central playing area, which served as an inner stage (see plate 19). This stage, framed by pillars and a triangular portico and raised two steps above the main-stage, had walls arranged in perspective. On it were represented private, intimate encounters, while scenes that took place in public, in the streets, gardens and palace of Illyria, were set on the undifferentiated main-stage. On each side of the inner stage were two practical doors, and next to them two archways, behind which perspective scenery was placed. Possibly following ancient Greek precedent, the scenery indicated that one of these archways led to the harbour and coast, the other to a park. Flanking the main-stage were two further entrances that indicated access to the streets of Illyria. The whole structure faced the audience.

Immermann was aware that his stage was unhistorical, but this did not concern him. What was important was the ideal environment he considered it to provide for the performance of Shakespeare, in contrast to a

[31] Immermann, *Werke*, vol. 4., p. 134. [32] Immermann, *Tagebücher*, p. 408.
[33] Schumacher, *Macbeth auf der deutschen Bühne*, p. 154.

DIE BÜHNE.

19 Immermann's stage for *Twelfth Night*, 1840

scenic stage behind the proscenium arch. This new stage gave an unwonted purity to the performance. As he wrote,

> Shakespeare, among all poets, is least tolerant of the admixture of modern pettiness. He always deals with greatness, wholeness, the unvarnished fates of the world and humanity, everything illusory, operatic in design, falls from his limbs like bad lacquer from a beautiful statue; he must be brought into the most intimate proximity with the listeners, when the secrets that flow forth from the heart of his people will be understood.[34]

With this stage, Immermann achieved an intimacy that allowed the audience, which only comprised something over 200 people, to focus their attention fully on the actors. The width of the fore-stage enabled him to block those actors so that character relationships were more apparent than they could be on the narrower, deeper scenic stage. The 'clear, light groups'[35] of the actors helped clarify the complexity of the action. The stage was especially useful for scenes that required characters to eavesdrop on each other or to intrigue. Furthermore, the flexibility of the overall structure, which had seven entrances, allowed him to achieve unusually subtle effects. In particular, it is clear from his description of how he arranged the first visit of Viola to Olivia's house,[36] that by skilful use of

---

[34] Immermann, 'Zur Aufführung von Shakespeares Lustspiel *Was ihr wollt*', *Werke*, vol. 1, p. 691.
[35] *Ibid.*, p. 692.   [36] *Ibid.*, p. 693.

both the main-stage and the inner stage, he could show events occurring simultaneously. This allowed him to establish a vivid contrast between Olivia's anticipation of the visit and Viola's apprehension before they met, which made the meeting itself richer than it could have been on the scenic stage, where convention dictated that only one place at a time could be represented.[37]

Immermann died a few months after his production of *Twelfth Night* so any further experimentation was up to the ageing Tieck. Such an opportunity eventually occurred when, in 1841, he was summoned to join the Berlin court theatre as dramaturg. His first experiments in producing plays under conditions approximate to those of their original production were with Sophocles's *Antigone* and Euripides's *Medea*. Finally, in 1843, with the aid of the stage designer J. C. J. Gerst and the regisseur, Karl Stawitsky, Tieck produced the first performance in Germany of *A Midsummer Night's Dream*, drawing upon his knowledge of the Elizabethan theatre.

Tieck, as we have already seen, was more concerned to find an effective way to produce Shakespeare in the nineteenth century than to resurrect the exact form of the Elizabethan theatre. A revival for purely antiquarian reasons, he realised, would have little purpose and attract few audiences. He had stated as much in a review of *Romeo and Juliet* written during his Dresden days, in which he claimed to be trying

> to discover a medium, to set up a theatre that architecturally approximates to the older English one, without entirely banishing painting and decoration. Indeed it could be so arranged that these illusory means to which we have accustomed ourselves, could present themselves more magically and diversely, even with greater purpose and stage effect, so that they enhance the effect of the play instead of, as so often happens, weakening or negating it.[38]

In fact, to a lesser degree even than Immermann, Tieck did not attempt a precise reconstruction of the Elizabethan stage. In reality, he had less opportunity to do so as, unlike Immermann with *Twelfth Night*, he had to work within the confines of the scenic stage, first of the Potsdam court theatre, then of the Berlin court theatre. What he did do was to incorporate some features of his Fortune Theatre reconstruction into the arrangement of vertical space, while using this structure to house pictorial elements from the scenic stage. Gerst's permanent set consisted of three galleries as the

[37] Immermann's *Regiebuch* for *Twelfth Night* has been lost. However, as detailed a reconstruction of the staging as is possible is provided by Fellner in 'Immermann als Dramaturg', pp. 191–2.
[38] Tieck, '*Romeo und Julia* von Shakespeare, nach Schlegels Uebersetzung', *Kritische Schriften*, vol. 3, p. 173.

Waldszenerie im „Sommernachtstraum"

20 Tieck's production of *A Midsummer Night's Dream*, 1843

back wall of the stage.[39] Each gallery was divided by pillars into three sections. The middle section of the lowest storey provided a niche that resembled the inner stage of the Elizabethan theatre and was used for scenes that suited it, such as the one between Titania and Bottom. On both sides of this niche, stairways ascended to the middle gallery in an arrangement close to that in Tieck's

39 My account of this production follows closely that given by Heide Nüssel in *Rekonstruktionen der Shakespeare-Bühne auf dem deutschen Theater* (Cologne, 1967), pp. 34–44.

reconstruction of the Fortune Theatre. Access to the third gallery was by steps behind the scenery. Each section of the gallery could either be covered by a curtain, so that when all curtains were drawn the back wall provided a neutral background to the action, or single curtains could be drawn aside to reveal a small scenic backcloth of part of the forest. The palace was indicated by classical columns being lowered to frame the most prominent part, the middle section of the second gallery, to which the steps led directly. This became the main playing area for Theseus, while the upper gallery became a balcony in the palace.

The multiple playing areas created by this set allowed the action to be presented with a fluidity unique to its time, but while a particular area could be localised at any point in the action, it was not possible to confine the action just to that one area. Hence, the open stage and fore-stage were used for all scenes, the location they designated being changed according to the scenic indications on the back wall. The workshop of the mechanicals could not be accommodated by any of the scenic areas in the back wall of the stage, so it had to be realised through lowering, in front of the wall, a realistic backdrop as specific as anything that could be seen on the scenic stage.

The production was unusually popular – it was given 169 times before being abandoned in 1885[40] – which suggests that substantial concessions were made to the audience's taste for realistic spectacle. Also, as this was the production for which Felix Mendelssohn wrote his incidental music to *A Midsummer Night's Dream*, perhaps the most popular incidental music written for the theatre in the nineteenth century, considerable portions of the production included ballet, performed amidst attractively designed woodland scenery lowered from the flies (see plate 20). This served to disguise the architectural nature of the permanent set. Tieck, working in a more public arena than Immermann had done, had to compromise between the fullness of the scenic stage and the sparseness of the Elizabethan stage. His highly successful venture quickly established *A Midsummer Night's Dream* as one of the most popular plays in the repertoire, but it did not fulfil to the letter Tieck's ambition to reproduce a staging as sparse as that which he had imagined in his earlier novella.

THE MUNICH SHAKESPEARE-STAGE

The first sustained attempt to develop an approach to Shakespeare that did not encumber him with 'the heavy, exceedingly complicated apparatus and mechanism of the modern stage'[41] was the one initiated at the Munich court theatre in 1889. Savits and Lautenschläger, who had been commis-

[40] Stahl, *Shakespeare und das deutsche Theater*, p. 287.
[41] Karl von Perfall's memorandum to the Munich court theatre, 1889. Quoted by Stahl, *Shakespeare und das deutsche Theater*, p. 493.

21 Munich Shakespeare-stage

sioned to design the structure that came to be known as the 'Shakespeare-stage', first solved the problem of distance between the stage and audience by building a fore-stage over the wide orchestra pit of the Munich Residenztheater, leaving only a narrow gap between the front of the stage and the first row of the stalls. In this, a flight of stairs leading from the pit to the stage was placed. The broad, empty fore-stage extended behind the permanent proscenium arch of the theatre to a proscenium wall, about half-way up the scenic stage, which was elaborately decorated with painted Romanesque arches. In the centre of this wall was a square archway, eight metres wide, which framed a substantial inner stage that was raised three steps above the fore-stage. The scenery of this inner stage was arranged in perspective and whenever it was changed, the change was hidden by a curtain drawn across the archway in the proscenium wall. Although it appeared to be remarkably solid, the whole structure could be constructed or dismantled in two hours (see plate 21).

This stage seemed to offer a strikingly simple solution to the problems of staging Shakespeare effectively. By retaining a sizeable and clearly visible inner stage, Lautenschläger ensured the same sort of interaction between the intimate and public spheres of action as Immermann had achieved in his production of *Twelfth Night*, while the open fore-stage, which was intended

22 *King Lear*, Munich Shakespeare-stage

never to be cluttered with props, was an ideal platform for actors to draw audience attention solely to the roles they were playing. But, like Tieck before him, the director Savits, who was responsible for the physical production, was working in a public theatre and needed to attract audiences. This led him to compromise the original severity of the conception. While the proscenium wall and the walls at the side of that part of the fore-stage that was behind the proscenium arch remained unchanged throughout the performance, the scenery of the inner stage was changed regularly as the performance proceeded. For example, during the first production on the Shakespeare-stage, which was *King Lear* (see plate 22), an over-complicated, even fussy relationship between the fore-stage and the inner stage developed.

The start of the performance was announced by a trumpet call, whereupon the main curtain, which covered everything including the fore-stage, went up and Gloucester, Edmund and Kent came on to the fore-stage. At the end of their conversation, the curtain hiding the inner stage parted to reveal Lear on his throne, surrounded by courtiers. His daughters, accompanied by their husbands, entered through doors on each side of the arch to the inner stage, while the court formally arranged itself on the fore-stage, with men to the left and women to the right. At the end of the scene, the inner stage was again curtained off, only to open a few minutes later to reveal a room in Gloucester's palace with Edmund discovered. He then left the inner stage to deliver his monologue on the fore-stage. This interchange between the two areas continued with unbroken regularity throughout the production.[42] Some attempt was made to indicate the difference between outdoor and indoor scenes. Whenever the inner stage represented a scene outdoors, characters entered on to the inner stage directly and, when using the fore-stage, entered only from the doors on the extreme sides; this gave an impression of greater space. For indoor scenes, they used the doors to the side of the arch in the scenic wall and moved in more constricted patterns than in the outdoor scenes.

The primary flaw in Savits's Shakespeare-stage was the mixture of open and scenic staging techniques. Given audiences' preference for Meininger-esque realism, there were several complaints that the emptiness of the forestage detracted from rather than added to the play's impact. Critics commented too on the contradiction between the heavy, even oppressive scenic wall on to which the Romanesque arches had been graphically painted and the inner stage, especially when outdoor scenes were represented on it.[43] Because of these negative reactions, as the Shakespeare-stage continued to be used, both for Shakespeare and for other classic plays, attempts were made to neutralise the difference between the fore-stage and the inner stage. By 1890, for a production of Goethe's *Götz von Berlichingen*, the arch framing the inner stage was decorated with an elaborate fringe of foliage to soften the severe lines of the original. Also, plays were staged in a way that ignored the difference between the two stages, focusing attention mainly on the inner stage, so that ultimately the whole structure came to be treated as little more than a scenic stage with a peculiarly large fore-stage.

To accomplish a revolution, changes should be radical and complete. This Savits admitted only after his Shakespeare-stage, which was used periodically at the Residenztheater until 1906,[44] had finally been abandoned. He had hoped his direction would highlight the 'inner' or symbolic action of the play, but this could be accomplished only on a stage where scenery and spectacle were reduced to an absolute minimum. Only then would the audience be able to attend solely to the unity between words and gesture in the actor's performance. Savits considered too many concessions

---

[42] Hans Durian, *Jocza Savits und die Münchener Shakespeare-Bühne* (Emsdetten, 1937), pp. 59–61.
[43] A summary of the critical response to the Shakespeare-stage can be found in Durian, *Savits*, pp. 25–32.
[44] The Shakespeare plays produced on the Shakespeare-stage were *King Lear, Macbeth, Romeo and Juliet, The Winter's Tale, Julius Caesar, Cymbeline, Twelfth Night, Richard II, Henry IV Parts 1 and 2, Henry V, Henry VI, Parts 2 and 3* and *Richard III*.

had been made on the Munich Shakespeare-stage to the realistic scenic stage, while those in the company who opposed the whole idea, such as the actor Ernst von Possart, who became intendant in 1892, had no compunction about adapting it to more conventional scenic purposes. Even Savits could not entirely free himself from a lingering taste for the spectacular *coups de théâtre* of the scenic stage. For example, in a production of *Macbeth* in November 1891, staged with the leafy cover over the inner arch, Savits had the Witches perform behind gauzes and employed an elaborate dumb-show in which Duncan displayed the trust he had in Macbeth while Macbeth was delivering down on the forestage the soliloquy in which it becomes clear the Witches' prophecy is working on him. Later in the play, Savits made liberal use of thunder and other sound-effects to augment the dramatic impact. Such techniques suggest that the actor was far from being the sole medium in his productions. And yet because it was deliberately deprived of the technical sophistication of the scenic-stage, the Shakespeare-stage failed to provide the fullness of spectacle Savits's theatricality seemed to invite. Hence it satisfied neither the purists nor those who preferred the scenic stage.

Nevertheless, the wide spaces of the fore-stage did allow for some experimentation, which built on the advances in blocking made by Immermann over fifty years earlier. Stage plans of the productions that have survived indicate that Savits explored with much accomplishment the potentiality of blocking to express the play's action. In his production of *Julius Caesar*, for example, he did not place the crowd at the centre of the play as the Meininger had done. Instead, Caesar himself became the pivotal point of action. The assassination was accomplished with particular effect, as the space of the fore-stage was used to underline the motives of the characters, with the physical distance of each conspirator from Caesar's body reflecting the closeness of his personal relationship with him.[45] At such moments, Savits discovered on the Munich Shakespeare-stage the possibility of arranging actors in Immermann's 'clear lucid groups' so that their thoughts, impulses and motives were felt through the physical arrangement of the production. But some critics found the most important advantage of the new stage to be the ease with which scenes could be changed. The action of the play could now flow uninterruptedly and its natural rhythms, often broken by the long pauses or scenic editing of the Meininger productions, could be felt viscerally. As a result, the unity of Shakespeare's seemingly disunified dramas became apparent and to an unprecedented degree the audience could feel themselves held by Shakespeare's action.[46] On this stage, therefore, the dilemma that Schiller had

[45] Durian, *Savits*, p. 69.
[46] Eugen Kilian, 'Die Münchener Shakespeare-Bühne', *Shakespeare-Jahrbuch*, 32 (1896), 115.

considered Shakespeare's plays to pose to anyone who wished to perform them was resolved. An epic action held the audience with the same tenacity that a dramatic action could.

In a long and often bitter retrospective account of the Munich Shake-speare-stage,[47] Savits attributed its ultimate demise to several causes. First, as he recognised himself, in catering to current tastes for realistic spectacle, he defeated the object of the exercise. There was considerable support for his stage from audiences, he claimed, but he blamed the critics who attacked his work as being unwilling to allow the stage to return to something approaching its elemental form, an accusation not totally justified as several critics discussed seriously and responsibly his efforts at reform.[48] Savits also blamed the actors, claiming that many of them were uneasy at being exposed on a stage that was free from the usual clutter of props. The exposure so produced hindered rather than aided them in their attempts to achieve freedom of expression, as if this could only be guaranteed when easy escape could be made to the security of stage furniture.[49] But above all, Savits realised that, whatever the purity of his ambitions, he was incapable of reversing what he saw as an accelerating trend in the theatre towards spectacle. To do this, he felt there would have to be a revolution in the institution of theatre itself. Actors should have to be required constantly to perform on the open stage with no option to return, as his Munich actors did, to the comfort of the scenic stage. Throughout his efforts, he found himself hampered by the crippling spirit of the scenic stage:

> It is as if there reside in the mind and soul of both artist and spectator, out on the stage and in the auditorium, tedious, malicious spirits and goblins, demons of ostentatious scenery, nesting in all angles and corners. They play a thousand tricks on the new [theatrical] dispensation that offends them ... Against them, in the [old] theatre, the memory is defenceless.[50]

FURTHER DEVELOPMENTS OF THE SHAKESPEARE-STAGE

Savits retired a disappointed man, defeated by the 'malicious spirits and goblins' of spectacle, but his reformist efforts were not entirely in vain. Although Lautenschläger's stage or the modified version of it was finally retired from the Munich court theatre in 1906, experiments in devising an effective stage for the performance of Shakespeare did not stop entirely. From 1908 until the First World War, a further refinement of the

---

[47] Jocza Savits, *Von der Absicht des Dramas* (Munich, 1908).

[48] For an especially sympathetic assessment of Savits's work, see for example Alfred Mensi von Klarbach, 'Die Shakespeare-Bühne im Jahre 1898', *Shakespeare-Jahrbuch*, 35 (1898), 362–75.

[49] Savits, *Von der Absicht des Dramas*, pp. 225–6.   [50] *Ibid.*, p. 229.

Shakespeare-stage came to be used intermittently at the court theatre for the production of Shakespeare's drama. This was not simply a development of the one used by Savits. While it recalled in considerably simplified form the original Shakespeare-stage, its design had also been clearly influenced by the relief-stage of the Munich Artists' theatre, which had opened under the direction of the nationalist director Georg Fuchs in the summer of 1908. In designing the stage and auditorium for the Artists' Theatre Fuchs and his collaborator, the architect Max Littmann, were not concerned to find the ideal stage environment for the performance of Shakespeare. Rather, Fuchs wished to create a theatre that, by using techniques borrowed from the avant garde of the various arts, would arouse among the Germans a sense of national community and Christian heritage.[51] Fuchs also wished to create a theatre that could suitably display the formal, often dancelike movements that he felt the actor should use, as, under the influence of his friend the artist Peter Behrens, he considered the purest expression of theatre to be contained in movement and dance.[52] A deep scenic stage was inadequate for such a purpose as the pure lines of the dancer or the formal gestures of the actor would be blurred when seen against realistic painted scenery or against a distant backcloth or cyclorama. Initially, Fuchs had envisaged a broad shallow stage, divided into a fore-stage, a middle-stage and a rear-stage, each raised slightly above the other, with direct access between the fore-stage and the auditorium through a flight of steps that ran the width of the fore-stage.[53] The fore-stage was to be the main playing area, while the middle-stage, beneath a large proscenium arch, would be separated from the rear-stage by curtains. The rear-stage would include perspective scenery, only to be used when an impression of open space was required.

The Munich Artists' Theatre by no means fulfilled to the letter Fuchs's requirements. The auditorium was in the form of a wedge, designed like that of Wagner's Festival Theatre at Bayreuth, ostensibly to nullify the audience's sense of class divisions and to arouse a feeling of national identity. In fact, it provided an ideal space from which to view the relief-stage, since unlike in the conventional auditorium with its massed tiers, all audience-members watched the performance from a roughly equivalent angle. The stage itself was neither as broad nor as rigorously divided nor as close to the audience as Fuchs had originally imagined. Instead, it was separated from the auditorium by an orchestra pit and though some division between the middle- and rear-stage was indicated,

[51] Georg Fuchs, *Die Revolution des Theaters* (Munich, 1909), pp. 37–48. A good summary of Fuchs's proto-Fascistic ideas can be found in Peter Jelavich, *Munich and Theatrical Modernism* (Cambridge, Mass., 1985), pp. 187–208.

[52] See Peter Behrens, *Feste des Lebens und der Kunst* (Leipzig, 1900), pp. 23–4.

[53] Georg Fuchs, *Die Schaubühne der Zukunft* (Berlin, 1905), pp. 46–61.

23 Set for the prayer-scene, *Hamlet*, III, 3, Munich new
Shakespeare-stage

the final impression was of a unified stage close to the model of the scenic
stage.[54] What was distinctive in this theatre was the unusual width and
shallowness of the stage. Though it was not as broad nor as shallow as
Fuchs had initially envisaged – he had hoped the relationship between the
width and depth would be 10:6, whereas it was 10:9[55] – it did allow actors
to be arranged as they had been on Immermann's stage, in relief to the
audience, so that the relationships that grew between their characters could
be given clearer spatial expression than on a conventional scenic stage.

    Fuchs's direction of the Munich Artists' Theatre, which lasted less than a
year, did nothing for the cause of Shakespeare. His only Shakespearean
production, *Twelfth Night*, was a thorough disaster. Ironically, it was only
in the following year, 1909, when the master of realistic illusion Max
Reinhardt took over the direction of the theatre for the summer that the
full potential of the relief-stage was explored.[56] Nevertheless, Fuchs's
efforts were appreciated by his contemporaries in that his stage, like
Lautenschläger's and Savits's Shakespeare-stage, allowed the audience
freedom to use their imagination. Its influence can therefore be seen in the
final manifestation of the Shakespeare-stage in the Munich court theatre.

[54] Nüssel, *Rekonstruktionen*, p. 117.   [55] Jelavich, *Munich*, p. 205.
[56] Georg Schaumberg, 'Max Reinhardt und das Münchener Künstlertheater', *Bühne und Welt*,
    11, 2 (1908–9), 936–8.

24 Set for graveyard-scene, *Hamlet*, v, 1, Munich new
Shakespeare-stage

   The basic principle of the final form was best demonstrated in the first use
of the stage, in a production of *Measure for Measure* at the court theatre in
1908. Here an effective juxtaposition between private scenes that take place
mainly indoors and the outdoor, public events was achieved. This was done
by playing much of the action before a muted blue-grey curtain that
allowed the front part of the stage to become effectively a fore-stage. The
curtain was drawn back only for the public scenes, not for all scenes as had
been the practice on the Shakespeare-stage. As a result, according to Eugen
Kilian, the adapter of the play, it was possible to stage the text with virtually
no changes in the order of scenes and to use the varying sizes of the stage to
give scenes differing emphasis and tone.[57] Hence, the play began with the
Duke's departure being played on the fore-stage before the curtain, which
was then drawn back for the street-scenes. The curtain was drawn once
again as the Duke negotiated with Brother Thomas for the Friar's habit. As a
result, the contrast between the scenes of intrigue that occur in enclosed
places – rooms, prisons, cloisters – and the public life of the streets and
brothels was well established and the particular rhythm of the play caught
most effectively. Other Shakespearean plays were staged in this manner,[58]

[57] Eugen Kilian, 'Eine neue Shakespeare-Bühne', *Shakespeare-Jahrbuch*, 46 (1910), 74.
[58] *Coriolanus, Julius Caesar, Hamlet* and *Timon of Athens* were also given on the new Shakespeare-
      stage.

notably *Hamlet*. The stage allowed private moments, such as the prayer-scene (see plate 23), to be staged with simplicity and intimacy while more public events, such as the graveyard-scene (see plate 24) could still be played against illusionistic scenery. Indeed, illusionistic scenery would not disappear from the German stage as a norm for another decade, with the coming of the expressionists. Nevertheless, perhaps this final arrangement of the Munich Shakespeare-stage, in catching more effectively than any other stage the peculiar rhythms of Shakespeare's drama, brought the production of his plays closer to the ideal initially articulated by *Sturm und Drang* than the spectacular and realistic productions of the nineteenth century had done.

10

Shakespeare at the Deutsches Theater: the 'colossus' restored?

The last Berlin theatre season before the outbreak of the First World War was distinguished by a unique occurrence, several performances of a cycle of ten plays by Shakespeare at the Deutsches Theater. Night after night, between November 1913 and May 1914, packed houses attended productions, all staged by the theatre's artistic director, Max Reinhardt, of *A Midsummer Night's Dream, Much Ado About Nothing, Hamlet, The Merchant of Venice, King Lear, Romeo and Juliet, Henry IV Parts 1 and 2, Twelfth Night* and *Othello*. Arthur Kahane, one of Reinhardt's leading dramaturgs, reporting on the cycle in the *Shakespeare-Jahrbuch* for 1914, claimed that 'never before on German stages devoted to the serious drama, have such successes, such attendance figures, such receipts been achieved as at these performances'.[1] Suddenly Shakespeare was not only a playwright of vast prestige but a commercial success as well. This was due almost entirely, according to Kahane, to the 'complete dissociation from all existing tradition' of Reinhardt's direction of the plays.

In some regards, Kahane's enthusiasm was not misdirected. From the purely statistical point of view, Reinhardt's Shakespeare-cycle was a formidable achievement, but whether its popularity was due to the total novelty of his directorial approach is questionable. In the theatre, widespread public acclaim is usually given to those whose work both satisfies expectations that audiences have cultivated over several years and includes some novelty of approach that sets the drama in a new light. Reinhardt's enthusiastic following may well have been because he combined these two elements with exceptional skill. But what perhaps made his work of particular importance to the German theatre was the completeness of his vision of Shakespeare. To a degree greater than any of his predecessors, he might have moved towards realising on stage those ideal visions that Shakespeare's plays had kindled in the imagination of the writers of *Sturm und Drang*. For all their modernity, Reinhardt's productions were therefore

---

[1] Arthur Kahane, 'Max Reinhardts Shakespeare-Zyklus im Deutschen Theater zu Berlin', *Shakespeare-Jahrbuch*, 50 (1914), 107.

a momentous step towards consummating a perception of the theatre's potential, suggested by Shakespeare's plays, that had been tantalisingly unfulfilled over the previous 150 years.

Reinhardt did not accomplish this on his own. Although his first successes in the opening years of the twentieth century had been in independent theatres, he was only able to capitalise fully on his early achievements when he took over the directorship of the Deutsches Theater in October 1905. By this time, with the possible exception of the Vienna Burgtheater, the Deutsches Theater was the most highly-regarded theatre in central Europe, due chiefly to the way in which the ambitions of the theatre's founder had been brought to remarkably full realisation.

THE DEUTSCHES THEATER UNDER ADOLPHE L'ARRONGE

The Deutsches Theater had been founded in 1883 by the playwright and theatre manager Adolphe L'Arronge, in collaboration with two of the leading virtuosi of the day, Friedrich Haase and Ludwig Barnay, and two actor-directors, Siegwart Friedmann and August Förster. The theatre's aims were various. Administratively it was to be an oligarchy like the Comédie Française, where senior actors – 'sociétaires' – made collective decisions in place of the traditional all-powerful director. Like the Comédie Française, the Deutsches Theater should have a national purpose, to commemorate 'the illustrious foundation of the German Reich', something that would be achieved by gathering to the theatre 'the intellectual and artistic powers'[2] of the nation. Unlike previous theatres with a similar function, the Deutsches Theater was to be independent, supported solely by the box-office and the generosity of investors and subscribers. Artistically, L'Arronge aspired to emulate the Meininger by creating a permanent ensemble, which would be devoted primarily to the play rather than to the display of the skills of the individual actor. As he wrote in a letter to the brothers Hart,

> Each person must renounce the vanity of playing only great and prominent roles, for the most particular obligation of our arrangement is that each person must be ready to subordinate himself to the whole and use his artistic capabilities even in the smallest duty. Our single guiding principle is to create, through the harmonious co-operation of valuable and significant artistic powers, an ensemble that makes prepared performances into genuine artistic achievements of the stage.[3]

---

[2] Adolphe L'Arronge, quoted in Alfred Dreifuss, *Deutsches Theater Berlin* (Berlin, 1983), pp. 52 and 54.

[3] Adolphe L'Arronge, letter to the brothers Hart, quoted in Julius Bab, *Das Theater der Gegenwart* (Leipzig, 1928), p. 38

Neither Haase nor Barnay were prepared to submit themselves to 'the most particular obligation' of L'Arronge's arrangement and they soon left the Deutsches Theater for other enterprises. August Förster, however, stayed on until 1888 and helped L'Arronge form a large company composed of some of the youngest and strongest actors in Germany, comprising in the 1885–6 season thirty-four men and twenty-one women. The formation of this ensemble L'Arronge considered to be his major achievement at the Deutsches Theater.[4]

When he founded the Deutsches Theater, L'Arronge did not intend to do what the Duke of Saxe-Meiningen may have had in mind when he founded his own ensemble, namely the successful and complete production of Shakespeare. Nevertheless, the advances made by the Meininger in the cause of Shakespeare were apparent by the prominence of his plays in the repertoire of the Deutsches Theater. Between 1883 and 1894, the years of L'Arronge's directorship, approximately one-third of all performances were of classic plays, and approximately one-tenth of all performances were of plays by Shakespeare.[5] However, under L'Arronge's direction, no important technical advances were made over those already accomplished by the Meininger. The large ensemble ensured performances that were efficiently acted throughout – as the Meininger had demonstrated, an important prerequisite for the successful production of Shakespeare. But there were also forces that militated against the unequivocal predominance of the ensemble, in effect those of rising young actors who, by force of personality and magnetism of stage presence, attracted the audience's adulation and came to be a prime drawing-power at the box-office.

The most celebrated of these was the Austrian Josef Kainz, who had spent three years with the Meininger and another three at the Munich court theatre before joining the Deutsches Theater as a founding member of the company. Kainz's rise to celebrity and lifelong fame occurred precipitately in November 1883 when he played the title role in Schiller's *Don Carlos* with striking passion and immediacy, with no overt concern to demonstrate consummate, virtuosic technique or to display his elegant demeanour and noble bearing. This performance led Otto Brahm, then drama critic for the *Vossische Zeitung*, to hail Kainz as a great renovator of acting after years of stale virtuosity. In later years Brahm came to see him as the first major modern interpreter of the classics.

---

[4] Adolphe L'Arronge, *Deutsches Theater und Deutsche Schauspielkunst*, 2nd edn (Berlin, 1896), p. 72.
[5] Figures based on statistics in Kurt Raeck, *Das Deutsche Theater zu Berlin unter der Direktion von Adolph L'Arronge* (Berlin, 1928). The Shakespeare plays performed were *Othello, King Lear, Much Ado About Nothing, Romeo and Juliet, Richard III, Hamlet, The Taming of the Shrew, Macbeth, Henry IV* and *The Winter's Tale*.

25 Kainz as Romeo

Kainz was the first to fulfil the modern demands of art in our tragedy – that is his great, his historic merit. Far from all hollow doctrine, entirely out of his own nature, from a nervous modern nature, he has seized hold of the problems of Shakespeare and Schiller and filled them, anew with the warm blood of life. Whatever had become dry tradition and declamation, he formed with a realistic directness that had been lost on the others. They were fumbling epigones, he an impudent modern.[6]

In Kainz's reanimation of classic roles, Brahm discerned qualities that would help the cause of naturalistic acting that he championed. Kainz seemed to form his characters from purely individual experience and perception, not from established models. As an actor he was subject to the slightest emotional fluctuations, which enabled him to explore in detail psychologically complex characters. He also projected an aura of 'nervousness' that appealed strongly to an age that felt itself to be unwelcomely pressured by an impersonal social world. Kainz's nervousness at one and the same time exalted the independence and therefore the prerogatives of the individual psyche and enacted the pressures to which it was subject. At this stage in his career, Kainz also radiated an energy that invigorated most people who saw him. Not surprisingly, with the exception of Don Carlos, his most celebrated role was Romeo. 'Romeo the child was discovered', wrote Brahm, 'young like the fourteen-year-old Juliet, boundless in his passion, a foolish, charming boy.'[7] This was not the solemn, responsible young man embodied by the Weimar actor, but a youth driven by his awakening sexual feelings, which were represented with clarity and lack of sentimentality (see plate 25). The lush poetry of the Schlegel translation was not indulged in for its own sake, but used to express vividly Romeo's erotic longings. In Kainz, poetry became dramatic.

His Juliet was, on several occasions, the young Agnes Sorma, whose ability to speak uncloying, unsentimental delivery of verse also contributed towards returning dramatic poetry to its original function as an expression of character. Sorma did not have the cold, classical, somewhat imposing beauty that often characterised actresses of the previous generation, of whom the stately Charlotte Wolter of the Burgtheater was the most splendid representative, but had a more appealing prettiness that allowed her to humanise her roles. She was, according to Martersteig, 'persevering in her girlish impulsiveness, charming with her amiable nature', and in most of the roles she played she disclosed 'the sunny light of a powerfully happy soul, even through the pain of tragedy'.[8] Both Sorma and Kainz

---

[6] Otto Brahm, 'Der Fall Kainz', *Theater, Dramatiker, Schauspieler*, ed. Hugo Fetting (Berlin, 1961), p. 134.
[7] *Ibid.*, p. 140.   [8] Martersteig, *19. Jahrhundert*, p. 672.

created an ambience of bouyancy and indestructibility, even in those roles normally regarded as exemplars of tragic determination.

THE DEUTSCHES THEATER UNDER OTTO BRAHM

In 1894, L'Arronge handed over the directorship of the Deutsches Theater to Otto Brahm, principally because he realised his tastes in modern drama did not accord with the public's. Brahm's sponsorship of productions of plays by Ibsen, Hauptmann, Strindberg and other naturalistic dramatists under the auspices of the Freie Bühne suggested he might be more capable of fulfilling the original ideals of the Deutsches Theater than its founder had been. In several respects, the trust L'Arronge placed in Brahm was justified as, during his ten-year tenure at the Deutsches Theater, Brahm consolidated the superior position of the theatre by making it into the foremost stage in Germany, possibly even Europe, for the plays of Ibsen, Hauptmann and Schnitzler. He also developed, before Stanislavski did, an ensemble of actors trained to portray to the most intimate details characters of a complex psychology. But disappointingly, Shakespeare was little more than an incidental concern of Brahm the theatre director.

When he took over the theatre, Brahm did not intend this decline in the importance of Shakespeare and other classic dramatists. As a dramatic critic during the 1880s, he had shown a keen appreciation of Shakespeare's work. Also sympathy for contemporary naturalist dramatists, which grew throughout this decade, drew him towards Shakespeare, the one classic writer whose work might be regarded as antecedent to the naturalists. In that well-established critical tradition that stretched back to the eighteenth century, Brahm saw Shakespeare as the creator not of significant action but of great and complex characters who could have a powerful emotional impact on their audience.[9] Consequently, his plays were of great value, as, if they were properly staged with close attention to character, they would be ideal vehicles for German actors to develop their powers of characterisation. Brahm saw Shakespeare as a powerful aid in his campaign to rid the German theatre of the empty pathos, hollow declamation and cloying sentimentality that still passed for acting among the ubiquitous epigones of the Weimar style. Of course, Shakespeare alone could not guarantee the transition to the more realistic style of acting that Brahm wished to see, as is clear from his acute descriptions of performances of Shakespeare he had covered when a critic. For example, while he granted that the American Edwin Booth, who gave guest appearances in Berlin in 1883, had considerable power, he deplored his playing of Iago as an elegant

---

[9] Fritz Martini, 'Shakespeare-Aufführungen im Spiegel der Kritik Otto Brahms und Alfred Kerrs', *Shakespeare-Jahrbuch* (Heidelberg, 1967), 124.

gentleman with none of the 'rough and hard' qualities of the original. When Booth played Othello at a subsequent performance, he could produce none of those eruptive outbursts that make the role so compelling.

> The Othello whose powerfully exploding passion devastates all around him and the dearest to him, and then drives him to commit murder on himself – him I saw less clearly and believed in less willingly.[10]

Above all, Brahm condemned inauthentic, artificial or inadequate emotions in the actors he wrote about. This was the most serious failing he set about to remedy as a director, first of the Freie Bühne, then of the Deutsches Theater.

One of the ways he intended to do this was by applying to the classics techniques of acting and characterisation that had been developed through the performances of Ibsen and Hauptmann.[11] As if to emphasise this, he began his directorship there by producing not a contemporary play but Schiller's *Kabale und Liebe* (*Intrigue and Love*), a universally popular classic whose sharp dramatic situations and melodramatic confrontations had suited well the pathos-laden, late-Weimar style. The production mirrored perfectly Brahm's prosaic personality that felt distaste for anything rhetorical. 'The man made a fuss about nothing,' wrote Alfred Kerr of him. 'All pathos was far from him; all complaisance too.'[12] But such a personality does not guarantee exciting theatre. Even though Brahm may have been right when he claimed in his biography of Schiller that the playwright wanted his work performed 'in a discrete style',[13] over a century of performance practice had accustomed audiences to seeing the play given in a declamatory manner that highlighted the symbolic quality of the characters and ignored their status as interesting individuals. Consequently, when they heard Rudolf Rittner as the hero Ferdinand deliver Schiller's vigorous and unmodern prose as if it were part of an everyday conversation and saw Josef Kainz, known as the most passionate Ferdinand in Germany, in the role of the unattractive intriguer Wurm, it was not surprising that they received unsympathetically Brahm's attempt to rid the classics of all elevated rhetoric. Brahm had over-compensated.

This is equally true of the only other production of a classic drama in which Brahm was directly involved, *The Merchant of Venice*, staged four weeks after *Kabale und Liebe*. The Shakespeare play made no better an impression than the Schiller had done, primarily because Brahm insisted on downplaying whatever situations were inherently theatrical and on having the verse delivered in subdued tones that sought to approximate to normal

[10] Brahm/Fetting, 'Der Fall Kainz', p. 84.
[11] Herbert Henze, *Otto Brahm und das Deutsche Theater in Berlin* (Berlin, 1930), p. 13.
[12] Alfred Kerr, *Die Welt im Drama*, 5 vols. (Berlin, 1917), vol. 5, p. 7.
[13] Otto Brahm, *Schiller*, 2 vols. (Berlin, 1888–92), vol. 1, p. 322.

conversation rather than to make the undeniably elevated language sound natural in the context of a stage performance. Moreover, the staging worked against the creation of an exciting theatrical aura. The trial-scene was blocked so as to isolate Shylock from his adversaries, who in their turn displayed total indifference to him.[14] As a result, the baneful forces Shylock embodied could not be displayed dramatically, as they were never seen to influence others. So, while Brahm may have welcomed Shakespeare as the creator of great and often complex characters, he suspected his theatricality and verbal richness as this militated directly against the sober theatre he wished to create.

> His inner aversion to all extravagance – even to verse – and his scepticism were the natural enemies of all those things that demand the flight of the imagination and rhythm; dialectic was more important to him than splendid and rapturous speech, the intellectual closer than the fantastic.[15]

Brahm's decisive failure to renovate the classics led to a pronounced split in the Deutsches Theater company. He assigned the direction of classic productions first to Cord Hachmann, then to the efficient but lustreless Emil Lessing, while he confined his activities to the production of contemporary drama. This created a disjointed situation, because while the public was interested in the new drama, their enthusiasm was kindled more by performances of the classics, which were now effectively in the hands of the theatre's two celebrities, Kainz and Sorma.[16] Ever more intensively, the two actors developed their optimistic vision of human potential, demon-strating, even at moments of tragic defeat, mastery over their physical and vocal powers and representing in their characters a strength that projected an image of the indestructibility of the human spirit.[17] As this redirected the audience's attention towards acting technique and personal magnetism, it encouraged the actors to practise a new, refreshed virtuosity that militated against the ensemble Brahm was cultivating. At the same time, the philosophy Brahm wished to articulate through his productions was diametrically opposed to that expressed by Kainz and Sorma. While they aspired to show human beings free from determining forces exercised by the physical and human environment, Brahm trained his most valued actors – Emanuel Reicher, Rudolf Rittner, Else Lehmann and Oscar Sauer – to represent their characters as determined, often irredeemably, by the environment in which they have grown and in which they live. This

[14] Henze, *Otto Brahm*, p. 28.   [15] *Ibid.*, p. 28.

[16] The seven Shakespeare plays performed at the Deutsches Theater between 1894 and 1899, the year of Kainz's departure from the company, were *Hamlet*, *The Merchant of Venice*, *Romeo and Juliet*, *Julius Caesar*, *The Taming of the Shrew*, *Henry IV* and *Richard III*.

[17] For a detailed description of Kainz's 'optimistic' interpretation of tragic figures, see Simon Williams, 'Josef Kainz: A Reassessment', *Theatre Research International*, 6 (1980–1), 195–216.

required an attention to the details of psychic and physical expression even more painstaking than any Kainz had practised in his early years at the Deutsches Theater. It also required representing a constant struggle with matter, showing the human condition as one that is inherently narrow and circumscribed. Julius Bab described this well in writing of Rittner and Lehmann. For him, they embodied most completely Gerhart Hauptmann's particular view of 'naturalism', which is

> whatever expresses itself formally as conscientious fidelity to reality, as being bound closely to the earth, that is in its inner essence a mode of living that indicates an unconditional surrender to the love of things, a deep state of being bound to the world, a humble submission to a higher power.[18]

These values were entirely opposite to those associated with Shakespeare when his plays were performed by Kainz and Sorma, which was Shakespeare as he existed in the eyes of the Berlin public.

Agnes Sorma left the Deutsches Theater in 1898, Kainz in 1899, because of a marked decline in the number of times the classics were performed.[19] After this the company produced contemporary works exclusively, until Brahm was forced to relinquish the directorship by L'Arronge, who was still the owner of the theatre. After an unimpressive interregnum of one year under Paul Lindau, L'Arronge appointed the most fashionable young stage director of the time, Max Reinhardt, to be the new director of the Deutsches Theater. One of the principal reasons for this appointment was Reinhardt's production a few months earlier at the Neues Theater of *A Midsummer Night's Dream*.

MAX REINHARDT

Influences on Reinhardt's early career in the theatre were various. One of his first biographers claimed that because Reinhardt had a penchant for the spectacular the most important was the Meininger.[20] However, while Reinhardt was not above filling his stage with detailed sets and properties, a more potent influence may well have been Dingelstedt. Reinhardt, who grew up in Vienna, would not have had an opportunity to see the Meininger,[21] but in 1891, when he was eighteen and a regular visitor to the fourth gallery of the Burgtheater, the company revived Dingelstedt's production of the history cycles. No doubt, the attention shown in this

---

[18] Julius Bab and Willi Handl, *Deutsche Schauspieler* (Berlin, 1908), p. 76.
[19] In the 1894–5 season there were 102 performances of nine classic plays, in 1895–6 seventy-seven of seven, 1896–7 twenty-two of two, and 1897–8, twenty-five of five.
[20] Max Epstein, *Max Reinhardt* (Berlin, 1918), p. 138.
[21] The last appearance of the Meininger in Vienna was in 1883, when Reinhardt was ten years old.

production to colour, line, form and shading as the prime expression of the drama must have appealed to the future director, whose own art would be composed of what Thomas Mann was to call 'magic attraction, the play of colours, clever fascination, the round dance, sound and dream'.[22] When Reinhardt joined the Deutsches Theater as an actor in 1894, two more influences began to work on him. Otto Brahm trained him to penetrate the psyches of his characters and to represent them with exactitude and credibility on stage. From Brahm, Reinhardt also learned the value of ensemble. But a greater influence may well have been Kainz. Not only was Kainz a close personal friend, but Reinhardt saw in his acting an ideal that he would later amplify to encompass the whole theatrical production. While Brahm may have deplored the tendency towards rhetoric in Kainz's acting during the 1890s, for Reinhardt this was the essence of his appeal. So much is clear from a letter he wrote, soon after he joined the Deutsches Theater.

> Apart from the impression of [Kainz's] appearance, which while not extraordinary is uncommonly attractive, from his various ingenious shadings [and] his strong temperament, there is the timbre of his voice, sometimes sensuous, sometimes audacious, defiant, *youthfully* powerful, that has an infinite charm. Above all the *tempo* and the clarity and purity of his speech are pleasures to the ear. *That* is pure rhetoric.[23]

For Reinhardt the appeal of Kainz's acting issued not from his ability to reveal all aspects of a character's psychic life, but from his capacity to use the externals of bodily movement and vocal timbre to suggest an inner world that could not be fully grasped. Reinhardt loved Kainz's acting because he played with appearance. He was deeply impressed by Kainz's Hamlet – to which he played the first Player – as in it he combined the conflicting styles of idealism, associated with the old virtuosi, and realism. Also he seemed to act from sources beyond normal experience. 'He created as if out of ecstasy, enraptured, inspired, transported.'[24] In contrast, Reinhardt found Reicher and Rittner good solely for realistic drama. They lacked the 'powerful outlines' required for performing the classics.

Reinhardt left the Deutsches Theater ensemble because he found Brahm's insistence on naturalism too limiting and because he had directorial ambitions of his own. These ambitions, which were satisfied in various theatrical ventures, were impelled by an idea of theatre which, while inspired by Kainz, also posited a function that was novel in Germany.

---

[22] Thomas Mann, 'Gedenkrede auf Max Reinhardt', in *Max Reinhardt in Berlin*, ed. Knut Boeser and Renata Vatková (Berlin, 1984), p. 65.
[23] Max Reinhardt, 'An Berthold Hold, 1. XI. 1894', in *Schriften*, ed. Hugo Fetting (Berlin, 1974), p. 38.
[24] *Ibid.*, p. 441.

By and large, from the earliest time of professional German theatre, as the Hamlet of *Der bestrafte Brudermord* argued,[25] whenever theatre wished to justify itself it did so by presenting itself as a means of educating citizens by teaching them moral lessons, by training their taste and by reinforcing the authority of whatever political and social entity sponsored or allowed the theatre. But Reinhardt thought of theatre differently. As he wrote in an early essay,

> what I have in mind is a theatre that once again gives beings joy, that leads them out of the grey misery of everyday life, out of themselves into a serene and pure air of beauty. I feel as if people have had enough of finding their own distress over and over again and that they long for lighter colours and an elevated life.[26]

In positing a philosophy of 'art for art's sake' Reinhardt's statement is not especially original. What is striking, however, is that Shakespeare's drama could only be staged in a way that realised practically the ideals of the writers of the late eighteenth century when such a purpose for theatre had been fully affirmed and the theatre itself brought to realisation. In other words, only when a particularly 'modern' conception of theatre was articulated and achieved were the ambitions of 150 years of theatrical theory and practice brought to fruition. This was Reinhardt's major contribution to the performance of Shakespeare in the German theatre.

Two attributes of Shakespeare's work above all had attracted and sometimes repelled eighteenth-century writers. One was his great and complex characters, which had stimulated theatrical practitioners from Schröder through to Brahm. It had led, as we have seen, to some notable advances in acting. The other attribute was that each of Shakespeare's plays seemed to represent a total world, in contrast to the more selective dramatic world of the French tradition. Shakespeare's world was difficult to reproduce because of the physical limitations of the stage and because in most theatres – the Burgtheater being a major exception – the leading actor remained the centre of audience attention. Only with the tours of the Meininger were the ensemble and physical production used to actualise the whole 'picture' or world of Shakespeare's drama. But the Meininger's attention to detail, however much it was intended to be in the service of the play, often had a disjunctive impact. The very exactitude of their scenic and costume design could direct the audience's attention away from the dramatic issues the design was supposed to materialise. The 'impressionist' art of the actor Kainz and, speculatively, of the earlier director Dingelstedt, combined with the ambition to create the illusion of a complete world on stage, were the bases of Reinhardt's work as a stage director.

---

[25] See p. 37.   [26] Reinhardt, *Schriften*, p. 64.

Few directors have felt more immediately the completeness of the world created by Shakespeare's imagination than Reinhardt. Later in life, during a famous speech on the actor, he described this in a characteristically enthusiastic manner:

> Shakespeare is the greatest and quite incomparable stroke of luck for the theatre. He was at once poet, actor and director. He painted landscapes and built architectural constructions with his words. His work is nearest to the creator's. He has created a magical, complete world; the earth with all its flowers, the sea with all its storms, the light of the sun, of the moon, of the stars; the fire with all its terrors and the air with all its spirits and in between human beings. Human beings with all their passions, human beings of an elemental magnificence and yet with the liveliest truth. Shakespeare's omnipotence is infinite, incomprehensible.[27]

No writer more completely exemplified Reinhardt's ideal of the artist as a second God,[28] whose art has a function similar to that of religion in that it allows the spectator to escape from the narrowness of his or her life by giving the imagination a freedom it is not able to exercise in everyday life. But to achieve this, there had to be few barriers between the play and its audience. The production must appeal easily and without offending their tastes. It must not just be presented as a museum piece from a different age and culture. 'Our calling', Reinhardt told his actors, 'is always to acquire anew the works we have inherited. That means giving birth to them anew in the spirit of our time. Our Shakespeare is *other* than the one of 400 years ago.'[29]

The spirit of the time in which Reinhardt's first and most celebrated production of *A Midsummer Night's Dream* was created was various. On the one hand the production was a product of the neoromantic movement that celebrated rich, image-laden poetry and a fantastic symbolic action. As such, it was part of the reaction against the sobriety of naturalism, a reaction reflected also in the plays of Hofmannsthal and the early Wedekind.[30] But, like several great works representative of their time, Reinhardt's *A Midsummer Night's Dream* satisfied the demands of the opposing ethos as well, in this case naturalism. The naturalistic aspect of the production was apparent from the opening scene in Theseus's court. In this, the material of the rich, coarsely-meshed Gobelin tapestries that constituted most of the set was repeated in the materials worn by the actors themselves,[31] thus establishing an identity between character and environ-

[27] *Ibid.*, p. 324.   [28] *Ibid.*, p. 304.   [29] *Ibid.*, p. 309.

[30] Gunther Rühle, 'Der *Sommernachtstraum* Max Reinhardts', *Shakespeare-Jahrbuch* (Heidelberg, 1976), 103–4.

[31] 'Aus dem Regiebuch *Ein Sommernachtstraum*, 1905', *Max Reinhardt in Berlin*, ed. Boeser and Vatková, p. 171.

ment that accorded closely with naturalist ideas on their interdependence. The majority of the action took place in and around the famous forest, built on a revolving stage. This forest, which appeared literally to be created of trees from the woods of northern Europe, has been described as 'the coronation of scenic naturalism'[32] because of its extraordinary air of reality and because the sometimes demonic, sometimes wraith-like fairies were dressed so as to appear literally creatures of the woodland. When they tormented the terrified mechanicals by playing mischievous tricks on them, they appeared to be both a physicalisation of the mechanicals' terror and a demonstration of the living forces of the forest.

But if Reinhardt followed naturalistic principles in observing the relationship between character and environment, the atmosphere of his production could not have been further from the 'grey on grey' world of Otto Brahm. His resourceful use of electric light meant that he could create numerous atmospheric effects, from the shimmer of blue light under glass to suggest a lake, through the glow-worms that accompanied the fairies' dance, to the moon and stars that cast all the woodland events in magical ambience. As a theatrical 'impressionist' therefore, Reinhardt used the stage to lead his audience to imagine an incorporeal world of infinite experience, spreading far beyond the confines of his stage.

The historical importance of the forest in the development of Shakespearean production consisted in Reinhardt's use of it to unify the various sub-plots of Shakespeare's complex action so that ultimately it appeared to be a symbolic expression of that whole action. It encapsulated the meaning of the play and in so doing provided a scenic completeness that complemented the completeness of the world conjured up by Shakespeare's text. 'In the beginning was the forest', wrote Heinz Herald,

> – with the exception of the . . . opening scene and the . . . finale – the stage for the whole play. It is its nourishing soil, its mother earth, everything originates from it, everything hides within it, everything flees, everything changes, everything finds itself, everything is reconciled. It has the closest relationship to each of the three groups of the play; for the spirits it is the natural element, for the human beings it is refuge, for the mechanicals the point of rendezvous.[33]

The forest acquired symbolic meaning for each of the three groups. The translucent lighting stood for the magical power of the fairies, the shifting perspectives created by the revolution of the stage prevented one from fully grasping the physical dimensions of the forest and therefore symbolised the deceptive emotions of the lovers, while the gnarled roots and

---

[32] Carl Niessen, *Max Reinhardt und seine Bühnenbildner* (Cologne, 1958), p. 15.
[33] Ernst Stern and Heinz Herald, *Reinhardt und seine Bühne* (Berlin, 1918), p. 38.

26 Set for Reinhardt's *A Midsummer Night's Dream*

treacherous rabbit-holes represented the hostility that the natural world can have for such as the mechanicals who cannot come to terms with it.[34]

The symbolic completeness of the forest was augmented by the skilful harmony of the physical production. The main stumbling-block for the successful presentation of Shakespeare on an illusionistic stage had been the long pauses that occurred whenever the scene was changed. These could necessitate a rearrangement of the text that could alter entirely the rhythm, even the meaning of the play. This problem was resolved by Reinhardt's resourceful use of the revolving stage so that one scene flowed into another. As a result, he could follow what he considered to be the natural rhythms and climaxes of the text and not the ones that the physical space might impose upon him. Also, as the forest had provided a visual complement to the multiple action of the play and had unified it, the movement of the revolving stage on which the forest stood augmented the impression of harmony (see plate 26). The gestures and movement of the actors and the dancing of the fairies were timed to accord with its movement. The sensation of total harmony was augmented by the interaction of Schlegel's poetry and Mendelssohn's music with the overall motion of the stage, actors and dancers. The physical and aural production, the use of space as an expression of the action and of light and sound as an emanation of this space were more complete than anything that had so far been seen in the German

---

[34] Heinrich Braulich, 'Max Reinhardts theatralische Vision von Mensch und Raum', *100 Jahre Deutsches Theater Berlin 1883–1983* (Berlin, 1983), pp. 66–7.

27 Eysoldt as Puck

theatre. No production had so completely realised the imaginative world that Shakespeare had suggested to Gerstenberg, the young Goethe, Herder and August Schlegel.

The novelty of this all-encompassing production was enhanced by the freshness of some of Reinhardt's conceptions. Some aspects of the scenery were reminiscent of the traditional nineteenth-century stage – in fact the lawn that covered the stage floor in the forest sequence had been taken from the Beerbohm Tree production, seen in Berlin some years previously.[35] Also, some of the costumes struck Ernst Stern as 'stereotypically theatre-Greek'.[36] But, on the whole, it looked radically different from previous productions of *A Midsummer Night's Dream*. In place of the conventional, lachrymose ballerinas in tutus who had passed for fairies in the production at the Berlin Court Theatre, Reinhardt had wood-spirits possessed by a demonic energy. The role of Puck was treated in a specially unorthodox manner. Normally represented as a mild pastoral creature with about as much menace as a Dresden shepherdess, in the hands of Gertrude Eysoldt, Puck became a disturbingly androgynous goblin, 'bristly, unkempt, shaggy, close to the animals; a form that reeked of black earth; a natural sound that had taken on form'[37] (see plate 27). Such changes made the sexual impulses that drive the lovers immediate and tangible, bringing to the fore their physicality, highlighting the way in which human beings are subject to those impulses rather than masters of them. But perhaps the most invigorating aspect of Reinhardt's production was the sense of play that infused it. The fairies played with the mechanicals and lovers, the lovers played with each other, and even Theseus seemed to play with them, for his opening ban on Hermia's love for Lysander was delivered not authoritatively but in a jesting tone that suggested strongly it was not unbreakable. From that dominant sense of play grew a lightness, a sense that the human world was not entirely limited by its physical being, that the lovers were not totally subject to their sexual desires, but that the imagination too was a potent force. Reinhardt's *A Midsummer Night's Dream* dispelled the sentimentality and wan romanticism that, despite Tieck's fine production some sixty-five years before, tended to permeate performances of the play. Instead, by creating a world infused by the sense of play, Reinhardt gave his audiences a stage-world that was new and yet moved towards fulfilling the potential that had first been sensed in Shakespeare's work a good 150 years before.

For some, Reinhardt never again equalled the achievement of *A Midsummer Night's Dream*. Alfred Kerr, his most persistent and cynical

[35] Oliver M. Sayler, *Max Reinhardt and his Theatre* (New York, 1924), p. 218.
[36] Ernst Stern, *Bühnenbildner bei Max Reinhardt* (Berlin, 1983), pp. 30–1.
[37] Hermann Bahr, quoted in Leonhard M. Fiedler, *Max Reinhardt* (Hamburg, 1975), p. 42.

critic, considered it to be the only Shakespeare play he directed with a proper regard for its structure.[38] From then on, Kerr considered Reinhardt's work to be fatally marred by a concern for the incidentals of production rather than the essence of action. He also found his work to be presented with such attention to good taste and emphasis on the overall harmony that it began to lose its effectiveness. He felt that Reinhardt frequently treated Shakespeare 'like someone who plays Beethoven with unctuous dexterity', rarely penetrating to the sometimes uncomfortable core of the play. Certainly Reinhardt, like all his predecessors, made no attempt to capture the invigorating roughness of Shakespeare's work.

By all accounts, Reinhardt's Shakespearean productions, which were the most acclaimed events of his early years as director of the Deutsches Theater, were notable for both the fullness with which the physical environment was realised and the technical proficiency with which it was accomplished. On the revolving stage were created structures that gave the illusion of a complete and self-contained world – Venice in *The Merchant of Venice*, Verona in *Romeo and Juliet* and a medieval town for both parts of *Henry IV*. Ernst Stern, Reinhardt's principal designer, used the revolving stage to create highly complex structures with several different playing areas and a multiplicity of 'surprising vistas and perspectives',[39] so that each composite setting for a production served as a physical correlate to the complexity of the play itself, a realisation of the variety of Shakespeare's world.

At times, such an approach, while ingenious, limited rather than released the full expressive potential of the play. The sheer multiplicity of settings required by, for example, *The Merchant of Venice*, created a cluttered environment that effectively summoned up the life and exuberance of Renaissance Venice, but failed to capture the broader contrasts in the play. Both the serene world of Belmont and Shylock's doleful realm were subsumed into the larger whole of a Venice that lived solely for enjoyment. Reinhardt's penchant for quasi-operatic spectacle may also have distracted attention from the issues at the heart of the play. For example, the arrival of the Prince of Arragon involved introductory trumpet-calls, the gathering of the servants, the unrolling of a carpet, the ceremonial placement of Portia and her retinue, the arrival of a magnificently decorated boat, the dignified disembarkation of the prince with his retinue in a replica of full Spanish ceremonial, the exchange of presents and the formal singing of tenors. After this, Portia began to speak her welcome.[40] Faced with such a

---

[38] Kerr, *Die Welt im Drama*, p. 105.   [39] Stern, *Bühnenbildner*, p. 42.
[40] The full stage directions for this scene from Reinhardt's *Regiebuch* are included in Heinrich Braulich, *Max Reinhardt: Theater zwischen Traum und Wirklichkeit*, 2nd edn (Berlin, 1969), pp. 86–7.

mass of stage business, Kerr's criticism might seem justified. Even Reinhardt's most enthusiastic critic, Siegfried Jacobsohn, often felt he overproduced. His initial production of *Twelfth Night*, given on the revolving stage, was a prime example of this. When the stage turned, Reinhardt was not content to allow even the briefest pause in the action but had to fill his stage with a wild pantomime of 'dancing maids. tippling servants, [and] comedians intent on masquerade'.[41] The atmosphere of festivity was so overwhelming that the imagination of the spectator was no longer allowed the free play it had been granted in *A Midsummer Night's Dream*.

These elaborate productions demonstrated that peculiar attribute of the theatre by which a complete representation of any play may defeat its own purposes by being too complete. In the theatre, sustaining the illusion depends partially on the willing effort of the audience and this effort can only be released when some part of the world on stage is absent. An effective realisation of the completeness of Shakespeare's plays must therefore include the illusion within the minds of each audience member that part of that world has been created from their own imagination. Reinhardt therefore found himself in a position analogous to that of the nineteenth-century stage director for whom realistic spectacle was inadequate to realise the fullness of Shakespeare's drama. He understood this himself when he acknowledged in an interview in 1915,

> I had gone far in the direction the Meininger had taken. I aspired towards a completion of decor. I engaged painters with famous names for my stage and wanted to make the illusion almost complete for the audience. With that I achieved a quite opposite effect. People came to see real trees on my stage; that was a novelty that impressed them more than the art we had to offer.[42]

Reinhardt was too much of a showman to renounce completely the acclaim such decorative staging could bring him, and he continued to provide it in gigantic projects like *The Miracle*. For Shakespeare, however, he turned to that alternative nineteenth-century tradition of the 'Shakespeare-stage' for a solution.

Simplification of decor had been apparent in some of his productions as early as 1906. Emil Orlik's designs for *The Winter's Tale* had been influenced by the ideas of Edward Gordon Craig,[43] while Carl Czeschka's designs for *King Lear* in 1908 did not set the play in any specific period but created the indefinite atmosphere of 'a wild fairy-tale from grey antiquity'.[44] But Reinhardt's tendency towards sparer, more abstract settings was not consolidated until 1909, when he began to direct at the Munich Artists' Theatre one of the final phases in the development of the Shake

[41] Siegfried Jacobsohn, *Max Reinhardt* (Berlin, 1910), p. 31.   [42] Reinhardt, *Schriften*, p. 265.
[43] Niessen, *Bühnenbildner*, pp. 18–23.   [44] Jacobsohn, *Max Reinhardt*, p. 37.

speare-stage. Given the extreme limitations of the stage, when *A Midsummer Night's Dream* was given there it was against a minimalist setting. No longer was there a Romantic forest but a set of 'four naked tree trunks, above them a few tendrils simulating branches, behind them a stretched out curtain for the horizon and before them a widely spread cloth for the green ground. The illusion succeeded completely'.[45] The setting could be imagined as a summit above a valley and created an aura of supernal lightness.

That the Artists' Theatre was beginning radically to influence Reinhardt's work was clear from his first directorial encounter with *Hamlet*. He had initially directed the play against splendid settings by Fritz Erler, 'which in their fine-toned gradation of rose, grey-white, sea-green and old gold created an atmosphere of oppression'.[46] However, as this scenery was cumbersome and awkward to change, when Reinhardt revived the play in 1910 at the Deutsches Theater, he incorporated into the production features from the Artists' Theatre that challenged the limitations of the proscenium stage in two ways. First, he built a fore-stage over the first few rows of the stalls to allow for a greater intimacy between the Hamlet of the soliloquies and his audience. Secondly, he discarded the realistic sets, at that time assumed to be an integral part of the proscenium stage, for a more abstract arrangement. What he did was apply the principle of the half-curtain, which had been developed by Savits, as the major scenic element of his production. Each scene was played before a curtain of a different colour that epitomised the mood of the scene; violet was the backdrop for Laertes' leave-taking from Polonius, dark green for Claudius at prayer, and red for Gertrude's bedroom.[47] The wider environment, represented by a cyclorama for the sky behind a balustrade, was to be filled out by the imagination of the spectators. The completeness of Reinhardt's production depended no longer on total physicalisation but on the imaginative play of the spectator's mind with the empty spaces before him, and greater efforts were made to use the actors rather than scenery as setting of the play (see plate 28).

Reinhardt's staging gave him an almost unprecedented opportunity to stage the original unadapted. Nevertheless, even though he did not rewrite, as several directors had done before him, he was capable of cuts that could drastically alter important aspects of the play. Interestingly, they often seem to serve the same purpose as the cuts that had been used well over a hundred years before. Take for example his *Hamlet*. Certainly his version is far fuller than the Heufeld/Schröder versions of the late eighteenth century, but it is still substantially abridged. As in the eighteenth century, when

---

[45] *Ibid.*, p. 1.   [46] Braulich, *Traum*, p. 117.   [47] Jacobsohn, *Max Reinhardt*, p. 54.

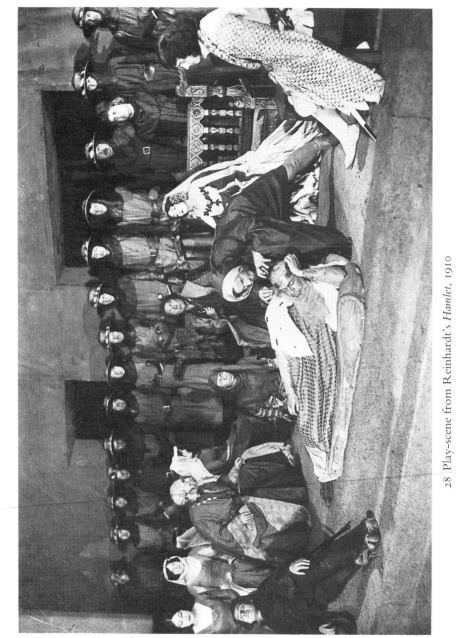

28 Play-scene from Reinhardt's *Hamlet*, 1910

characters' observations slow the action down, as for example Marcellus's speech on Christmas Eve, they are cut.[48] So too are speeches such as Rosencrantz's on the cease of majesty, which might break the hold the action has over the spectator's imagination by encouraging him or her to think about the action and its wider consequences and not solely to experience it on the director's terms. Elaborations, striking images, emphatic statements are cut where they turn the audience's attention to the language itself rather than to the action which the language expresses. Particularly noticeable among the cuts are those to the role of Claudius. This is trimmed so radically that he no longer appears to be a skilled political manoeuvrer; the intrigue between him and Laertes is so reduced that on the basis of the surviving lines it is impossible to understand what is going on. These cuts lessen the audience's attention of the world surrounding Hamlet in order to concentrate more exclusively on his predicament, as if the world is of importance mainly as a reflection of his state of mind. In Act v, most of Hamlet's narrative of the voyage to England is cut, for two possible reasons; first because it comes late in the evening and, as Kerr observed, Reinhardt had difficulty in sustaining the structure of a play, secondly because the account reveals aspects of Hamlet's character that may not sit easily with the sympathies of the audience. The sum total of these cuts amounts to a reduced *Hamlet*. 'Completeness' has been retained in that the play sustains its hold over the imagination of the audience, but this hold is strikingly reminiscent of the hold Schiller ideally felt any play should exercise over the audience. The outer, less subjective world of the Renaissance court has been considerably reduced and the particular viewpoint which the audience is encouraged to take of it has been nullified by the cutting of those passages that encourage them to contemplate rather than experience the action. For all his novelty of staging, there are still distinct vestiges of Schiller in Reinhardt's dramaturgy.

Whatever his shortcomings, Reinhardt did much to solve the discrepancy between physical production and the Shakespearean text, which had been a weakness in many nineteenth-century performances. He was possibly even more successful in resolving the tension that had grown up between the actor as an individual and the ensemble of which he was a part. In the nineteenth century, wherever ensemble had been aimed for, mediocre acting seemed to be the rule – again with the exception of the Burgtheater. Attempts to create an ensemble of leading actors in which each contributed his or her strengths to the creation of the whole had failed dismally, most notably in Munich at a series of performances sponsored by Dingelstedt in 1856, and later in 1880 in the same city, when the Munich

---

[48] William Shakespeare, *Hamlet, Prinz von Dänemark*, Illustrierte Klassiker des Deutschen Theaters nach Inszenierungen von Max Reinhardt (Berlin, n.d. [1912]), p. 19.

court theatre briefly revived the practice of 'model ensembles' composed solely of famous actors. Indeed L'Arronge's foundation of the Deutsches Theater was motivated in part by the desire to remedy this failure. It could be done only by training a company of young actors who had not fallen into the self-indulgent ways of the old virtuosi.

As we have seen, the fortunes of the Deutsches Theater ensemble were various in the pre-Reinhardt years, but the expectations that the theatre had created were the ground on which he could build. Perhaps his greatest achievement was to form an ensemble in which the powerful inner world of the individual actor and the demands of the outer world of the ensemble did not seem to violate each other. Reinhardt's habit of working out a production totally in his *Regiebuch* before going into rehearsal suggests that his method was despotic. But all accounts of his work with actors in rehearsal argue that he was consistently open to their suggestions and able to incorporate their individual vision. As Reinhardt moved away from dependence on spectacular scenery, the contribution of the actor came increasingly to the fore.

In the evolution of this powerful ensemble, which included at certain times almost all the important young actors of Germany, Shakespeare was a crucial aid to Reinhardt. In return, Reinhardt served his plays well. Once again, Shakespeare as the creator of great characters became vital to the development of the German theatre. As Heinz Herald observed in his discussion of Reinhardt as a director of Shakespeare, the unique stamp of a Shakespearean play is that each character feels profoundly his or her rights as a human being, and we too sense this. 'Antonio is right and Shylock is right, and whether we wish to or not, we love both.'[49] 'Love' may be too strong a word to use in this context, but there can be no doubting Herald's claim that the most forcible conflicts in Shakespeare are between characters who consider themselves to be acting on their rights as human beings, rights the audience also recognises. In order to represent such conflicts effectively, complete characterisation was therefore necessary. From his years with Otto Brahm, Reinhardt learnt how to develop a character that was thoroughly worked through psychologically and realised on stage exactly. But while such complexity could be understood and appreciated by audiences in modern naturalistic plays with small casts or in classic productions such as those given by Kainz and Sorma, when the lead characters were the main focus of interest, naturalistic completeness was difficult to achieve when all actors of a large-cast play attempted it.

Reinhardt solved the problem by asking his actors not to explore their characters as if they were real human beings, as this would involve much

[49] Heinz Herald, *Max Reinhardt* (Berlin, 1915), p. 68.

29 Moissi as Hamlet

Albert Bassermann
als „Hamlet."

Verl. Herm. Leiser, Berlin Wilm.

30 Bassermann as Hamlet

work that was irrelevant to the production and in performance might retard the progress of the action. Instead, he encouraged them to discover images around which their roles could be organised, or he would discover these images for them. His success was dependent not so much on the novelty of this proceeding as on the accuracy and originality of these images and on his ability to choose a single detail to suggest a whole realm of experience. He helped Eduard von Winterstein, one of his leading actors, to create an extremely successful Iago after Winterstein had asked Reinhardt not to give him the role because he disliked the character. Had he adopted a naturalistic approach, such an objection might have been sustainable, but Reinhardt encouraged Winterstein to approach the role through the impressionist technique of suggestion, by telling details rather than by full realisation:

> Reinhardt understood wonderfully how to intimate the whole situation, a character, with the intonation and timbre of a single word. I learnt this from him. Already in the first scene with Rodrigo this Iago stood fully formed in all the deeply-grounded malice of his character, I might even say it came clearly to light in the first outcry: 'One Michael Cassio, a Florentine!' In these single lines the whole character of Iago revealed itself to me – and later, I hope, to the spectator.[50]

In essence, this was Reinhardt's approach to the actor, which allowed him once he had assembled a thoroughly competent company, to create performances in which even the smallest role was played with a more satisfying fullness than had previously been the case in the German theatre. Moreover, as the actor did not become as deeply involved in the role as the naturalist actor was liable to do, he or she seemed constantly to be playing with it and endowing it with lightness. Hence productions still seemed to be exercises in imaginative freedom. In this way, Reinhardt continued the legacy he had inherited from Kainz.

Such an approach to acting is perhaps most suited to the performance of comedy. Alfred Kerr constantly argued that Reinhardt was incapable of directing tragedy properly as he could not intensify the action.[51] Reinhardt himself also expressed a preference for comedy, especially broad physical farce such as that of the mechanicals in *A Midsummer Night's Dream*. But receipts at the Deutsches Theater show that his productions of tragedy were equally popular. Again, this is possibly due to the continuation of the influence of Kainz. One of Kainz's greatest achievements had been to introduce a lightness of tone into tragedy after the solemn, overstated interpretations of the earlier generations of actors. This invited the

[50] Eduard von Winterstein, quoted in Paul Koeppler, 'Shakespeare-Inszenierungen aus den Jahren 1905–1938', *Maske und Kothurn*, 19, 2 (1973), 147.
[51] Kerr, *Die Welt im Drama*, p. 130.

sympathetic participation of the audience in the performance instead of asking them to detach themselves, to stand outside admiring the actor's technique. Such was the case with Reinhardt's leading actors too. For example, his two great Hamlets, Alexander Moissi and Albert Bassermann, gave interpretations of the role that were as diametrically opposed as Brockmann's and Schröder's had been back in the eighteenth century. Moissi played Hamlet as 'as melancholic, gentle boy' (see plate 29), using his mellifluous voice to draw his audience to him. Bassermann made Hamlet a more positive figure, 'a heroic man, who was shaken by rage at the commonness of the world around him, and whose drive to act was crippled only because he regarded the world of contemplation with the same passion as he did the world of action' (see plate 30).[52] Moissi always enchanted his audiences; his attractive and yielding personality suggested a man of delicate sensibility, which made him from the start an ideal Reinhardt actor. Bassermann was harsher. He had been one of Brahm's finest naturalistic actors, so he tended to state rather than suggest. However, as he learnt the economy of Reinhardt's method, he too was able to evolve a sense of playing with the character and drew the audience to participate in its experience with him. The two different interpretations could be incorporated into the same production on different nights without audiences being aware of any discrepancy. While this may argue against the integrity of Reinhardt's work to the extent that no interpretative point of view was followed, it is a perfect example of how he created on stage a world so complete that it could accommodate widely differing interpretations.

Reinhardt's work might not represent the culmination of 150 years of Shakespearean performance in the German theatre. He certainly did not achieve on stage the full world of Shakespeare as envisioned by Herder and Goethe. But he went far towards assembling Herder's 'ruins of the colossus' into a coherent structure that was nearing completion.

[52] Julius Bab, *Albert Bassermann* (Leipzig, 1929), pp. 164–5.

Appendix: Shakespeare on the German stage, a timeline 1586–1914

All plays are entered under the title by which they are most commonly known. However, they frequently appeared in Germany with different titles and, until the late eighteenth century at least, in versions radically different from those in the First Folio. Entries in capital letters indicate the first performance of the play in Germany. When two first performances of the same play are indicated, the first will either indicate a version of the play radically different from the Shakespearean original or, in the case of performances at Biberach, an amateur performance.

1586 Group of English actors perform before the Elector of Saxony

1592 English Comedians perform at Duke of Brunswick's court. Robert Browne's troupe performs at Frankfurt fair

1604 ROMEO AND JULIET performed in Nördlingen

1608 Possible performance of THE MERCHANT OF VENICE at Graz

1620 *Titus Andronicus* published in collection of English tragedies and comedies

1625 Possible performance of HAMLET in Hamburg

1626 John Green performs at Dresden court. Possible Shakespeare plays include
. *Romeo and Juliet, The Merchant of Venice*, JULIUS CAESAR, *Hamlet*, KING LEAR

1660 Possible performance of THE COMEDY OF ERRORS, Dresden

1661 OTHELLO performed in Dresden

1693 THE TAMING OF THE SHREW performed in adaptation by Christian Weise at Zittau

1710 Earliest known publication date of *Hamlet* (*Der besträfte Brudermord*)

1741 Publication of Borck's translation of *Julius Caesar*, in alexandrines. First complete translation of any Shakespeare play in Germany

1758 Publication of Grynaeus's translation of *Romeo and Juliet* in blank verse

1761 THE TEMPEST performed in Biberach. Probably the first play ever to be performed in Germany under Shakespeare's name

1762 Publication of first volume of Wieland's prose translations. By 1766, published twenty-one plays in eight volumes

1769 ANTONY AND CLEOPATRA performed in Biberach

1761 Weisse's *Richard III* first performed by Koch in Hamburg

1767 Weisse's *Romeo and Juliet* first performed by Koch in Leipzig

1771   Pelzel's adaptation of THE MERRY WIVES OF WINDSOR first performed in Vienna

(Dec.) MACBETH performed in Biberach

1772   Stephanie's *Macbeth* first performed in Vienna

1773   (Jan.) Heufeld's HAMLET first performed in Vienna

(Dec.) *Hamlet* performed in Biberach

Publication of Herder's 'Shakespeare Essay' in *Von deutscher Art und Kunst*

1774   (Feb.) OTHELLO performed in Biberach

(Dec.) ROMEO AND JULIET performed in Biberach

Publication of Lenz's 'Observations on the Theatre', as introduction to translation of *Love's Labour's Lost*

1775   (Feb.) AS YOU LIKE IT performed in Biberach

(Apr.) *Othello* in Schmid's translation performed by Döbbelin in Berlin

Publication of first volume of Eschenburg's translations. By 1777, all plays published in 12 volumes

1776   (Sep.) Schröder produces *Hamlet* in Hamburg, with Brockmann as Hamlet

(Nov.) Schröder produces *Othello* in Hamburg

1777   RICHARD II produced in Prague

(Nov.) Schröder produces THE MERCHANT OF VENICE in Hamburg

(Nov.) Schröder produces Grossmann's adaptation of *The Comedy of Errors* in Hamburg

(Dec.) Brockmann begins celebrated guest appearances as Hamlet in Berlin

(Dec.) Schröder produces MEASURE FOR MEASURE in Hamburg

1778   TIMON OF ATHENS produced in Prague

Schröder acts Hamlet for first time

(Jul.) Schröder produces KING LEAR in Hamburg

(Nov.) Schröder produces *Richard II* in Hamburg

(Dec.) Schröder produces HENRY IV in Hamburg

1779   (Jun.) Schröder produces *Macbeth* in Hamburg

1780   Schröder tours Germany. Plays Hamlet and Lear at Mannheim

1781   Schröder hired by Vienna Burgtheater, to 1785. Introduces major roles to Vienna

(May) Meyer produces CORIOLANUS in Hamburg

1782   (Dec.) THE TWO GENTLEMEN OF VERONA performed in Biberach

1783   *The Merchant of Venice* produced in Mannheim, with Iffland as Shylock

1784   Burger's translation of *Macbeth*, first performed in Göttingen

1785   JULIUS CAESAR produced in Mannheim

1788   Fleck first acts Shylock, in Berlin

1789   *Timon of Athens* produced in Mannheim

1791   *Coriolanus* produced in Mannheim

Goethe appointed director of Weimar court theatre, to 1817. Produces KING JOHN

1792   Schröder produces MUCH ADO ABOUT NOTHING in Hamburg

1795   Publication of first parts of *Wilhelm Meisters Lehrjahre*; completed 1796

1797   A. W. Schlegel publishes first volume of translations of Shakespeare; completed by Tieck in 1833

1799 First production of Schlegel's translation of *Hamlet*, at Berlin court theatre

1800 First production of Schiller's *Macbeth* in Weimar

1803 Goethe produces *Julius Caesar* at Weimar

1809 Wolff first acts *Hamlet* in Schlegel's version in Weimar

Ludwig Devrient joins Breslau town theatre, to 1815. First performs Lear and Shylock

1812 Goethe's *Romeo and Juliet* produced in Weimar

1814 Schreyvogel appointed to Vienna Burgtheater, to 1832

1815 Ludwig Devrient joins Berlin court theatre, until death in 1832

1816 Wolff's success as Hamlet in Berlin

Schreyvogel produces ROMEO AND JULIET at the Burgtheater

1817 Ludwig Devrient performs Falstaff (*Henry IV*) in Berlin

1822 Schreyvogel produces *King Lear* at the Burgtheater; first performance of Heinrich Anschütz in title role

1828 Ludwig Devrient's last major Shakespearean role, Richard III

1838 Seydelmann at Berlin court theatre, to 1843. Roles include Richard III and Shylock

1840 Immermann's production of *Twelfth Night* in Düsseldorf

1842 CYMBELINE produced at Burgtheater

1843 Tieck produces A MIDSUMMER NIGHT'S DREAM in Berlin

1849 Laube appointed director of Burgtheater, to 1867

1850 Laube's first production of Shakespeare at the Burgtheater, *Julius Caesar*

1851 Dingelstedt appointed director of Munich court theatre, to 1857

1852 ANTONY AND CLEOPATRA produced at Dresden court theatre

1854 Dawison leaves Burgtheater for Dresden court theatre, to 1864. Major roles include Hamlet, Othello, Shylock

1855 (Mar.)Dingelstedt produces *Macbeth* in Munich

(Nov.) Dingelstedt produces THE TEMPEST in Munich

1857 Dingelstedt appointed director of Weimar court theatre, to 1867

1859 Dingelstedt produces THE WINTER'S TALE at Weimar

1864 Dingelstedt produces the HISTORY CYCLES in Weimar

1870 Dingelstedt appointed director of Burgtheater, to 1881

1871 Mitterwurzer joins Burgtheater for second time, to 1880. Major roles include Shylock, Iago, Richard III, Macbeth

1873 Dingelstedt begins to produce history plays in Vienna, to 1874

1874 First season of Meininger in Berlin. Productions include *Julius Caesar*, *Twelfth Night*, *The Merchant of Venice*

1876 The Meininger first perform *Macbeth*, in Berlin

1878 The Meininger first perform *The Winter's Tale*, in Berlin

1883 Adolphe L'Arronge founds the Deutsches Theater, Berlin. Josef Kainz joins the company

1889 Shakespeare-stage inaugurated in Munich with production of *King Lear*

1890 Last European tour of the Meininger

1894 Otto Brahm appointed director of Deutsches Theater, to 1904

1905   Max Reinhardt's first production of *A Midsummer Night's Dream*
Reinhardt appointed director of Deutsches Theater
1908   New Shakespeare-stage inaugurated in Munich with production of
       Measure for Measure
1909   Max Reinhardt produces summer season at Munich Artists' Theatre
1913   Max Reinhardt's cycle of ten Shakespeare plays at Deutsches Theater

Select bibliography

Abeles, Frederick, 'Shakespeare-Aufführungen am Burgtheater unter Laube' (unpublished dissertation, University of Vienna, 1935).

Adams, Graham C., 'The Ottoneum: A Neglected Seventeenth-Century Theatre', *Shakespeare Studies*, 15 (1982), 243–68.

Alexander, R. J., 'George Jolly [Joris Jolliphus] der wandernde Player und Manager. Neues zu seiner Tätigkeit in Deutschland, 1648–1660', *Kleine Schriften der Gesellschaft für Theatergeschichte*, 29/30 (1978), 31–48.

Altmann, Georg, *Heinrich Laubes Prinzip der Theaterleitung*. Schriften der Literar-historischen Gesellschaft Bonn, 5 (Dortmund, 1908).

Ludwig Devrient: Leben und Werke eines Schauspielers. Deutsche Lebensbilder (Berlin, 1929).

Amundsen, Gerhard, *Die neue Shakespeare-Bühne des Münchener Hoftheaters* (Munich, 1911).

Anschütz, Heinrich, *Erinnerungen aus dessen Leben und Wirken* (Leipzig, n.d., [1900]).

Asper, Helmut G., 'Ludwig Tieck inszeniert *Was ihr wollt*. Beschreibung und Analyse einer Fiktion', *Shakespeare-Jahrbuch* (Heidelberg, 1974), 134–47.

Atkinson, Margaret Edith, *August Wilhelm Schlegel as a Translator of Shakespeare* (Oxford, 1952).

Bab, Julius, *Das Theater der Gegenwart*, Illustrierte theatergeschichtliche Monographien, 1 (Leipzig, 1928).

Albert Bassermann, Biographien deutscher Schauspieler (Leipzig, 1929).

Die Devrients (Berlin, 1932).

Kränze der Mimen (Emsdetten, 1954).

Bab, Julius, and Willi Handl, *Deutsche Schauspieler* (Berlin, 1908).

Baesecke, Anna, *Das Schauspiel der englischen Komödianten in Deutschland*. Studien zur englischen Philologie, 87 (Halle, 1935).

Bang, Hermann, *Josef Kainz* (Berlin, 1910).

Barnay, Ludwig, *Erinnerungen*, 2 vols., 2nd edn (Berlin, 1903).

Bartels, Adolf, *Chronik des Weimarischen Hoftheaters* (Weimar, 1908).

Batley, E. M., 'Rational and Irrational Elements in Lessing's Shakespeare Criticism', *Germanic Review*, 45 (1970), 5–25.

Bauer, Roger, 'Die europäische Shakespeare-Rezeption im 18. Jahrhundert', *Shakespeare-Jahrbuch* (Heidelberg, 1985), 151–63.

Bauman, Thomas, 'Opera versus Drama: *Romeo and Juliet* in Eighteenth-Century Germany', *Eighteenth-Century Studies*, 11, 2 (1977–8), 186–203.

Behrens, Peter, *Feste des Lebens und der Kunst* (Leipzig, 1900).

Bergmann, Gosta, M., 'Der Eintritt des Berufregisseurs in die deutschsprachige Bühne', *Maske und Kothurn*, 12 (1966), 63–91.

Beutler, Ernst (ed.), *Goethes Rede zum Schäkespears Tag*, Schriften der Goethe-Gesellschaft, 50 (Weimar, 1938).

Bircher, Martin, 'Die früheste deutsche *Coriolan*-Übersetzung im Fragment des Zürchers Johann Jakob Kitt (1747–1796)' *Shakespeare-Jahrbuch* (Heidelberg, 1968), 121–40.

Blackall, Eric A., *Goethe and the Novel* (Ithaca and London, 1976).

Blättner, Fritz, 'Das Shakespeare-Bild Herders', in *Vom Geist der Dichtung* (Hamburg, 1949), pp. 49–64.

Blessin, Stefan, 'Die radikal-liberale Konzeption von *Wilhelm Meisters Lehrjahre*', *Deutsche Vierteljahrschrift für Literaturwissenschaft und Geistesgeschichte*, 49 (Sonderheft) (1975), 190–225.

Blinn, Hansjürgen (ed.), *Shakespeare-Rezeption. Die Diskussion um Shakespeare in Deutschland I: Ausgewählte Texte von 1741 bis 1788* (Berlin, 1982).

Bloch, P. A., 'Schillers Shakespeare-Verständnis', in *Festschrift Rudolf Stamm*, ed. E. Kolb and J. Hasler (Bern, 1969), pp. 81–101.

Bobinger, Julius, 'Entwicklungstendenzen deutscher Shakespeare-Bearbeitungen im 18. Jahrhundert', in *Grossbritannien und Deutschland*, ed. Ortwin Kuhn (Munich, 1974), pp. 334–46.

Böckmann, P., 'Der dramatische Perspektivismus in der deutschen Shakespeare-Deutung des 18. Jahrhunderts', *Formensprache Studien zur Literarästhetik* (Hamburg, 1966), pp. 45–97.

Boehtlingk, A., *Shakespeare und unsere Klassiker*, 3 vols. (Leipzig, 1909–10).

Boeser, Knut, and Renata Vatková (eds.), *Max Reinhardt in Berlin*, Statten der Geschichte Berlin, 6 (Berlin, 1984).

Bolte, Johannes, '*Der Jude von Venetien*', *Shakespeare-Jahrbuch*, 22 (1887), 189–201.

Die Singspiele der englischen Komödianten und ihrer Nachfolger in Deutschland, Holland und Skandinavien, Theatergeschichtliche Forschungen, 7 (Hamburg and Leipzig, 1893).

Der Danziger Theater im 16. und 17. Jahrhundert, Theatergeschichtliche Forschungen, 12 (Hamburg and Leipzig, 1895).

Schauspiele am Hofe des Landgrafen Moritz von Hessen-Cassel, Akademie der Wissenschaften, Berlin. Philosophisch-historische Klasse. Sitzungsberichte 1931, 3 (Berlin, 1931).

Bonds, Mark Evan, 'Die Funktion des *Hamlet*-Motivs in *Wilhelm Meisters Lehrjahre*', *Goethe-Jahrbuch*, 96 (1979), 101–10.

Booth, Michael R., 'The Meininger Company and English Shakespeare', *Shakespeare Survey*, 35 (1982), 13–20.

Borcherdt, Hans Heinrich, 'Schiller's Bühnenbearbeitungen Shakespearescher Werke', *Shakespeare-Jahrbuch*, 91 (1955), 52–64.

Boyd, J., *Goethe's Knowledge of English Literature*, Oxford Studies in Modern Languages and Literature (Oxford, 1932).

Braekman, W., 'The Relationship of Shakespeare's *Titus Andronicus* to the German Play of 1620 and to Jan Vos's *Aran en Titus*', *Studia Germanica Gandensia*, 9 (1967), 9–118 and 10 (1968), 7–65.

Brahm, Otto, *Schiller*, 2 vols. (Berlin, 1888–92).

Theater, Dramatiker, Schauspieler, ed. Hugo Fetting, (Berlin, 1961).

Brandl, Alois, 'Ludwig Fulda, Paul Heyse, und Adolf Wilbrandt über die Schlegel-Tiecksche Shakespeare-Übersetzung', *Shakespeare-Jahrbuch* 37 (1901), xxxvii–lv.

'Edward Young: *On Original Composition*: Ein Beitrag zur Geschichte der Shakespeare-Kritik im achtzehnten Jahrhundert', *Shakespeare-Jahrbuch*, 39 (1903), 1–42.

'Englische Komödianten in Frankfurt a.M.', *Shakespeare-Jahrbuch*, 40 (1904), 229–30.

Braulich, Heinrich, *Max Reinhardt: Theater zwischen Traum und Wirklichkeit*, 2nd edn (Berlin, 1969).

'Max Reinhardts theatralische Vision von Mensch und Raum', *100 Jahre Deutsches Theater Berlin 1883–1983* (Berlin, 1983), pp. 66–70.

Brauneck, Manfred (ed.), *Spieltexte der Wanderbühne I, Englische Comedien und Tragedien*, Ausgaben deutscher Literatur des XV. bis XVIII. Jahrhunderts (Berlin, 1970).

Brennecke, Ernest (ed.), *Shakespeare in Germany, 1590–1700*, Curtain Playwrights (Chicago, 1964).

Brown, Jane K., 'The Theatrical Mission of the *Lehrjahre*', in *Goethe's Narrative Fiction*, ed. William J. Lillyman (Berlin and New York, 1983).

Bruford, Walter Horace, *Theatre, Drama and Audience in Goethe's Germany* (London, 1950).

Brüggemann, Fritz (ed.), *Die Aufnahme Shakespeares auf der Bühne der Aufklärung in den sechziger und siebziger Jahren*. Deutsche Literatur, 14, Erklärung, 11 (Leipzig, n.d. [1937]).

Brunkhorst, Martin, 'Natur und Wahrheit: Probleme der Hamlet-Rolle im 18. Jahrhundert', *Shakespeare-Jahrbuch* (Heidelberg, 1973), 38–52.

Shakespeares Coriolanus in deutscher Bearbeitung, Komparatistische Studien, 3 (Berlin and New York, 1973).

Brunner, Karl, 'Die erste deutsche *Romeo*-Übersetzung', *Archiv für deutsche Sprache und Literatur*, 153 (1928), 188–201.

Bühnenbild und Raumgestaltung in den Inszenierungen Max Reinhardts (Salzburg, 1972).

Bullough, Geoffrey, *Narrative and Dramatic Sources of Shakespeare*, 8 vols. (London and New York, 1957–75).

Burckhard, Max, *Anton Friedrich Mitterwurzer* (Vienna, 1906).

Carlson, Marvin, 'Montigny, Laube, Robertson: The Early Realists', *Educational Theatre Journal*, 24 (1972), 227–36.

The German Stage in the Nineteenth Century (Metuchen, 1972).

Goethe and the Weimar Theatre (Ithaca and London, 1979).

Chambers, E. K., *The Elizabethan Stage*, 4 vols. (Oxford, 1923).

Claus, Horst, *The Theatre Director Otto Brahm*, Theatre and Dramatic Studies, 10 (Ann Arbor, 1981).

Cohn, Albert, '*König Lear* 1692 und *Titus Andronicus* 1699 in Breslau aufgeführt', *Shakespeare-Jahrbuch*, 23 (1888), 266–81.

Cohn, Albert (ed.), *Shakespeare in Germany in the Sixteenth and Seventeenth Centuries. An Account of English Actors in Germany and the Netherlands and of the Plays Performed by Them during the Same Period* (London and Berlin, 1865; reprinted Wiesbaden, 1967).

Costenoble, Karl, *Aus dem Burgtheater*, 2 vols. (Vienna, 1889).

Creizenach, Wilhelm (ed.), *Die Schauspiele der englischen Komödianten*, Deutsche National-Literatur, 23 (Berlin and Stuttgart, n.d. [1889]).

Daffis, Hans, *Hamlet auf der deutschen Bühne bis zur Gegenwart*, Literarhistorisches Forschungen, 1 (Berlin, 1912).

David, J. J., *Mitterwurzer*, Das Theater, 13 (Berlin and Leipzig, n.d. [1905]).

Deetjen, Werner, 'Shakespeare-Aufführungen unter Goethes Leitung', *Shakespeare-Jahrbuch*, 68 (1932), 10–35.

Delius, Nikolaus, *Die Tieck'sche Shakespearekritik* (Bonn, 1846).

Devrient, Eduard, *Aus seinen Tagebüchern*, ed. Rolf Kabel, 2 vols. (Weimar, 1964).
   Geschichte der deutschen Schauspielkunst, ed. Rolf Kabel and Christoph Trilse, 2 vols. (Munich and Vienna, 1967).

Dietrich, Margret (ed.), *Das Burgtheater und sein Publikum* (Vienna, 1976).

Dingelstedt, Franz, *Studien und Copien nach Shakespeare* (Budapest, Vienna and Leipzig, 1858).
   Theater, 4 vols. (Berlin, 1877).
   Literarisches Bilderbuch, Allgemeiner Verein für deutsche Literatur, ser. 4 (Berlin, 1878).

Dobbek, Wilhelm, 'Herder und Shakespeare', *Shakespeare-Jahrbuch*, 91 (1955), 25–51.

Dreifuss, Alfred, *Deutsches Theater Berlin* (Berlin, 1983).

Drews, Wolfgang, *Die grossen Zauberer*, 3rd edn (Vienna and Munich, 1953).
   König Lear auf der deutschen Bühne bis zur Gegenwart, Germanische Studien, 114 (Berlin, 1932).

Durian, Hans, *Jocza Savits und die Münchener Shakespeare-Bühne*, Die Schaubühne, 19 (Emsdetten, 1937).

Eckardt, Ludwig, 'Shakespeares englische Historien auf der Weimarer Bühne', *Shakespeare-Jahrbuch*, 1 (1865), 362–91.

Eckermann, Johann Peter, *Gespräche mit Goethe in den letzten Jahren seines Lebens, 1823–1832*, 2 vols. (Leipzig, n.d.).

Ehrentreich, Alfred, 'Die Shakespeare-Bühne in neuer Sicht', *Neusprachliche Mitteilungen auf Wissenschaft und Praxis*, 19 (1966), 91–101.

Eisenberg, Ludwig, *Adolf Sonnenthal* (Dresden, 1896).
   Grosses biographisches Lexikon der deutschen Bühne im 19. Jahrhundert (Leipzig, 1903).

Eloesser, Arthur, *Das Theater in Berlin* (Stuttgart, 1906).

Engel, Eva J., 'Lessing, Christoph Friedrich Nicolai and Moses Mendelssohn: Advocates of Shakespeare', in *Lessing and the Enlightenment*, ed. Alexej Ugrinsky (Westport, Conn., 1986), pp. 25–34.

Epstein, Max, *Max Reinhardt* (Berlin, 1918).

Erken, Günther, 'Deutschland', 'Das Werk auf der Bühne: Deutschland', and 'Die deutschen Übersetzungen', in *Shakespeare-Handbuch*, ed. Ina Schabert (Stuttgart, 1972), pp. 662–90, 759–74 and 833–53.

Ermann, Kurt, *Goethes Shakespeare-Bild*, Studien zur deutschen Literatur, 76 (Tübingen, 1983).

Evans, Marshall Blakemore, '*Der bestrafte Brudermord* and Shakespeare's *Hamlet*', *Modern Philology*, 2, 3 (1905), 433–50.

    Der bestrafte Brudermord: sein Verhältnis zu Shakespeares Hamlet, Theatergeschichtliche Forschungen, 19 (Hamburg and Leipzig, 1910).

    'Elizabethan Ghosts and Herzog Julius of Braunschweig', *Journal of English and Germanic Philology*, 22 (1923), 195–216.

Falckenberg, Otto, 'Zur Frage der Inszenierung des *Sommernachtstraums*', *Shakespeare-Jahrbuch*, 77 (1941), 116–23.

Fasolt, Theodore, *Bogumil Dawison* (Dresden, 1857).

Fellner, Richard, *Geschichte einer deutschen Musterbühne* (Stuttgart, 1888).

    'Karl Immermann als Dramaturg', *Karl Immermann, eine Gedächtnisschrift zum 100. Geburtstage des Dichters* (Hamburg and Leipzig, 1896).

Fetting, Hugo, *Conrad Ekhof*, Beiträge zur deutschen Theatergeschichte (Berlin, 1954).

Fiedler, Leonhard M., *Max Reinhardt*, Rowohlts Monographien, 228 (Hamburg, 1975).

Findlay, Ian, 'The Porter's Scene in Schiller's *Macbeth*', *Modern Language Notes*, 88 (1973), 980–7.

Fischer, Rudolf, 'Shakespeare und das Burgtheater, eine Repertoirestudie', *Shakespeare-Jahrbuch*, 37 (1901), 123–64.

Flemming, Willi (ed.), *Das Schauspiel der Wanderbühne*, Deutsche Literatur, ser. 13, Barockdrama, 4 (Leipzig, 1931).

    (ed.), *Die deutsche Barockkomödie*, Deutsche Literatur, ser. 12, 3 (Leipzig, 1931).

    Goethe und das Theater seiner Zeit (Stuttgart, 1968).

Francke, Otto, 'Jocza Savits', *Shakespeare-Jahrbuch*, 52 (1916), 153–8.

Frenzel, Karl, *Berliner Dramaturgie*, 2 vols. (Erfurt, n.d.).

    'Die szenische Einrichtung der Shakespeareschen Dramen', *Shakespeare-Jahrbuch*, 36 (1900), 256–66.

Freudenstein, Reinhold, *Der bestrafte Brudermord. Shakespeares Hamlet auf der Wanderbühne des 17. Jahrhunderts*, Britannica et Americana, 3 (Hamburg, 1958).

Fuchs, Georg, *Die Schaubühne der Zukunft*, Das Theater, 15 (Berlin, 1905).

    Die Revolution des Theaters (Munich and Leipzig, 1909).

Funck, Z., *Aus dem Leben zweier Schauspieler: August Wilhelm Ifflands und Ludwig Devrients* (Leipzig, 1838).

Gardiner, Jeffrey B., and Albert R. Schmitt, 'Christoph Martin Wieland: "Theorie und Geschichte der Red-Kunst und Dicht-Kunst. Anno 1757". An Early Defense of Shakespeare', *Lessing Yearbook*, 5 (1973), 219–41.

Gebhardt, Peter, *August Wilhelm Schlegels Shakespeare-Übersetzung. Untersuchungen zu seinem Übersetzungsverfahren am Beispiel des Hamlet*, Palaestra, 257 (Göttingen, 1970).

Genast, Eduard, *Aus dem Tagebuche eines alten Schauspielers*, 4 vols. (Leipzig, 1862).

Genée, Rudolf, *Geschichte der Shakespeare'schen Dramen in München* (Leipzig, 1870).

Die Entwicklung des szenischen Theaters und die Bühnenreform in München (Stuttgart, 1889).

Gericke, R., 'Zu einer neuen Bühnenbearbeitung des *Macbeth* (von Dingelstedt)', *Shakespeare-Jahrbuch*, 6 (1871), 19–82.

Gerstenberg, Heinrich Wilhelm von, *Briefe über Merkwürdigkeiten der Literatur*, ed. Alexander von Weilen, Deutsche Literaturdenkmale des 18. und 19. Jahrhunderts, 29–30 (Heilbronn, 1890).

Gidion, Heidi, 'Eschenburgs Shakespeare-Übersetzung', *Shakespeare-Jahrbuch* (Heidelberg, 1971), 35–47.

Gille, Klaus F. (ed.), *Goethes Wilhelm Meister: Zur Rezeptionsgeschichte der Lehr- und Wanderjahre*, Texte der deutschen Literatur in wirkungsgeschichtlichen Zeugnissen, 3 (Königstein, 1979).

Gillies, A., 'Herder's Essay on Shakespeare: *Der Herz der Untersuchung*', *Modern Language Review*, 32 (1937), 262–80.

Girard, René, *Lenz, 1751–1792: Genèse d'une dramaturgie du tragi-comique* (Paris, 1968).

Glossy, Karl, *Aus der Briefmappe eines Burgtheaterdirektors* (Vienna, 1925).

Goethe, Johann Wolfgang von, *Goethes Werke*, ser. 1, 55 vols. (Weimar, 1887–1918).

ser. 2, 13 vols. (Weimar, 1890–1904).

ser. 4, 50 vols. (Weimar, 1887–1912).

Goethes Gespräche, 5 vols. (Zurich and Stuttgart, 1965–87).

Die Briefwechsel zwischen Goethe und Zelter, ed. Max Hecker, 4 vols. (Leipzig, 1913).

Gottsched, Johann Christoph, *Versuch einer kritischen Dichtkunst, Ausgewählte Werke*, 11 vols. (Berlin and New York, 1973), vol. 6, pt. 2.

Gregori, Ferdinand, *Josef Kainz*, Das Theater, 3 (Berlin and Leipzig, 1901).

'Shakespeare auf der modernen Bühne, I. Adolf von Sonnenthal: König Lear. II. Josef Kainz: Romeo', *Shakespeare-Jahrbuch*, 40 (1904), 84–94.

Grimm, Reinhold, *et al.* (eds.), *Der deutsche Shakespeare* (Basel, Hamburg and Vienna, 1965).

Grohmann, Walter, *Das Münchener Künstlertheater*, Schriften der Gesellschaft für Theatergeschichte, 47 (Berlin, 1935).

Gross, Edgar, *Johann Friedrich Ferdinand Fleck*, Schriften der Gesellschaft für Theatergeschichte, 22 (Berlin, 1914).

Grube, Karl, *Die Meininger*, Das Theater, 9 (Berlin and Leipzig, 1904).

Grube, Max, 'Shakespeare und die Bühnenkunst', *Shakespeare-Jahrbuch*, 34 (1898), 418–39.

The Story of the Meininger, trans. Ann Marie Koller, Books of the Theater Series, 4 (Coral Gables, Florida, 1965).

Grünbaum, Anita, 'Von Tiecks *Sommernachtstraum*-Inszenierung zur Aufführung in Stockholm', *Kleine Schriften der Gesellschaft für Theatergeschichte*, 20 (1964), 36–58.

Grynaeus, Simon, *Romeo and Juliet*, ed Ernst Heinrich Mensel (Northampton, Mass., 1933).

Guglia, Eugen, *Friedrich Mitterwurzer* (Vienna, 1896).

Gundolf, Friedrich, *Shakespeare und der deutsche Geist*, 8th edn (Berlin, 1927).

Gudlike, Karl S., 'Heinrich Wilhelm von Gerstenberg und die Shakespearedeutung der deutschen Klassik und Romantik', *Journal of English and Germanic Philology*, 58 (1950), 91–108.

'Lichtenbergs Shakespeare-Auffassung', *Shakespeare-Jahrbuch*, 96 (1960), 90–105.

'Richtungskonstanten in der deutschen Shakespeare-Deutung des 18. Jahrhunderts', *Shakespeare-Jahrbuch*, 98 (1962), 64–92.

'Shakespeare im Urteil der deutschen Theaterkritik des 18. Jahrhunderts', *Shakespeare-Jahrbuch* (Heidelberg, 1967), 37–69.

'Themen der deutschen Shakespeare-Deutung von der Aufklärung bis zur Romantik', in *Wege zur Literatur* (Berne, 1967), pp. 109–32.

'Hallers Shakespeare-Bild', *Seminar*, 6, 2 (1970), 91–110.

'Repertoire: Deutsches Theaterleben im Jahre 1776', in *Literarisches Leben im achtzehnten Jahrhundert in Deutschland und in der Schweiz* (Bern and Munich, 1975), pp. 290–6.

Haake, August, *Theater-Memoiren* (Mainz, 1866).

Hadamowsky, Franz, *Die Josefinische Theaterreform und das Spieljahr 1776/77 des Burgtheaters*, Quellen zur Theatergeschichte, 2 (Vienna, 1978).

Hadamzcik, Dieter, *F. L. Schröder und das Burgtheater* (Berlin, 1961).

Haeussermann, Emil, *Das Wiener Burgtheater* (Vienna, Munich and Zurich, 1975).

Hahn, Karl-Heinz, 'Zur Weimarer *Hamlet*-Inszenierung des Jahres 1809', *Natur und Idee*, ed. Helmut Holtzhauer (Weimar, 1966), pp. 92–114.

Handl, Willi, *Schauspieler des Burgtheaters* (Vienna and Frankfurt, 1955).

Hardén, Maximilian, *Köpfe*, 9th edn (Berlin, 1910).

Hartleb, Hans, *Deutschlands erster Theaterbau: Geschichte der englischen Komödianten unter Landgraf Moritz dem Gelehrten von Hessen-Cassel* (Berlin and Leipzig, 1936).

Hauffen, Adolf, 'Schröders Bearbeitung des *Kaufmann von Venedig*s', *Vierteljahrschrift für Literaturgeschichte* 5 (1892), 87–97.

Haym, Rudolf, *Herder* (Berlin, 1958).

Hecht, Hans, 'Shakespeare und die deutsche Bühne der Gegenwart', *Germanisch-Romanische Monatsschrift*, 2 (1910), 288–99 and 348–57.

Heine, Carl, *Das Schauspiel der deutschen Wanderbühne vor Gottsched* (Halle, 1889).

Henze, Herbert, *Otto Brahm und das Deutsche Theater in Berlin* (Berlin, 1930).

Herald, Heinz, *Max Reinhardt: Ein Versuch über das Wesen der modernen Regie* (Berlin, 1915).

Herder, Johann Gottfried, *Werke*, vol. 1 (Munich, n.d. [1953]).

Herrig, Hans, *Die Meininger: ihre Gastspiele und deren Bedeutung für das deutsche Theater* (Dresden, 1879).

Herrmann, Wilhelm, *Thalias liebster Sohn: Iffland und Mannheim* (Mannheim, 1960).

Herz, Emil, *Englische Schauspieler und englisches Schauspiel zur Zeit Shakespeares in*

Deutschland, Theatergeschichtliche Forschungen, 18 (Hamburg and Leipzig, 1903).

Heun, Hans Georg, 'Goethes Kritik an Shakespeares *Romeo und Julia*', *Shakespeare-Jahrbuch*, 98 (1962), 201–15.

Shakespeares Romeo und Julia in Goethes Bearbeitung (Berlin, 1965).

Hille, Gertrud, *Die Tieck-Semper'sche Rekonstruktion des Fortunatheaters: Ein Beitrag zur Geschichte der Bühnenreform des 19. Jahrhunderts* (Berlin, 1929).

Hilton, Julian, 'Shakespeare: The Emancipator of German Drama', *History of European Ideas*, 2, 3 (1981), 203–20.

Hirsch, Adolf von, *Bogumil Dawison* (Leipzig, 1866).

Hoffmann, Paul F., *Friedrich Ludwig Schröder als Dramaturg und Regisseur*, Schriften der Gesellschaft für Theatergeschichte, 52 (Berlin, 1939).

Hoffmeier, Dieter, *Ästhetische und methodische Grundlagen der Schauspielkunst F. L. Schröders*, Studienmaterial für die Künstlerischen Lehranstalten. Theater und Tanz, 1955, 4 (Dresden, 1955).

Die Einbürgerung Shakespeares auf dem Theater des Sturm und Drangs, Schriften zur Theaterwissenschaft 3, 2 (Berlin, 1964).

'Die Meininger: Historismus als Tageswirkung', *Material zum Theater*, 54 (1974), 3–47.

Hoffmeister, Gerhart, 'The English Comedians in Germany', *German Baroque Literature. The European Perspective*, ed. Gerhart Hoffmeister (New York, 1983).

Holmes, T. M., and H. M. Waidson, 'The Shakespearean Strain', *The German Theatre: A Symposium*, ed. Ronald Hayman (London, 1975), pp. 27–58.

Huesmann, Heinrich, *Shakespeare-Inszenierungen unter Goethe in Weimar*, Österreichische Akademie der Wissenschaften. Philosophisch-historisch Klasse. Sitzungsberichte, 256, 2 (Vienna, 1968).

Hüttner, Johann, 'Theatre Censorship in Metternich's Vienna', *Theatre Quarterly*, 10 (1980), 61–9.

Immermann, Karl, *Werke*, ed. Benno von Wiese, 5 vols. (Frankfurt, 1971–3).

Zwischen Poesie und Wirklichkeit: Tagebücher 1831–1840, ed. Peter Hasubeck, Winkler Weltliteratur Dünndruck Ausgabe (Munich, 1984).

Inbar, Eva Maria, 'Shakespeare in der Diskussion um die aktuelle deutsche Literatur, 1773–1777: Zur Entstehung der Begriffe "Shakespierendes Drama" und "Lesedrama"', *Jahrbuch des Freien Deutschen Hochstifts* (1979), 1–39.

'Shakespeare-Rezeption im deutschen bürgerlichen Drama des 18. Jahrhunderts', *Germanisch-Romanische Monatsschrift*, n.s. 30, 2 (1980), 129–49.

Shakespeare in Deutschland: Der Fall Lenz, Studien zur deutschen Literatur, 67 (Tübingen, 1982).

'Zur Funktion der Fussnoten in Wielands Shakespeare-Übersetzung', *Literaturwissenschaftliches Jahrbuch der Görres Gesellschaft*, 21 (1980), 57–73.

Isaacs, J. (ed.), *William Poel's Prompt-Book of Fratricide Punished*, The Society for Theatre Research Pamphlet Series, 5 (London, 1956).

Isaacsen, Hertha, *Der junge Herder und Shakespeare*, Germanische Studien, 93 (Berlin, 1930).

Iser, Wolfgang, 'Der Kaufmann von Venedig auf der Illusionsbühne der Meininger', Shakespeare-Jahrbuch, 99 (Heidelberg, 1963), 72–94.

Itkonen, Kyösti, Die Shakespeare-Übersetzungen Wielands (1762–1766), Studia philologia Jyvaskylaensia, 7 (Jyvaskylä, 1971).

Jacobs, Monty (ed.), Deutsche Schauspielkunst (Leipzig, 1913).

Jacobsohn, Siegfried, Max Reinhardt (Berlin, 1910).

Jelavich, Peter, Munich and Theatrical Modernism (Cambridge, Mass., 1985).

Joachimi-Dege, Marie, Deutsche Shakespeare-Probleme im 18. Jahrhundert und im Zeitalter der Romantik, Untersuchungen zur neueren Sprach- und Literaturgeschichte, 12 (Leipzig, 1907).

Jolles, F., 'Shakespeares Midsummer Night's Dream in Deutschland: einige Betrachtungen über den Vorgang der Assimilation', German Life and Letters, 16 (1963), 229–37.

Jurgens, Woldemar, 'Dingelstedt, Shakespeare und Weimar', Shakespeare-Jahrbuch, 55 (1919), 75–85.

Kagler, K. G., 'Weshalb immer noch die Shakespeare-Übertragungen der Romantiker vorzuziehen sind', Shakespeare-Jahrbuch, 92 (1956), 90–5.

Kahane, Arthur, 'Max Reinhardts Shakespeare-Zyklus im Deutschen Theater zu Berlin', Shakespeare-Jahrbuch, 50 (1914), 107–20.

Kaulfuss-Diesch, Carl H., Die Inszenierung des deutschen Dramas an der Wende des 16. und 17. Jahrhunderts (Leipzig, 1905).

Kerr, Alfred, Die Welt im Drama, 5 vols. (Berlin, 1917).

Kilian, Eugen, 'Die scenischen Formen Shakespeare's in ihrer Beziehung zu der Aufführung seiner Dramen auf der modernen Bühne', Shakespeare-Jahrbuch, 28 (1893), 90–110.

'Die Münchener Shakespeare-Bühne', Shakespeare-Jahrbuch, 32 (1896), 109–32.

'Shakespeare auf der modernen Bühne', Shakespeare-Jahrbuch, 36 (1900), 228–48.

'Schreyvogels Shakespeare-Bearbeitungen', Shakespeare-Jahrbuch, 39 (1903), 87–120; 41 (1905), 135–62; 43 (1907), 53–97.

'Eine neue Shakespeare-Bühne', Shakespeare-Jahrbuch, 46 (1910), 69–83.

Aus der Praxis der modernen Dramaturgie. Die dramaturgischen Blätter, 2nd ser. (Munich, 1914)

Kindermann, Heinz, 'Shakespeares Tragödien im Spielplan des frühen Burgtheaters', Österreich und die angelsächsische Welt, ed O. Hietsch (Vienna, 1961).

Theatergeschichte Europas, 10 vols. (Salzburg, 1957–74).

'Shakespeare und das Burgtheater', Sitzungsberichte, 245, Abt. i der Österr. Akademie der Wissenschaften (Vienna, 1964).

Klarbach, Alfred Freiherr Mensi von, 'Die Shakespeare-Bühne im Jahre 1898', Shakespeare-Jahrbuch, 35 (1898), 362–75.

Klein, Ursula, 'Die frühromantische Kritik und Shakespeare', Shakespeare-Jahrbuch (Weimar), 110 (1974), 153–63.

Kliewer, Erwin, A. W. Iffland: Ein Wegbereiter in der deutschen Schauspielkunst, Germanische Studien, 195 (Berlin, 1937).

Klingemann, August, Kunst und Natur, 3 vols. (Brunswick, 1823–38).

Knudsen, Hans, *Goethes Welt des Theaters* (Berlin, 1949).

Deutsche Theatergeschichte, Kroners Taschenausgabe, 270, 2nd edn (Stuttgart, 1970).

Koeppler, Paul, 'Shakespeare-Inszenierungen aus den Jahren 1905–1938', *Maske und Kothurn*, 19, 2 (1973), 143–50.

Koffka, Wilhelm, *Iffland und Dalberg* (Leipzig, 1865).

Kollek, Peter, *Bohumil Dawison: Porträt und Deutung eines genialen Schauspielers*, Die Schaubühne, 70 (Kastellaun, 1978).

Koller, Anne Marie, *The Theater Duke: Georg II of Saxe-Meiningen and the German Stage* (Stanford, 1984).

Korninger, Siegfried, 'Shakespeare und seine deutschen Übersetzer', *Shakespeare-Jahrbuch*, 92 (1956), 19–44.

Krengel-Strudthoff, Inge, 'Das antike Rom auf der Bühne und der Übergang vom gemalten zum plastischen Bühnenbild. Anmerkungen zu den *Cäsar*-Dekorationen Georgs II von Meiningen', *Bühnenformen – Bühnenräume – Bühnendekorationen: Beiträge zur Entwicklung des Spielorts*, ed. Rolf Badenhausen and Harald Zielske (Berlin, 1974).

Kuckhoff, Amin-Gerd, 'Shakespeare und ein Anfang: Zur Shakespeare-Rezeption in der Zeit der Entwicklung des bürgerlichen deutschen Nationaltheaters', *Shakespeare-Jahrbuch* (Weimar), 116 (1980), 42–52.

Kühne, Gustav, *Portraits und Silhouetten*, 2 vols. (Hannover, 1843).

L'Arronge, Adolph, *Deutsches Theater und Deutsche Schauspielkunst*, 2nd edn (Berlin, 1896).

Larson, Kenneth E., 'Wieland's Shakespeare: A Reappraisal', *Lessing Yearbook*, 16 (1984), 229–49.

Laube, Heinrich, *Theaterkritiken und dramaturgische Aufsätze*, ed Alexander von Weilen, 2 vols., Schriften der Gesellschaft für Theatergeschichte, 7 and 8 (Berlin, 1906).

Schriften über das Theater, ed Eva Stahl-Wisten (Berlin, 1955).

Leeuwe, Hans de, 'Shakespeares Shylock: europäische Darsteller einer berühmte Rolle', *Kleine Schriften der Gesellschaft für Theatergeschichte*, 23 (1969), 3–22.

Leister, Edda, and Grisela Prossnitz (eds.), *Max Reinhardt: Sein Theater in Bildern* (Velbert bei Hanover, 1968).

Max Reinhardt in Europa, Max-Reinhardt-Forschungs- und Gedenkstatte Publikation, 4 (Salzburg, 1973).

Leitzmann, Albert, 'Dodds' *Beauties of Shakespeare* als Quelle für Goethe und Herder', *Shakespeare-Jahrbuch*, 55 (1919), 59–74.

Lessing, Gotthold Ephraim, *Werke*, ed. Karl Eibl *et al.*, vol. 4 (Munich, 1973).

Legband, Paul (ed.), *Das Deutsche Theater in Berlin* (Munich, 1909).

Leuca, George, 'Wieland and the Introduction of Shakespeare into Germany', *German Quarterly*, 28 (1955), 247–55.

Lewinsky, Josef (ed.), *Vor den Kulissen*, 2 vols. (Berlin, 1881).

Lichtenberg, Georg C., 'Impressions of Garrick', trans. John Nowell, *History Today*, 22 (1972), 161–8.

Liebscher, Otto, *Franz Dingelstedt: Seine dramaturgische Entwicklung und Tätigkeit bis 1857* (Halle, 1909).

Limon, Jerzy, *Gentlemen of a Company: English Players in Central and Eastern Europe, 1590–1660* (Cambridge, 1985).

Lindau, Paul, *Nur Erinnerungen*, 2 vols. (Stuttgart and Berlin, 1919).

Linzer, Martin, *Die Düsseldorfer Musterbühne* (Berlin, 1956).

Litzmann, Berthold, *Friedrich Ludwig Schröder*, 2 vols. (Hamburg, 1890 and 1894).

Litzmann, Berthold (ed.), *Schröder und Gotter* (Hamburg and Leipzig, 1887).

Löden, Brigitte, *Max Reinhardts Massenregie auf der Guckkastenbühne von 1905 bis 1910*, Europäische Hochschulschriften, ser. 20, Film- und theaterwissenschaftliche Studien, 3 (Bern, 1976).

Lothar, Rudolf, *Sonnenthal, Das Theater*, 8 (Berlin, n.d. [1904]).

Das Wiener Burgtheater (Vienna, n.d.[1934]).

Low, Alfred D., *Jews in the Eyes of the Germans* (Philadelphia, 1979).

Lüdecke, Henry, 'Zur Tieck'schen Shakespeare-Übersetzung', *Shakespeare-Jahrbuch*, 55 (1919), 1–29.

Ludwig Tieck und das alte englische Theater, Deutsche Forschungen, 6 (Frankfurt, 1922).

Ludvik, D., 'Zur Chronologie und Topographie der "alten" und "späten" englischen Komödianten in Deutschland', *Acta Neophilologia*, 7 (1975), 47–65.

Macey, Samuel L., 'The introduction of Shakespeare into Germany in the Second Half of the Eighteenth Century', *Eighteenth-Century Studies*, 5 (1971), 261–9.

Mann, Otto, *Geschichte des deutschen Dramas* (Stuttgart, 1963).

Martersteig, Max, *Pius Alexander Wolff* (Leipzig, 1879).

Das deutsche Theater im 19. Jahrhundert, 2nd edn (Leipzig, 1924).

Martini, Fritz, 'Shakespeare-Aufführungen im Spiegel der Kritik Otto Brahms und Alfred Kerrs', *Shakespeare-Jahrbuch* (Heidelberg, 1967), 123–46.

Maurer-Schmoock, Sybille, *Deutsches Theater im 18. Jahrhundert*, Studien zur deutschen Literatur, 71 (Tübingen, 1983).

McNamee, Lawrence F., 'The Meininger Players and Shakespeare', *Drama Survey*, 3, 2 (1964), 264–75.

Meissner, Johann (ed.), *Die englischen Comoedianten zur Zeit Shakespeares in Österreich*, Beiträge zur Geschichte der deutschen Literatur und des geistigen Lebens in Österreich, 4 (Vienna, 1884).

Menhennet, Alan, *Order and Freedom: Literature and Society in Germany from 1720 to 1805* (London, 1973).

Mentzel, Elizabeth, *Geschichte der Schauspielkunst in Frankfurt am Main* (Frankfurt, 1882).

Merschberger, Prof. Dr, 'Die Anfänge Shakespeares auf der Hamburger Bühne', *Shakespeare-Jahrbuch*, 25 (1890), 205–72.

Meyer, F. L. W., *Friedrich Ludwig Schröder*, 2 vols. (Hamburg, 1819).

Minor, Jakob, *Aus dem alten und neuen Burgtheater* (Zurich, 1920).

Moormann, Maria, *Die Bühnentechnik Heinrich Laubes*, Theatergeschichtliche Forschungen, 30 (Leipzig, 1917).

Mueller, D. M., 'Wieland's *Hamlet* Translation and Wilhelm Meister', *Shakespeare-Jahrbuch* (Heidelberg, 1969), 198–212.

Muenzer, Clark S., *Figures of Identity: Goethe's Novels and the Enigmatic Self* (University Park and London, 1984).

Müller, J. H. F., *Abschied von der k. k. Hof- und National-Schaubühne* (Vienna, 1802).

Müller, Joachim, *Shakespeare und ein deutscher Anfang: Die von Borcksche Überset-
zung des Julius Caesar von 1741 im Streitfeld von Gottsched und J. E. Schlegel*,
Sitzungsberichte der Sachsischen Akademie der Wissenschaften zu Leipzig.
Philologisch-historische Klasse, 119, 5 (Berlin, 1977).

Murad, Orlene, *The English Comedians at the Court in Graz, 1607–1608*, Salzburg
Studies in English Literature, Elizabethan and Renaissance Studies, 81
(Salzburg, 1978).

Niessen, Carl, *Deutsches Theater und Immermanns Vermächtnis*, Die Schaubühne, 35
(Emsdetten, 1940).

   Max Reinhardt und seine Bühnenbildner (Cologne, 1958).

   'Goethe und die romantische Shakespeare-Bühne', *Kleine Schriften zur Theaterwissenschaft und Theatergeschichte* (Emsdetten, 1971), pp. 63–70.

Nüssel, Heide, *Rekonstruktionen der Shakespeare-Bühne auf dem deutschen Theater*
(Cologne, 1967).

Oechelhauser, Wilhelm, 'Shakespeare auf dem Wiener Burgtheater', *Shakespeare-
Jahrbuch*, 4 (1869), 349–67.

Oppel, Horst, *Das Shakespeare-Bild Goethes* (Mainz, 1949).

   'Shakespeare in Deutschland', *Englisch-deutsche Literaturbeziehungen*, vol. 1,
   Grundlage der Anglistik und Amerikanistik, 1–2 (Berlin, 1971), pp. 98–125.

Osborne, John, 'From Political to Cultural Despotism: The Nature of the
Saxe-Meiningen Aesthetic', *Theatre Quarterly*, 5 (1975), 40–54.

   The Meiningen Court Theatre, 1866–1890 (Cambridge, 1988).

Osborne, John (ed.), *Die Meininger: Texte zur Rezeption* (Tübingen, 1980).

Pascal, Roy, 'The Stage of the Englische Komödianten: Three Problems', *Modern
Language Review*, 35, 3 (1940), 367–76.

   The German Sturm und Drang (Manchester, 1953).

   'Constancy and Change in Goethe's Attitude to Shakespeare', *Publications of the
   English Goethe Society*, new ser., 34 (1964), 153–74.

Pascal, Roy (ed.), *Shakespeare in Germany, 1740–1815* (Cambridge, 1937).

Petersen, Julius, 'Ludwig Tiecks *Sommernachtstraum*-Inszenierung', *Neues Archiv
für Theatergeschichte*, vol. 2, Schriften der Gesellschaft für Theatergeschichte,
41 (Berlin, 1930), pp. 163–98.

   'Schiller und Shakespeare', *Euphorion*, 32 (1931), 145–65.

Phelps, Leland R., 'Goethe's Adaptation of *Romeo and Juliet*', in *Creative Encounter*
(Chapel Hill, 1978), pp. 17–24.

Pichler, Anton, 'Die Shakespeare-Aufführungen des Mannheimer Hof- und
Nationaltheaters 1779–1871', *Shakespeare-Jahrbuch*, 9 (1874), 295–309.

Plard, Henri, 'Shakespeare mis en scène par Goethe', *Revue d'Histoire du Théâtre*, 16
(1964), 351–62.

Price, L. M., *English Literature in Germany* (Berkeley, 1953).

Prölss, Robert, 'Shakespeare-Aufführungen in Dresden vom 20. Oct. 1816 bis
Ende 1860', *Shakespeare-Jahrbuch*, 15 (1880), 173–210.

   Das herzogliche Meiningen'sche Hoftheater (Leipzig, 1887).

Raeck, Kurt, *Das Deutsche Theater zu Berlin unter der Direktion von Adolph l'Arronge*
(Berlin, 1928).

Reinhardt, Max, *Schriften*, ed. Hugo Fetting (Berlin, 1974).

Reissland, Ingrid and Volker, 'Historienmalerei und Illusionismus: Die Theaterd-ekorationen des Meininger Hoftheaters in der 2. Hälfte des 19. Jahrhunderts', *Bildende Kunst*, 10 (1985), 454–8.

Rellstab, Ludwig, 'Ludwig Devrient', *Gesammelte Schriften*, vol. 9 (Leipzig, 1860).

Richter, Albrecht Kurt (ed.), *Beiträge zum Bekanntwerden Shakespeares in Deutsch-land*, 3 vols. (Breslau, 1909 and 1910; Oppeln, 1912).

Richter, Helene, *Schauspieler-Charakteristiken*, Theatergeschichtliche Forschungen 27 (Leipzig and Hamburg, 1914).

   Kainz (Vienna and Leipzig, 1931).

Roberts, David, 'Wilhelm Meister and Hamlet: The Inner Structure of Book III of *Wilhelm Meisters Lehrjahre*', *Publications of the English Goethe Society*, ser. 2, 45 (1975), 64–100.

Roennecke, Rudolf, *Franz Dingelstedts Wirksamkeit am Weimarer Hoftheater* (Greifswald, 1912).

Rohmer, R., 'Lessing und Shakespeare', *Shakespeare-Jahrbuch*, (Weimar, 1967), 40–53.

Rosenthal, Friedrich, *Schauspieler aus deutscher Vergangenheit*, Amalthea-Bucherei, 8 (Zurich, 1919).

   Unsterblichkeit des Theaters (Munich, 1924).

Rötscher, Heinrich Theodor, *Seydelmanns Leben und Wirken* (Berlin, 1845).

Rowe, Nicholas, 'Life of Shakespeare', *The Plays of William Shakespeare*, ed. George Steevens (London, 1774).

Rühle, Gunther, 'Der *Sommernachtstraum* Max Reinhardts', *Shakespeare-Jahrbuch* (Heidelberg, 1976), 100–14.

Sarlos, Robert K., 'Dingelstedt's Celebration of the Tercentenary: Shakespeare's Histories as a Cycle', *Theatre Survey*, 5, 2 (1964), 117–31.

Sauer, Thomas G., *A. W. Schlegel's Literary Criticism in England, 1811–1846*, Studien zur Literatur der Moderne, 9 (Bonn, 1981).

Savits, Jocsza, *Von der Absicht des Dramas* (Munich, 1908).

   Shakespeare und die Bühne des Dramas (Bonn, 1917).

Sayler, Oliver M., *Max Reinhardt and his Theatre* (New York, 1924).

Schanze, Helmut, 'Shakespeare-Kritik bei Friedrich Schlegel', *Germanisch-Romanische Monatsschrift*, 15 (1965), 40–50.

Schaumberg, Georg, 'Max Reinhardt und das Münchener Künstlertheater', *Bühne und Welt*, 11, 2 (1908–9), 936–8.

Schiller, Friedrich von, *Schillers Werke*, Nationalausgabe, 47 vols. (Weimar, 1943–).

Schink, Johann Friedrich, *Dramaturgische Fragmente*, 4 vols. (Graz, 1781).

Schirmer, Walter F., 'Shakespeare und der junge Goethe', *Publications of the English Goethe Society*, 17 (1947), 26–42.

Schlegel, August Wilhelm, *Kritische Schriften und Briefe*, 7 vols. (Stuttgart, 1962–74).

Schlegel, August Wilhelm, and Ludwig Tieck, trans., *Shakespeares dramatische Werke*, 12 vols. (Berlin, 1839–40).

Schlegel, Johann Elias, *Ausgewählte Werke* (Weimar, 1963).

Schmidt, Friedrich Ludwig, *Denkwürdigkeiten*, ed. H. Uhde (Hamburg, 1875).

Schöffler, P., 'Shakespeare und der junge Goethe', *Shakespeare-Jahrbuch*, 76 (1940), 11–33.

Schreyvogel, Josef, *Die Bühnenbearbeitungen von Romeo und Julia und König Lear* (Vienna, 1841).

    Josef Schreyvogels Tagebücher: 1810–1823, ed. Karl Glossy, 2 vols., Schriften der Gesellschaft für Theatergeschichte, 2 and 3 (Berlin, 1903).

Schreyvogl, Friedrich, 'Heinrich Laube als Theaterdirektor', *Maske und Kothurn*, 2 (1956), 193–8.

    Das Burgtheater: Wirklichkeit und Illusion (Vienna, 1965).

Schrickx, Willem, 'English Actors at the Courts of Wolfenbüttel, Brussels and Graz during the Lifetime of Shakespeare', *Shakespeare Survey*, 33 (1980), 153–68.

    'English Actors' Names in German Archives and Elizabethan Theatre History', *Shakespeare-Jahrbuch* 118 (1982), 146–57.

    '"Pickelherring" and the English Actors in Germany', *Shakespeare Survey*, 36 (1983), 135–47.

Schröder, Friedrich Ludwig, *Hamburgisches Theater*, 4 vols. (Hamburg, 1785), vol. 4.

    Maass für Maass (Schwerin and Wismar, 1790).

    Dramatische Werke, ed. Eduard von Bulow, 4 vols. (Berlin, 1831), vol. 4.

Schröder, Rudolf Alexander, 'Goethe und Shakespeare', *Shakespeare-Jahrbuch*, 84/86 (1950), 17–39.

Schumacher, Erich, *Macbeth auf der deutschen Bühne*, Die Schaubühne, 23 (Emsdetten, 1938).

Schütze, Johann Friedrich, *Hamburgische Theatergeschichte* (Hamburg, 1794).

Schwarz, Hans-Gunther, 'Lenz und Shakespeare', *Shakespeare-Jahrbuch* (Heidelberg, 1971), 85–96.

Seydelmann, Karl, *Aus seinen Rollenheften und Briefen*, Studienmaterial für die künstlerischen Lehranstalten, Theater, 2 (Berlin, 1955).

    Rollenhefte Karl Seydelmanns, ed. Max Grube, Schriften der Gesellschaft für Theatergeschichte, 25 (Berlin, 1915).

Shakespeare und das deutsche Theater. Eine Dokumentation der Deutschen Shakespeare-Gesellschaft West, des Kurpfälzischen Museums der Stadt Heidelberg und des Instituts für Theaterwissenschaft der Universität Köln (Cologne, 1964).

Singer, Herta, 'Die Akustik des alten Burgtheaters', *Maske und Kothurn*, 4 (1958), 220–9.

Sonnenfels, Josef von, *Briefe über die Wienerische Schaubühne* (repr. Vienna, 1884).

Speidel, Ludwig, *Schauspieler* (Berlin, 1911).

Stadler, Ernst, *Wielands Shakespeare*, Quellen und Forschungen, 107 (Strassburg, 1910).

    'Reinhardt und Shakespeare: 1904–1914', *Shakespeare-Jahrbuch*, 99 (1963), 95–109.

Stahl, Ernst Leopold, 'Der Düsseldorfer Dramaturg', in *Festschrift für Eugen Kilian zu seinem 25 jährigen Bühnenjubiläum* (Munich, 1918).

Shakespeare und das deutsche Theater (Stuttgart, 1947).

Stamm, Rudolf, 'Probleme der Shakespeare-Übersetzung', *Zwischen Vision und Wirklichkeit* (Bern and Munich, 1964), pp. 63–84.

Steck, Paul, *Schiller und Shakespeare. Idee und Wirklichkeit*, Europäische Hochschulschriften, 14 (Frankfurt, Berne and Las Vegas, 1977).

Stellmacher, Wolfgang, 'Grundfragen der Shakespeare-Rezeption in der Frühphase des Sturm und Drang', *Weimarer Beiträge*, 10 (1964), 323–45.

'Der junge Herder und Shakespeare', *Shakespeare-Jahrbuch* 103 (Weimar, 1967), 54–67.

Herders Shakespeare-Bild: Shakespeare-Rezeption im Sturm und Drang. Dynamisches Weltbild und bürgerliches Nationaldrama. (Berlin, 1978).

'Shakespeare-Rezeption in der deutschen Klassik und Romantik', *Shakespeare-Jahrbuch*, 121 (Weimar, 1985), 114–34.

Stellmacher, Wolfgang (ed.), *Auseinandersetzung mit Shakespeare: Texte zur deutschen Shakespeare-Aufnahme, 1790–1830*, Deutsche Bibliothek, 12 (Berlin, 1985).

Auseinandersetzung mit Shakespeare: Texte zur deutschen Shakespeare-Aufnahme von 1740 bis zur französischen Revolution, Deutsche Bibliothek, 7 (Berlin, 1976).

Stern, Ernst, *Bühnenbildner bei Max Reinhardt* (Berlin, 1983).

and Heinz Herald, *Reinhardt und seine Bühne* (Berlin, 1918).

Stifter, Adalbert, *Der Nachsommer* (n.p. n.d. [1956]).

Styan, J. L., *Max Reinhardt*, Directors in Perspective (Cambridge, 1982).

Suerbaum, Ulrich, 'Der deutsche Shakespeare', in *Festschrift Rudolf Stamm*, ed. Eduard Kolb and Jörg Hasler (Berne and Munich, 1969), pp. 61–80.

Tenczhert, Joachim, 'Die Meininger und ihre Zeit', *Theater der Zeit*, 8 (1953), 25–34.

'Meininger und Meiningerei. Über Wirkung und Folgen einer Theaterreform', *Theater der Zeit*, 8 (1953), 30–6.

Terfloth, John, 'The pre-Meiningen Rise of the Director in Germany and Austria', *Theatre Quarterly*, 6 (1976), 64–86.

Thurn, Rudolf Payer von, 'Joseph Schreyvogels Beziehungen zu Goethe', *Jahrbuch der Grillparzer Gesellschaft*, 10 (1900), 96–128.

Tieck, Ludwig, *Dramaturgische Blätter*, 2 vols. (Leipzig, 1826 and 1852).

Kritische Schriften, 4 vols. (Leipzig, 1848).

Das Buch über Shakespeare, ed. Henry Lüdecke (Halle, 1920).

'Der junge Tischlermeister', in *Romane* (Munich, n.d.).

Tittmann, Julius, *Die Schauspiele der englischen Komödianten in Deutschland*, Deutsche Dichter des 17. Jahrhunderts, 13 (Leipzig, 1880).

Tornius, V., *Goethe als Dramaturg* (Leipzig, 1909).

Troizkij, S., *Karl Seydelmann: Die Anfänge der realistischen Schauspielkunst* (Berlin, 1949).

Ulrici, Hermann, 'Ludwig Devrient als König Lear', *Shakespeare-Jahrbuch*, 2 (1867), 292–7.

Victor, Walther, 'Zwischen zwei Welten Goethes und Shakespeares', in *Goethe – gestern und morgen. Gedanken, Gedenken, Gedichte*, 2nd edn (Berlin, 1970), pp. 207–23.

Vincke, Gisbert, 'Zur Geschichte der deutschen Shakespeare-Übersetzung', *Shakespeare-Jahrbuch*, 16 (1881), 254–73.

'Zur Geschichte der deutschen Shakespeare-Bearbeitung', *Shakespeare-Jahrbuch*, 17 (1882), 82–99.

Völcker, Bruno, *Die Hamletdarstellungen Daniel Chodowieckis*, Theatergeschichtliche Forschungen, 29 (Leipzig, 1916).

Wahle, Julius, *Das Weimarer Hoftheater unter Goethes Leitung* (Weimar, 1892).

Walter, Friedrich (ed.), *Archiv und Bibliothek des Grossh. Hof- und Nationaltheaters in Mannheim: 1779–1839*, 2 vols. (Leipzig, 1899).

Walzel, Oskar, 'Der Kritiker Lessing und Shakespeare', *Shakespeare-Jahrbuch*, 65 (1929), 23–48.

Weigand, H., 'Shakespeare in German Criticism', in *The Persistence of Shakespeare Idolatry*, ed. H. M. Schueler (Detroit, 1964).

Weilen, Alexander von, 'Laube und Shakespeare', *Shakespeare-Jahrbuch*, 43 (1907), 98–137.

Hamlet auf der deutschen Bühne bis zur Gegenwart (Berlin, 1908).

Weilen, Alexander von (ed.), *Der erste deutsche Bühnen-Hamlet: die Bearbeitungen Heufelds und Schröders* (Vienna, 1914).

Wertheim, Ursula, 'Philosophische und ästhetische Aspekte in Prosastücken Goethes über Shakespeare', *Goethe*, 26 (1964), 54–76.

Widmann, Wilhelm, *Hamlets Bühnenlaufbahn (1601–1877)*, Schriften der deutschen Shakespeare-Gesellschaft, ser. 1 (Leipzig, 1931).

Wiecke, Thomas, 'Meiningen und die Meininger: Acht Thesen', *Theater der Zeit*, 29, 6 (1974), 10–11.

Wieland, Christoph Martin, *Gesammelte Schriften*, ed. Ernst Stadler, 10 vols. (Berlin, 1911).

Wiese, Benno von, *Karl Immermann* (Bad Homburg, 1969).

Williams, Simon, 'Josef Kainz: A Reassessment', *Theatre Research International*, 6 (1980–1), 195–216.

German Actors of the Eighteenth and Nineteenth Centuries: Idealism, Romanticism and Realism, Contributions in Drama and Theatre Studies, 12 (Westport, Conn. 1985).

Winds, Adolf, *Hamlet auf der deutschen Bühne*, Schriften der Gesellschaft für Theatergeschichte, 12 (Berlin, 1909).

Geschichte der Regie (Berlin and Leipzig, 1925).

Wolff, Max J., 'Die Tragödie von *Romeo und Julietta*', *Shakespeare-Jahrbuch*, 47 (1911), 92–105.

Wolffheim, Hans, (ed.), *Die Entdeckung Shakespeares: Deutsche Zeugnisse des 18. Jahrhunderts* (Hamburg, 1959).

Würtenberg, G. (ed.), *Shakespeare in Deutschland*, Deutsche Ausgaben, 265 (Bielefeld, 1931).

Würzbach, Alfred von, *Bogumil Dawison* (Vienna, 1871).

Young, Edward, *Complete Works: Poetry and Prose*, ed. James Nichols (Hildesheim, 1968).

Index